Transfer Thinking in Translation Studies

Playing with the Black Box of Cultural Transfer

Translation, Interpreting and Transfer

4

"Translation, Interpreting and Transfer" takes as its basis an inclusive view of translation and translation studies. It covers research and scholarly reflection, theoretical and methodological, on all aspects of the core activities translation and interpreting, but also similar rewriting and recontextualization practices such as adaptation, localization, transcreation and transediting, keeping Roman Jakobson's inclusive view on interlingual, intralingual and intersemiotic translation in mind. The title of the series, which includes the more encompassing concept of transfer, reflects this broad conceptualization of translation matters.

Series editors
Luc van Doorslaer (KU Leuven / University of Tartu)
Haidee Kotze (Utrecht University)

Editorial board
Lieven D'hulst (KU Leuven)
Daniel Gile (University Paris 3, Sorbonne Nouvelle)
Sara Ramos Pinto (University of Leeds)

Advisory board
Pieter Boulogne (KU Leuven)
Elke Brems (KU Leuven)
Leo Tak-hung Chan (Lingnan University, Hong Kong)
Dirk Delabastita (University of Namur)
Dilek Dizdar (University of Mainz)
Yves Gambier (University of Turku)
Arnt Lykke Jakobsen (Copenhagen Business School)
Reine Meylaerts (KU Leuven)
Franz Pöchhacker (University of Vienna)
Heidi Salaets (KU Leuven)
Christina Schäffner (Aston University, Birmingham)

Transfer Thinking in Translation Studies

Playing with the Black Box of Cultural Transfer

Edited by
Maud Gonne, Klaartje Merrigan,
Reine Meylaerts & Heleen van Gerwen

LEUVEN UNIVERSITY PRESS

© 2020 by Leuven University Press / Presses Universitaires de Louvain / Universitaire Pers Leuven. Minderbroedersstraat 4, B-3000 Leuven (Belgium).

All rights reserved. Except in those cases expressly determined by law, no part of this publication may be multiplied, saved in an automated datafile or made public in any way whatsoever without the express prior written consent of the publishers.

ISBN 978 94 6270 263 9
e-ISBN 978 94 6166 372 6
D / 2020 / 1869 / 63
https://doi.org/10.11116/9789461663726
NUR: 610
Cover: Daniel Benneworth-Gray
Typesetting: Crius Group

This book is dedicated to Lieven D'hulst,
an enthusiastic colleague, passionate professor,
eminent researcher, and dear friend,
in honor of his unwavering commitment and
dedication to translation studies,
his mentorship and support of aspiring scholars,
and his contagious desire to transfer knowledge
and sympathy in Belgium and beyond.

Table of Contents

Introduction: Transfer thinking in translation studies: Playing with the black box of cultural transfer — 9
Maud Gonne & Reine Meylaerts

Reclaiming the past: Translations from the Anglo-Saxon for the twenty-first century — 33
Susan Bassnett

From Britain to Brussels and back again: On the transfer of national images and linguistic interactions in Charlotte Brontë's *The Professor* and its first Dutch and French translations — 49
Dirk Delabastita & Maud Gonne

The figure of the translator in two Francophone African classics — 79
Jean-Marc Moura

Short remarks about titles: Translation, transfer... and trade — 91
Yves Chevrel & Isabelle Nières-Chevrel

Transfer in news translation — 113
Christina Schäffner

Russian bears on the move, or how national images are transferred — 133
Pieter Boulogne & Luc van Doorslaer

Legal transfer and translation: The translation of legal and administrative texts in Flanders and Northern Italy during the French Revolution and the Napoleonic period — 157
Michael Schreiber

Language and translation policies in state-building processes: The case of Lithuania — 181
Dainora Maumevičienė, Ramunė Kasperavičienė & Yves Gambier

Transfer troubles 207
Andrew Chesterman

About the editors 225

About the authors 227

Index 233

Introduction

Transfer thinking in translation studies: Playing with the black box of cultural transfer

Maud Gonne & Reine Meylaerts

1. Opening up the field of translation studies: From translation to transfer to the 'tradosphere'

Since its emergence in the 1980s in the framework of Franco-German intercultural history (Espagne and Werner 1987), the notion of cultural transfer has spread, without any real terminological consensus, in different research fields of the humanities, including literary studies, cultural history, policy studies and translation studies (see e.g., Appadurai 1996, Saunier 2013). Used as a tool to study a large array of movements of texts, ideas, objects, people, knowledge, images, and so on, transfer seems to always induce a dynamic of *transformation* and mediation, and to account for a certain materiality that researchers can retrace from the past. In cultural history, for example, transfer is a means to unravel the historical vectors of cultural circulation, with a particular focus on the construction of cultural identities and asymmetrical power relationships. According to Michel Espagne, transfer refers to any passage of a cultural object from one context to another resulting in a transformation of its meaning (i.e., a dynamic of re-semanticization), which can only be fully recognized by taking into account the historical vectors of the passage (Espagne 2013, 1).

The notion of transfer made its way into the field of translation studies in the 1990s via polysystem theory (see e.g., Even-Zohar 2005), in which transfer appeared as a crucial aspect of a (cultural or literary) system's survival and maintenance, and covered a great variety of translation-like practices and forms. Even-Zohar defined transfer as a "process whereby imported goods are integrated into a home repertoire, and the consequences generated by this integration" (Even-Zohar 1997, 359). This is a target-oriented view: transfer is seen both as a state and a process, linked to the effect of integration on the transferred goods (**Chesterman**, 208). According to the Israeli scholar, translation (proper) is only one of several different types of movement that can be observed between and within (cultural, literary) systems. In 1990, he called upon translation studies scholars to move towards transfer theory:

> Our accumulated knowledge about translation indicates more and more that translational procedures between two systems (languages/literatures) are in principle analogous, even homologous, with transfers within the borders of the system. The hypothesis of analogy/ homology has been formulated before, notably by Jakobson (1959), but no consequences have ever been drawn for translation theory. Shall we go on ignoring this hypothesis or would it not be wiser to acknowledge the implicit practice whereby translation is discussed in terms of transfer and vice versa ? In other words, would it not be profitable to think and work explicitly rather than implicitly in terms of a transfer theory ? If so, where will inter-systemic translation be located, and with what consequences ? Sooner or later, I believe, it will turn out to be uneconomical to deal with transfer and translation separately. (Even-Zohar 1990b, 73)

Since then, the concept has been regularly used and adapted (i.e., transferred) in translation studies research, as "Even-Zohar's transfer theory is beneficial in that it places translation in a larger context and does not detach it from other related phenomena" (Weissbrod 2004, 38). Nevertheless, the idea was never to eliminate translation studies, but to recognize the particularities of translation in comparison with other similar practices and to "change our conception of the translated text in such a way that we may perhaps be liberated from certain postulated criteria" (Even-Zohar 1990b, 74).

Various other researchers explicitly responded to Even-Zohar's call (Weissbrod 2004; Göpferich 2007; Göpferich 2010; D'hulst 2012). Susanne Göpferich (Göpferich 2010, 374-377), in dialogue with the transdiscipline of *Transferwissenschaft* – a field of research investigating access to knowledge in the broadest sense of the term (see Wichter and Antos 2001) – redefined the concept of transfer as the transformation of texts and other media according to functionalist objectives, in other words, with the intention to obtain a target text or product that can fill specific functions in the target culture. In this framework, translation is seen "as a more constrained mode of transfer associated with equivalence or invariance requirements" (Göpferich 2010, 374).

As discussed by **Andrew Chesterman** in this volume, Lieven D'hulst (2012) took Even-Zohar's call an important step further by opening up the concept of transfer. He proposed a (re)location of translation history, from assumed translation to assumed transfer, as a "*tool* to identify and describe the forms, meanings and functions of a broad spectrum of exchange activities taking place both between and within cultures" that researchers should "assume" as transfers (D'hulst 2012, 150). The concept of 'assumed transfer' aims to do justice to the interaction and reciprocity of cultural exchanges (and the changes they induce), to take into account as many elements as possible (verbal or not) which characterize the processes of transfer, and to reflect the historical evolution of these practices. In other words, transfer is not unidirectional: "a transferred product may itself give way to another product using a different carrier, then back again" (D'hulst 2012, 140). Transfer covers a variety of associated modes of knowledge dissemination – including (self-) translation, adaptation, plagiarism, and so on – whose meaning changes over time, depending on and merging with adjacent concepts.

D'hulst also adds a crucial aspect, largely neglected in Even-Zohar's systemic approach, namely the mediating/transferring agents: "it [transfer] needs mediators or agents manipulating these products (translators, critics, historians, etc.)" (D'hulst 2012, 140). Mediators being (sometimes simultaneously) smugglers and customs officers, they entertain paradoxical relationships with borders, at the same time creating (see e.g., Pym 1998), enforcing (see e.g., Leerssen 2014) and surpassing them.

> The smugglers, as we understand them (...) promote exchanges and often create their own norms, circuits, channels and forms (...) The custom officer, however, occupied an existing position, wanting to fulfil the dominant norm and hindering exchanges. (Roig-Sanz and Meylaerts 2018, 3)

This specific implementation of the transfer concept is inspired by the development of the concept of 'entangled history' (Werner and Zimmermann 2006). Starting from the idea that the study of cultural transfer often presupposes the existence of homogenous and separate nations, even when the historical context problematizes this distinction, the concept of 'entangled history' has attempted to emphasize the reciprocity and crossover (but also the asymmetry) of cultural transfers, in other words, the impact of transfer on all entities involved and transformed in the transfer process (persons, practices or objects crossed over). Consequently, the entities or objects of research are not only considered in relation to each other, but also through each other, in terms of interactions and circulation.

By combining these different perspectives, transfer can become an umbrella concept, referring to the multidirectional and transformative process of exchange (verbal and non-verbal) between and within cultures, and requiring the presence of a mediator. However, one could object that if every cultural process is a transfer process, nothing is transfer anymore. It is important to stress in this respect that this enlargement does not mean that everything is transfer, but that a great many things have a transfer *dimension* and can be better understood through this transfer dimension. Moreover, many empirical studies on mediators, or institutional networks, have demonstrated the operationality of the concept of transfer (see e.g., Béghin and Roland 2014; Gonne 2017; Meylaerts et al. 2018; Meylaerts 2020) to describe the complex circulation of cultural goods and texts or literary models across national, linguistic and cultural borders, and in particular, to apprehend processes of cultural/national identity building. In sum, transfer has played, and still plays, an important role in opening up the field of translation studies.

The evolution of the field indeed continues, and transfer is one of the driving forces in this evolution (see below). In this respect, translation studies has experienced some challenging times lately. The need to further broaden the scope of the discipline has been extensively debated among translation studies scholars. This is particularly well illustrated by the scientific orientation of recent translation studies' international congresses, which envisioned translation as a life process, inexorably connected with ecological and development concerns, such as the 2019 EST "Living Translation: process, product, people" conference and the 2021 IATIS "Cultural ecology of Translation" conference. It also transpires through the appointment of a sign-language interpreting scholar (Jemina Napier) as CETRA chair professor in 2019. Observers can easily glimpse translation studies entering into a new interdisciplinary and societal dialogue.

As a response to the proliferation of multimodal and hyper-objects, massively distributed in time and space, new trends in translation studies aim to redefine the specificity of translation as a complex and unpredictable process (rather than as a product), connecting much more than texts (linguistic bias), and overtaking the binaries (source-target) that have traditionally delimited the field of study. From an ecotranslational (Cronin 2017) or biosemiotics (Marais 2019) point of view, translation becomes an all-encompassing concept to think the interconnectedness of all human and non-human activities, and to apprehend the emergence of social-cultural phenomena. In fact, "once you decide that translation is a process rather than a product, you can find evidence of that process virtually everywhere" (Pym 2014, 146). Therefore, Michael Cronin uses the term 'tradosphere' to refer to all translation systems on the planet; all the ways in which information circulates between living and non-living organisms and is translated into a language or a code that can be processed or understood by the receiving entity (Cronin 2017, 71).

While these new translation studies' approaches give testimony to a significant change in paradigm, they have, nonetheless, been criticized for two reasons. First of all, and echoing the previously mentioned critique on transfer: if everything is translation, nothing is translation any more. This is precisely what **Chesterman** (219) refers to: "if one can see anything as translation or the result of translation – parks, churches, government organizations etc. – does the concept retain any meaning? Does metaphorization have no limits?" Here again, however, and as Cronin argues in his review of Marais' *(Bio)Semiotic theory of translation* (2019) (Cronin 2020): not everything *is* a translation, but a great many things have a translational *dimension* and can be better understood if this dimension is taken into account. This should be taken into consideration by translation studies if the discipline wants to stay relevant in the twenty-first century digital age, characterized by an exponential growth of multimodal and hyper-objects, thus dethroning the (literary) text as the primary product of translation. Secondly, these new translation studies approaches are also criticized for their limited operational and explanatory power. However, these approaches must be taken for what they are: a "meta-theory or a philosophy of translation, which should be able to explain any particular approach to translation, whether more narrowly linguistic or whether broadly sociological/ideological, whether focused on one mode or medium or whether multimodal or multimedial, whether the interest is more neo-structural or whether the interest is ideological, critical or ideational" (Marais 2019, 178). They do not pretend to offer ready-made methods to explore the translation worlds they are opening. Rather, it is the opening itself that is important for translation studies to remain relevant in the twenty-first century.

The umbrella term 'transfer', as discussed above, can also be seen as an attempt to unite various (intersemiotic, intralingual, interlingual) translational practices under one single interdisciplinary methodological framework in order to better embrace the complexity of (inter)cultural processes. In view of its alleged vagueness, the notion of transfer has struggled to claim its place in translation studies. Furthermore, the poor metaphorical potential of the term (see **Chesterman** in this volume) has prevented scholars from making extensive use of it alongside other correlated notions such as transculturation, cultural translation, mediation, transediting, etc. Moreover, the traditional use of the expression 'linguistic transfer' to indicate the invariant displacement of semantic and/or formal content, persists. Still, its successful development in neighboring historical subdisciplines (see e.g., Middell 2014, Roig-Sanz and Meylaerts 2018), where it is used to study how cultural practices can overcome traditional geographic and linguistic barriers, has invited further interdisciplinary dialogue, notably with translation history (D'hulst 2012). As a result, the notion of transfer in a narrow (linguistic) sense has been opened up toward the socio-cultural settings in which translation (as a process that never stands on its own) is performed and translations (as products) function (see **Schäffner**, 113-114).

In a time of paradigm shifts, this book aims to explore the potential and interdisciplinary power of transfer as a concept and an analytical tool to travel in the 'tradosphere', that is to say, to overcome the binary tensions of the discipline, and to account for complex, non-linear (see also below) and transmedial cultural dynamics, and for the interconnectedness of different discursive and institutional practices, including translation. It constitutes an important challenge and opportunity for a translation studies field in mutation to (re-)define its scope across a variety of modes of signification.

2. A tool to play with the black box of cultural processes

The contributions in *Transfer thinking* display a variety of research angles (literary studies, imagology, translation studies, translator studies, periodical studies, postcolonialism ...) and study a variety of non-linear and entangled, transfer processes, which cross linguistic and cultural boundaries and cannot be reduced to simple movements from a source to a target (culture, text). **Chesterman** critically discusses the metaphorical definition of translation as transfer and its hidden assumption of movement. He states that "in translation there is also a sense in which texts do *not* move – a literal sense, moreover. (...) a text in culture A that is translated into culture B is not, after this process, by definition absent from culture A" (210). This is why he considers the assumption of movement to be often misleading.

The transfer processes studied in this volume apply to different objects and aspects, ranging from literary texts (**Delabastita and Gonne, Bassnett, Moura**), legal texts (**Schreiber**), news (**Schäffner**), images (**Boulogne and van Doorslaer**) and identities (**Maumeviciene, Kasperaviciene and Gambier**); to ideologies (**Schreiber**), power asymmetries (**Moura**), titles (**Chevrel and Nières-Chevrel**) and heterolingualisms (**Delabastita and Gonne**). By embracing a process-oriented way of thinking, all these contributions aim to open the 'black box' of transfer in the widest sense. For Edgar Morin (Morin 2005, 49), the traditional scientific paradigm (also called 'the paradigm of simplicity') consists in considering the inputs and outputs of a system, without entering into the mystery of the black box; that is, without having access to (or omitting to consider) the internal functioning of the system. However, according to the French mathematician and philosopher René Thom (1980, 303), all the major technical and scientific achievements of humanity consist of unveiled black boxes, and the only conceivable way of unlocking a black box is to play with it. For our purpose, the black box consists of a transfer space, a space where elements interact, transform and combine to offer complex, hybrid objects that we consume and study as culture.

Every chapter in this book 'plays' with this black box in a different way, attempting to unravel or reveal the complex processes underlying cultural objects by retracing (sometimes genetically) the historical factors and power struggles behind transfers, as well as the intertwinement of multilayered (discursive) practices which constrain the circulation of culture in (more or less recent) history.

3. Non-linearity and entanglements

Traditionally, translation studies links translation to, at least, the existence of one specific source text, and the transfer of (some elements of) the source text into a target text, the translation. While this kind of conceptualization has the advantage of being simple and straightforward, it often leads to an oversimplification of what translation as a product, and transfer as a process, really entails. As has been discussed above, new trends in translation studies aim to redefine translation as a complex, multidirectional and partly unpredictable transfer process (rather than as a product), connecting much more than texts and overtaking the binaries of 'source' versus 'target'. However, multidirectional transfer relationships are difficult to reconstruct: they vary in shape and content, and keep a loose bond with their source (D'hulst 2018, 241). Still, they offer a much more profound understanding of cultural exchange in all its manifestations. Transfers can thus be described as (historical) processes from which the final state cannot be deduced: they change in quality and direction, run continuously or discontinuously, accelerate, end abruptly, gradually die off or last forever (Eisenberg 2005, 100).

The contributions in this volume are, each in their own way, illustrations of this broad conceptualization of transfer. While studying the emergence of Anglo-Saxon as an area of study, both academic and popular, in the nineteenth century and its maintenance thanks to a renewed interest in Old Norse and the Vikings in popular series such as *Game of Thrones*, **Susan Bassnett** discovers "centuries of transcribing, editing, commentary, and other forms of rewriting [that] call into question our understanding of the 'original'" (**Bassnett**, 40). Working with transfer as an analytical tool indeed forces researchers to go beyond simplistic source-target thinking. This is not to say that we should forget about them altogether – transfers do need source and target poles (D'hulst 2012) – but, as Marais (2014, 17) argues, merely untangling source from target does not allow us to better understand the complex nature of phenomena anchored in languages, literatures, cultures, and societies. Source and target are both needed and relate to one another in often surprising ways.

In a similar fashion, the bilingual (French-Dutch and French-Italian) legal texts that form the corpus of **Michael Schreiber**'s contribution on the translation of legal and administrative texts in Flanders and Northern Italy during the French Revolution and the Napoleonic Period, illustrate the analytic need to overcome straightforward distinctions between 'source' and 'target' texts. In Schreiber's case study, 'source' and 'target' appear together in one and the same legal publication wherein the target text functions as a support for the reader to gradually improve his/her knowledge of the source language, which, in turn, would eventually make the target language, and thus the translation, superfluous. This strategy served the language policy of imposing French as the national language in the annexed territories during the period under study. Moreover, on a microstructural level, the textual and syntactic structure of the source text is maintained in the target text, blurring once again the distinction between 'source' and 'target'. In more general terms, the 'source' is present in the 'target'; every translation contains non-translated elements.

This is also particularly well illustrated by the contribution of **Dirk Delabastita and Maud Gonne** that discusses the transfer of cultural representations and linguistic interactions staged by Charlotte Brontë in her novel *The Professor* (1857) and its 'back'transfers as evidenced by the first French (1858) and Dutch (1859) translations. The entangled story of *The Professor* – a young Englishman who leaves Great Britain to work as a teacher in Belgium, where he finds professional and romantic happiness before returning to England – takes shape in a novel that displays a great amount of French heterolingualisms and (stereotyped) images of the continentals, in particular the French and (both Flemish- and French-speaking) Belgians. Belgium, which finds itself at the crossroads of nations and languages, turns out to be an ideal site for intercultural mediations and transfers, which become instrumental in defining what it means to be 'English'. Because multidirectional transfers are already at play in an unstable source text that blends French and English, the 'back' translation generates an inextricable ambiguity that can only be "grasped in a wider historical context of international interactions, and onto which a set of cultural images and axiological oppositions are grafted" (**Delabastita and Gonne**, 75).

Back transfers are even more directly at work in the contribution of **Yves Chevrel and Isabelle Nières-Chevrel**, which explores how translations of titles reflect back on the original titles. This is the case for the American bestseller *From the Tablets of Sumer: Twenty-Five Firsts in Man's Recorded History* by Samuel Noah Kramer, published in 1956. The following year, Arthaud published an edition with a more concise title, *L'Histoire commence à Sumer*, which was translated into German as *Die Geschichte beginnt mit Sumer* (1979), and into Spanish as *La historia empieza en Sumer* (1985), before it finally made its way back into English, three decades later, as *History Begins at Sumer: Thirty-Nine Firsts in Recorded History* (1988). Through the analysis of title translations in a wide variety of languages and (literary) genres, this article shows the vast potential of the little discipline of *titrologie* to rethink traditional conceptions of transfer and translation.

Complex entanglements in the circulation of cultural products are also evident in **Pieter Boulogne and Luc van Doorslaer**'s travel in the footsteps of the 'Russian bear', used here as an auto- and hetero-image of Russia. The association of Russia with a bear is not the result of a linear transfer process, but is based on various back and forth transfer processes between Russia and the West, which, in turn, reflect the evolution of a complex geopolitical context. The transnational circulation of the Russian bear via European (mainly English) press was a form of mockery of the Russo-French coalition during the Napoleon wars, a form of criticism during the Crimean war, and promoted fear under communist Russia. Nowadays, the image of the hibernating bear prevails. The softer, national, auto-image of the strong bear did not develop independently but in dialogue with the hetero-image. From this confrontation emerged an entangled dialogue between Russia and the West, which remains relevant to apprehend international configurations today.

Past transfers are not the only ones that are difficult to reconstruct. As **Christina Schäffner** shows, research in news translation is also faced with the challenge that traditional labels of 'source text' and 'target text' hardly ever apply. Journalists continually translate, copy and adapt from various (international) delocalized sources, making it impossible to establish clear relationships between texts. Moreover, non-linearity induces unpredictable output (see also below). Effects are not proportional to their causes: they can be bigger or smaller than expected. This is illustrated by the genetic reconstruction of the quote "you can stick your corpses up your arse", supposedly said by Peter Handke. What appears to have been a wrong quote, was transferred across different languages and target audiences, thus creating a reality and transfer process of its own: "adapting texts to suit the target audience and/or the ideological position of the newspaper can result in an altered point of view and a different conceptualization of social reality for the target readers" (**Schäffner**, 120).

4. Transmediality and chains of interconnected transfer techniques

Translation studies has traditionally focussed on interlingual translation, at the expense of intra- and intersemiotic translational relationships. Written material has been privileged over oral production. Besides, "the imbalance between research on literary translation or general printed translation and research on other types of interlinguistic transfer (e.g., interpreting, specialized or multimodal translation) persists and is probably even more acute in the subfield of translation history" (Buzelin 2018, 344). However, translation (proper) never stands on its own and cannot always be distinguished from related practices: "it is hardly feasible to mark clear boundaries between translating and other writing activities: to start with, the very act of translating includes forms of non-translating (borrowing, adaptation, rewriting, etc.)" (D'hulst 2014, 1261). Research into different types of translation, into a variety of genres, and into different contexts and settings has led to a rethinking of traditional concepts (**Schäffner**, 114).

When reconstructing complex transfer chains, transfer techniques and media overlap and alternate constantly: borrowing, copying, adapting, rewriting, (self-)translating, proofreading, plagiarizing, multilingual writing (see Genette 1982). We can also add transmedial or intersemiotic adaptation, rewriting, reinterpreting, re-semanticization, and so on. As an umbrella concept, transfer should be able to account for the variety of modalities and the interconnectedness of the different techniques through which information, knowledge and ideas flow, be they verbal or not, written or oral.

Transmedial re-semanticization and reinterpretation processes accompanied the circulation of the image of the Russian bear, from written material in the west (Gottfried Leibniz, Francesco Algarotti and William Shakespeare used the bear to refer to Russia) to Russian folk tales (**Boulogne and van Doorslaer**). Old English poetry such as *Beowulf*, originating in the oral Germanic tradition, was composed in various dialects and underwent a process of intralingual translation by generations of anonymous scribes before being retranslated, adapted, reinterpreted and manipulated into modern English, and becoming a source of inspiration for fantasy literature, cinema and TV series (**Bassnett**). In the case of news translation (**Schäffner**), the term 'transediting' (Stetting 1989) covers the collaborative work of people assuming different roles and engaging in language transfer, cultural adaptation, proofreading, revising, naturalizing, editing and other textual processes that are carried out repeatedly and cyclically (Kang 2007, 238).

Transmediality is also widespread in children's literature, and in fields largely determined by and dedicated to the market and economic profit. Taking the example of the proliferation of titles in mass culture, **Chevrel and Nières-Chevrel** describe the transfer chain, directed by Walt Disney Studios, of *Winnie-the-Pooh* in France between 1966 and 1974: three medium-length films, based on two childhood classics by the English writer Alan Alexander Milne, resulting in the publication of six new book titles:

> The children's market is riddled with works adapted into films that are themselves, in return, readapted into books. Titles thereby end up designating only one of the many possible variants of the same commodity. The economic value of titles in children's publishing is all the greater because, in the minds of parents and children, names of collections or series end up supplanting the name of the author, who is sometimes forgotten, and more often just ignored. (**Chevrel and Nières-Chevrel**, 106)

When reconstructing transfer chains, scholars are often confronted with oral, non-literate production and performances. Yet, there is a persistent lack of attention for orality that is mainly due to the literacy bias of modernity, which privileges writing over orality (see e.g., Bandia 2011). **Jean-Marc Moura** addresses this issue in his study of two Francophone African novels, *L'étrange Destin de Wangrin* by Ahmadou Hampâté Bâ and *Une vie de Boy* by Ferdinand Oyono, which both include a representation of an interpreter in a colonial context. Moura's case study is located at the interface between orality and writing and illustrates the idea of a double transposition process which involves, on the one hand, translating oral narrative cultures into written form and, on the other hand, translation between distant cultures (Bandia 2010, 265). The difficult passage from oral expression to writing, in a historical process of asymmetrical colonial powers, is textualized and problematized amongst others through the use – for Bâ – and the non-use (non-transfer) – for Oyono – of transfer techniques such as glossaries of African words and expressions.

The role of orality and transmediality cannot be overestimated in court interpreting and theater and opera translation, two important domains in state-building processes in Lithuania (see **Dainora Maumeviciene, Ramune Kasperaviciene and Yves Gambier**). While in the 1930s Lithuanian was decreed the official language in Lithuanian courts, the rights of non-Lithuanian speakers were nonetheless preserved through the use of court interpreters. If not only speech, but also facial expressions, gestures and other types of body language become a part of the message (and thus of its transfer) during court trials, similar types of multimodality are at play in theater and opera translation as well, where meaning is conveyed through the interplay of light and movement, gestures, expressions, body language, sound and music, speech and surtitles. Every opera or piece of theater is a multisemiotic message, in which image, sound and speech interact in a dynamic way to convey meaning. It is this interaction that makes them powerful elements in the construction of cultures and societies.

By considering not only Jakobson's three types of translation, but also transmedial processes and chains of interconnected transfer practices, the contributions in this book allow us to better comprehend the complexity of cultural transfer processes and gain access to the often hidden parts of the black box of cultural transfer through which our cultural products are shaped and acquire meaning.

5. From translators to mediators

Gaining access to this black box also requires us to take into account the agent of transfer, in particular the figure of the translator. Since the 1980s, translation studies has opened up this concept and has focused on the translator as a mediator between two cultures or texts (see Katan 2013). It was Taft who coined the expression 'cultural mediator' to refer to a "person who facilitates communication, understanding, and action between persons or groups who differ with respect to language and culture" (Taft 1981, 53). In the context of refugees, asylum seekers, health care and other public services, Katan proposes the concept of 'intercultural mediator' for people who "translate, interpret and do whatever else is necessary to reduce the linguistic, cultural and institutional barriers in favour of their client" (Katan 2013, 90). A similar plurality of roles and contexts characterizes the agents of cultural transfer and their role in complex transfer processes, for which we propose to use the very same concept of '(inter)cultural mediator'. This mediator category includes many more features than merely the translating one:

> The concept of cultural mediator refers to strikingly flexible and multi-functional actors who negotiated their way – sometimes pragmatically, sometimes with financial and/or ideological motives, sometimes quite unconsciously – between different cultures and language groups. They often simultaneously assumed different roles, combining activities as editors, art dealers, writers of chronicles, (self-)translators, multilingual writers, art and literary critics and playwrights, and they transferred a

variety of cultural objects, for example via exhibitions, translations, musical performances, artistic and literary chronicles or essays. They did this using a plethora of interrelated discursive transfer techniques (translation, adaptation, plagiarism, summary, censorship, etc.) and, by doing so, they manipulated in many ways cultural products within or between nations or regions. (Gonne and Lobbes 2014, 1249)

More often than not, translation is thus just one part of a mediator's activities and in some cases it may even be entirely absent. Once again, if translation studies wants to open itself up and access the black box of cultural transfer, it needs to go beyond reductive conceptualizations of transfer agents. In the case of literary translation, "[w]e all know that authors may interact with the translators of their work, that authors may write about translators and vice versa or that translators may turn into authors. We also know that authors may be(come) self-translators or write in two languages. And we know how dynamic the relations are between writing and translating in the world of multimedia" (D'hulst 2014, 1262). The contributions in this volume give ample evidence of these plural roles. It is well-known, for example, that Ezra Pound was a poet, critic, translator and publisher, and that these activities interacted with one another in dynamic ways. The "Old English scholar and translator Michael Alexander" described Pound as a genius and dedicated "his own collection of translations of Old English poetry, entitled *The Wanderer: Elegies, Epics, Riddles. Poems from England's Ancient Origins*" (**Bassnett**, 41) to him. Also, when writing *The Professor*, Charlotte Brontë acted both as an English author, and a French translator via the numerous heterolingual components present in the novel. Both activities, however, are an integral part of the same process and literary purpose (**Delabastita and Gonne**). Similar interactions and overlaps can be observed in other cultural processes and non-literary contexts. In **Chevrel and Nières-Chevrel's** contribution, the titles of translated books, both in the field of literature and in other domains, are the result of a complex translation process in which translator, publisher and author roles constantly interact and overlap. The intricate relation between translatorship and authorship has even been enshrined in French law, where "under the current French Intellectual Property Code, a translator is also considered an author". Moreover, the authors raise an interesting question: "in the case of a new original translation, is a new translator then allowed to use the title of an earlier translation?" (**Chevrel and Nières-Chevrel**, 94) As shown by **Schäffner**, news production is guided by professional standards and ethics, such as production speed, readability of the texts, and factual accuracy. Journalists act as intercultural mediators: translating, summarizing, paraphrasing, interpreting, and so on, without considering their work as such. This plurality of roles can easily span fields that tend to be seen as very distant from each other. For example, in each of the 21 ruling governments during the independence period in Lithuania (1918-1940), there was at least one minister who was also a translator, and engaged in other transfer roles and political fields of expertise (**Maumeviciene, Kasperaviciene and Gambier**). Further back in history, then, **Schreiber** reveals that translations of regional decrees in Flanders and Northern Italy during the French Revolution and the Napoleonic Period were published by "administrative employees, not by full-time translators" since there were "no official translation offices" at the regional level (163).

In other words, the different chapters in this book illustrate, each in their own way, that it makes little sense to isolate the translator category, in other words to split up the agents' activities in separate parts, according to scholarly or disciplinary boundaries and viewpoints. On the contrary, it is precisely the combination of each mediator's actions and roles that constitutes its specificity, more so than the sum of all these activities taken separately. As such, the various chapters show the potential of the mediator concept to play with the black box of transfer and to help us understand the complexity of cultural transfer. A mediator plays a kind of macro-role, becomes an attraction pole, which is built out of more than the sum of his or her separate roles and activities. At the same time, each individual role or activity cannot be fused or confused with the whole (see also below). The interactions between the different roles are crucial to understand both the mediator who performs a 'macro-role', as well as different subroles.

One of the consequences of this combination and interaction of roles is that, contrary to any preconceived image we may have of mediators, they do not occupy a perfect inbetween or third space. They are not a finite and separate entity acting between target and source cultures; rather, they are part of both the so-called 'target', and the 'source'. Moreover, mediators do not invalidate the boundaries they transgress. Instead, they make use of, shift, specify and define these lines. This is, for instance, the case in the French translation of *The Professor*: the translator, Henriette Loreau, though acting as a mediator of Brontë's fiction for French readers, domesticates the original heterolingual dialogue. She dissolves all of Brontë's heterolingual French into an "homogeneously, seamlessly and elegant" target-language text (**Delabastita and Gonne**, 69). That is to say, the boundaries between source and target texts and cultures are simultaneously reinforced and weakened. The reinforcement is the result of a domestication strategy, whereas the weakening results from the sheer act of mediation, and from the fact that the French dialogues are transposed as such in translation. The latter is a good illustration of the fact that every translation also contains elements of non-translation and that the 'source' (text) is a part of the 'target' (text). We do not need to resolve or choose between these binary oppositions, but rather analyze and conceive the complex interrelationships between them. 'Source' and 'target' both constitute the reality of translation and, from a complexity perspective, are related to one another 'at the edge of chaos': the creative space or moment where new meanings are created, boundaries are tested and conceptualisations are questioned (see e.g., Marais 2014).

Sometimes, multifaceted mediators are the subject of fictionalization, which is the case for Crimsworth, the professor in Brontë's book, who is typically represented as both a conciliatory mediator (e.g., between antagonist characters) and a prejudice maker, despising continental values (**Delabastita and Gonne**, 61). In *L'étrange Destin de Wangrin* and *Une vie de Boy* as well, the mediating characters not only act as translators, but also form a bridge between two cultures, thus trying to connect Europeans and natives. Wangrin is not only an interpreter, he is also a rich tradesman who is able to deal with French colonizers as well as his own people. In the end, however, he forgets his native customs, sinks into alcoholism and dies miserably (**Moura**, 81).

According to the multipolar model for studying cultural mediators (D'hulst et al. 2014), subject poles that cluster combinations of attributes (such as teacher, translator and interpreter in Crimsworth's case, or interpreter and tradesman in Wangrin's case), are linked to activity poles corresponding to institutional or discursive transfer actions, such as translating, teaching, writing, interpreting, which dialectically interact with each other and also interact within larger cultural and institutional poles (such as the Franco-British opposition or the colonizer-colonizing opposition). The combination of activities may change their mutual properties and the relationships between them may vary through time.

Shifting focus from the translator towards the mediator does not mean that we should not study the specificity of the translator role, but that we have to consider it in relationship to other roles that form a whole, which helps us better understand the larger transfer processes between and within cultures, the overall purpose of these processes, and the historical evolution of these combinations.

6. Emergence and transformation

Transfer induces transformations (Espagne and Werner 1987; Even-Zohar 1990b; Espagne 2013). According to **Chesterman,** however, transfer, such as translation, corresponds more to an additive than a transformational equation. Indeed, when transferred, the source text (or object) does not disappear into a new form: "alongside (not instead of) one text, another is created that is relevantly similar to the first one" (**Chesterman**, 212). Therefore, he prefers to think of this process in terms of a memetic metaphor. This does not prevent us from observing that what connects these products (texts or objects) has a reinterpretative, re-semanticizational and transformative character, and that new meaning emerges from these connections, for both the source and target texts or objects. In sum, as examples from the various chapters in this book illustrate, since transfer can be defined as an emergent phenomenon, both the transformational and additive equation are part of transfer.

The notion of emergence refers to the process through which a system or organization emerges out of the interaction of its parts. In this system or organization the whole is typically more than the sum of its parts, but at the same time each separate part cannot be fused or confused with the whole. The *product* of transfer can be conceptualized as an emergent phenomenon, resulting from the interaction between its parts (the words in a translated text, or the verbal, visual and auditive images in a film, etc.) and creating something new which, at the same time, is similar to its source. Emergence is also crucial to understand the *process* of transfer, which is characterized by non-linear change or non-linear causality. This means that similar changes need not lead to similar results, and that small changes may lead to major consequences, whereas major interventions may have minor consequences for the resulting product. In other words, the same transfer strategies can have very different effects (or vice versa: very different transfer strategies can have the same effect), according to the situation and context. As a result, the consequences of cultural transfer are highly unpredictable because every transfer process produces both changes and invariabilities between the source and target text or object, which interact upon each other and with their context in complex ways. Traditionally, mainly the changes have been conceptualized, at the expense of the invariabilities and the interactions between both. Transfer "makes use of specific procedures or techniques to impose formal (…), semantic (…) and functional changes (…) on the transferred products" (D'hulst 2012, 140). This is what **Chesterman** refers to as the "inevitability of change", the "obligatory and optional shifts, the effect of agency, a change of skopos (purpose), and much else" (211).

The contributions in this volume illustrate transfer as an emergent process and product. **Moura,** for example, reveals that "[b]ecause of the specificities of the colonial and social histories of Belgium and the Netherlands, the same Dutch translation (*De huisjongen*) inevitably evoked different associations among Flemish and Dutch readers" (86). Formal and functional changes are very visible in **Chevrel and Nières-Chevrel**'s contribution. Titles serve a conative function since they have to constantly seduce a new public, and they undergo deletion, reduction or elucidation procedures precisely to maintain this conative function. Their meaning can also change through the use of different cover illustrations for the same title, resulting in a different appropriation by successive generations of readers. But not surprisingly, "the most straightforward solution to introduce a translated book" is simply by "taking over the original title. *Manhattan Transfer* (Dos Passos), *Berlin Alexanderplatz* (Döblin), *Peterburg* (Belyi), also transcribed as Petersburg or Pétersbourg, are urban places easily identifiable, which, in turn, have become familiar places, in part because of these titles". Also, a literal translation of a title such as *Le Rouge et le Noir* "does not prevent the fact that questions are persistently raised about the meaning of the title" (**Chevrel and Nières-Chevrel**, 98).

With the metaphor of the 'intelligent builder', **Bassnett** reminds us that selection is entirely part of the transfer process. She considers the chain of intralingual translations of literature written in Old English (or Anglo-Saxon) into modern English as a form of (re)interpretation. In one of her case studies, she analyzes the mysterious and enigmatic ending of *Wulf and Eadwacer* by comparing various new translations. In a women-centered translation of this dramatic monologue, Jane Holland (2008) and Jane Draycott (2010) made semantic changes: a "transgressive translation" for twenty-first century readers but "mindful of the conventions of Old English poetry" and echoing elements of that prosody at the same time (45). Importantly, however, Bassnett rightfully concludes that "every translation is a re-imagining of a poem, and every reading of a poem is itself an act of translation." Moreover, "as no individual reader remains the same, each reading becomes a different – not merely another – reading. The same poem cannot be read twice" (45). Or, as we indicated earlier, many things (e.g., reading) have a translational dimension.

An interplay of semantic, functional and formal changes and invariabilities is also observable in the circulation of the Russian bear image. The foreign national image of the Russian bear has been taken over from the West "but only after an adaptation process, in accordance with national interests and under the influence of the existing, more admirative images of bears" (**Boulogne and van Doorslaer**, 151). Alongside its muzzled and aggressive hetero-image, the bear grew into a positive and reliable image: the sweet friend of Masha in a Russian children animation that spread all over the world. As illustrated by the spread of the Russian bear, transfer is a crucial element in the construction and emergence of identities. As mentioned earlier, transfer serves the maintenance and survival of cultural systems, especially when a polysystem has not yet been crystallized, when a literature is either "peripheral" or "weak" and when there are turning points or (literary) vacuums (Even-Zohar 1990a,

48): survival through evolution, maintenance through change – these are complex paradoxes that should be analyzed and understood, not resolved. On a more systemic level, **Maumeviciene, Kasperaviciene and Gambier** see translation and transfer policy (i.e., the import of 'foreign' elements) as a crucial element for nation-building and Lithuanian identity-(re)presentation processes. In Lithuania, theater and opera translations were suitable forms of resistance against Soviet ideology and communism:

> During the period of the independent Republic of Lithuania, many performances and librettos were translated into Lithuanian. However, in annexed Lithuania, many art directors wisely staged performances and plays with metaphorically hidden Soviet-ideology criticism and used translations of scenarios to twist and manipulate the meaning and the message they aimed to deliver to the audience. However, many such performances were banned and art directors had to leave Lithuania due to their persecution. (**Maumeviciene, Kasperaviciene and Gambier**, 196).

Similarly, in his study of the translation of legal documents in the Southern Netherlands and Italy during the Napoleonic period, **Schreiber** observes that translations retained legal structures that did not exist in the target cultures. The Southern Netherlands and Italy were among the countries to adopt the *phrase unique* structure for several legal text types, in provenance from the Code Napoléon. In this case, transfer implied invariability and change and with it, a long-lasting French political and ideological influence. This is not always the case. As **Delabastita and Gonne** show, the back-transfer in Dutch and French of *The Professor* triggered less functional and semantic changes than expected. It barely altered the axiological oppositions present in the source text. But at the same time, Brontë's work was notoriously unsuccessful. In other words, few changes can have major consequences.

Finally, transfer is a transformational process that maintains a complex relationship with the emergence of borders. Transformation implies that the new context is different enough to impose a change. The bigger the transformation, the greater the border. Are boundaries prior to transfers? This is what **Schäffner** stresses in her chapter on news translation: "journalists do perform mediation activities which cross linguistic and cultural boundaries" (117). Or do transfer techniques show us where boundaries are emerging, are being redrawn or reinforced? Transfer might indeed also create boundaries (Pym 1998, 93), for example, by erasing multilingual dialogue (**Delabastita and Gonne**).

7. Limits and promises for translation studies

All the contributions in this volume contribute to 'thinking' transfer; some even question if translation can be seen as a form of transfer (**Chesterman**). The various chapters play with the black box of transfer to reconstruct parts of (past and present) complex dynamics of cultural emergence. By doing so, they contribute to the opening of the translation studies field towards a greater consciousness of its interdisciplinary and conceptual power. However, transfer as a concept and a tool does not escape criticism (see D'hulst 2018). The hidden assumption of invariance (illustrated by the transfer of a football player by **Chesterman**, 210) and the implicit acceptance of transfer as a unilateral movement between an active target culture and a passive source culture contradict the idea of entanglements, where dynamic cultures interact in many different directions.

The transfer metaphor, indeed, seems to imply a displacement rather than a transformation and a duplication. It is true that in Economics, for instance, transfer refers to a one-way payment to an entity (person or organization). In Psychology, transference (*transfert* in French) is the unidirectional process of projecting one's feelings onto someone else. In times of COVID-19, medical transfer implies cooperation across borders in order to move patients from one hospital to a less overwhelmed one. But even in these contexts, can we really assume that these transferred entities do not leave anything at their starting point, and that they are not transformed by their journey to another destination? Let's take the football player example again. We could suggest that, besides a lot of money, the football player did not only leave an empty position behind, but also some expertise and prestige in the club (s)he departed from. And even if the receiving club expects the transferred player to preserve the same (or better) skills as (s)he displayed in the previous team, this cannot guarantee that the change of (sportive, cultural, linguistic, familiar) environment will not (immediately) alter the player's psychological state and football proficiency. In a later phase, Chesterman indeed recognizes that the environment of the new club will have an effect on the new player, "so the assumption of invariance is not completely maintained" (**Chesterman**, 216).

Another problematic aspect of transfer thinking is the difficulty to reconstruct transfer processes that are only partly observable (cf., the black box). Moreover, transfer seems to be judged only a posteriori. What is then the degree of integration and the required time interval, before we can call an imported item a transfer (**Chesterman**, 208)? While it is important to recognize the challenges in reconstructing transfer processes and to refrain from simplifications and quick conclusions, the various chapters in this volume testify to the importance of comparison as an analytical tool. A nuanced comparison of (chains of) products remains an important analytical part of the study of transfer processes.

Transfer as a tool and concept is also full of promises for a translation studies field in mutation, generating more powerful generalizations (**Chesterman**) as well as more accurate descriptions, amongst others, by overcoming source-target (**Delabastita and Gonne**), written-oral (**Moura**) and verbal-nonverbal biases (**Boulogne and van Doorslaer**). It allows us to reconstruct (even if only partly) how complex relationships (from past and present) take root and how they produce "something new which changes tradition, the new constellation, the consequences and side-effects of the meeting between cultures, the dynamics of development and the feedback effects" (Eisenberg 2005, 99-100). The transfer metaphor opens new research perspectives towards the emergence of hitherto unseen phenomena that rethink, in a refreshing way, the complex articulation of the singular and the universal.

Finally, the twenty-first-century digital revolution urges us to rethink translation studies in terms of process rather than in terms of product. In the digital world, objects are constantly copied, changed, translated and moved around in an unpredictable dynamic in which source and target distinctions appear to be illusory. Through a continuous process of refreshing and updating, sources are more fragile and unstable than ever. Reflections on the sustainability of access to (digital) knowledge, in a context of rapid technological innovations, should include transfer thinking, since the programming techniques of encoding, decoding and recoding are nothing else than transfer processes, dependent on the many decisions made by a large group of (mediating) agents. A good understanding of the processes of transmedial selection, transformation, reinterpretation and recontextualization is more than ever needed to allow the dissemination of knowledge and to make sense of the world we live in. For a field entering a new age, translation studies will have to think flexibly, in order to think transfer.

References

Appadurai, Arjun. 1996. *Modernity at Large: Cultural Dimensions of Globalization*. Minneapolis: University of Minnesota.

Bandia, Paul. 2011. "Orality and translation." In *Handbook of Translation Studies*, edited by Yves Gambier and Luc van Doorslaer, 108-112. Amsterdam: John Benjamins.

Béghin, Laurent, and Hubert Roland, eds. 2014. *Médiation, traduction et transferts en Belgique francophone. Textyles* 45.

Buzelin, Hélène. 2018. "Sociological models and translation history." In *A History of Modern Translation Knowledge*, edited by Lieven D'hulst and Yves Gambier, 337-346. Amsterdam: John Benjamins.

Charle, Christophe. 2010. "Comparaisons et transferts en histoire culturelle de l'Europe. Quelques réflexions à propos de recherches récentes." *Les cahiers Irice* 5 (1): 51-73.

Cronin, Michael. 2017. *Eco-translation: translation and ecology in the age of the anthropocene*. Abingdon: Routledge.

— 2020. "Review Of A (Bio)Semiotic Theory of Translation: The Emergence of Socio-Cultural Reality." *Translation Studies*. doi: 10.1080/14781700.2020.1719539.

D'hulst, Lieven. 2012. "(Re)Locating Translation History: From Assumed Translation to Assumed Transfer." *Translation Studies* 5 (2): 139-155.

— 2018. "Transfer Modes." In *A History of Modern Translation Knowledge*, edited by Lieven D'hulst and Yves Gambier, 135-142. Amsterdam: John Benjamins.

D'hulst, Lieven, Maud Gonne, Tessa Lobbes, Reine Meylaerts, and Tom Verschaffel. 2014. "Towards a Multipolar Model of Cultural Mediators within Multicultural Spaces. Cultural Mediators in Belgium, 1830-1945. " *Revue Belge de Philologie et d'Histoire* 92 (4. Special issue guest-edited by Tessa Lobbes and Maud Gonne: Belgian Cultural Mediators, 1830-1945. Crossing Borders, Borders Resisting.): 1255-1275.

Eisenberg, Christiane. 2005. "Cultural Transfer as a Historical Process: Research Questions, Steps of Analysis, Methods." In *Metamorphosis. Structures of Cultural Transformations*, edited by Jürgen Schlaeger, 99-111. Tübingen: Gunter Narr.

Espagne, Michel. 1994. "Sur les limites du comparatisme en histoire culturelle." *Genèses* 17: 112-121.

— 2013. "La notion de transfert culturel." *Revue Sciences/Lettres 1*: 1-21. doi: 10.4000/rsl.219.

Espagne, Michel, and Michael Werner. 1987. "La construction d'une référence culturelle allemande en France: Genèse et histoire (1750-1914)." *Annales* 4 (July-August 1987): 969-992.

Even-Zohar, Itamar. 1990a. "The Position of Translated Literature within the Literary Polysystem." *Poetics Today* 11 (1): 45-51. doi: 10.2307/1772668.
— 1990b. "Translation and Transfer." *Poetics Today* 11 (1): 73-78.
— 1997. "The Making of Culture Repertoire and the Role of Transfer." *Target* 7 (2): 355-363.
— 2005. *Papers in Culture Research*. Tel Aviv: Tel Aviv University.
Genette, Gérard. 1982. *Palimpsestes. La Littérature au second degré*. Paris: Le Seuil.
Gonne, Maud. 2017. *Contrebande littéraire et culturelle à la Belle Époque: Le « hard labour » de Georges Eekhoud entre Anvers, Paris et Bruxelles*. Leuven: Leuven University Press.
Gonne, Maud, and Tessa Lobbes. 2014. "Introduction." *Revue Belge de Philologie et d'Histoire*. 92 (4. Special issue guest-edited by Tessa Lobbes and Maud Gonne: Belgian Cultural Mediators, 1830-1945. Crossing Borders, Borders Resisting.): 1249-1253.
Göpferich, Susanne. 2007. "Translation Studies and Transfer Studies." In *Doubts and Directions in Translation Studies*, edited by Yves Gambier, Miriam Shlesinger and Radegundis Stolze, 27–39. Amsterdam: John Benjamins.
— 2010. "Transfer and Transfer Studies." In *Handbook of Translation Studies*, edited by Yves Gambier and Luc van Doorslaer, 374-377. Amsterdam: John Benjamins.
Joyeux-Prunel, Béatrice. 2003. "Les transferts culturels. Un discours de la méthode." *Hypothèses. Publications de la Sorbonne* 1 (6): 149-162.
Kang, Ji-Hae. 2007. "Recontextualization of News Discourse: A Case Study of Translation of
News Discourse on North Korea." *The Translator* 13 (2): 219-42.
Katan, David. 2013. "Intercultural mediation." In *Handbook of Translation Studies*, edited by Yves Gambier and Luc van Doorslaer, 84-91. Amsterdam: John Benjamins.
Leerssen, Joep. 2014. "Networks and Patchworks: Communication, Identities, Mediators." In *Revue Belge de Philologie et d'Histoire* 92 (4. Special issue guest-edited by Tessa Lobbes and Maud Gonne: Belgian Cultural Mediators, 1830-1945. Crossing Borders, Borders Resisting.): 1395-1403.
Marais, Kobus. 2014. *Translation theory and development studies: a complexity theory approach*. New York: Routledge.
— 2019. *A (Bio)Semiotic Theory of Translation. The Emergence of Social-Cultural Reality*. New York: Routledge.
Meylaerts, Reine, Lieven D'hulst, and Tom Verschaffel, eds. 2018. *Cultural Mediation in Europe, 1800-1950*. Leuven: Leuven University Press.
— 2020. "Cultural Mediators and Their Complex Transfer Practices." In *Cultural Organizations, Networks and Mediators in Contemporary Ibero-America*, edited by Diana Roig Sanz and Jaume Subirana, 46-62. New York: Routledge.

Middell, Matthias, ed. 2014. *Cultural Transfers, Encounters and Connections in the Global 18th Century*. (*Global History and International Studies* 6). Leipzig: Leipziger Universitätsverlag.

Morin, Edgar. 2005. *Introduction à la pensée complexe*. Paris: Éditions du Seuil.

Pym, Anthony. 1998. *Method in Translation History*. Manchester: St. Jerome.

— 2014. *Exploring Translation Theories (second edition)*. New York: Routledge.

Roig-Sanz, Diana, and Reine Meylaerts. 2018. "General Introduction. Literary Translation and Cultural Mediators. Toward an Agent and Process-Oriented Approach." In *Literary Translation and Cultural Mediators in 'Peripheral' Cultures. Customs Officers or Smugglers?*, edited by Diana Roig-Sanz and Reine Meylaerts, 1-37. London: Palgrave Macmillan.

Saunier, Pierre-Yves. 2013. *Transnational History*. Basingstoke: Palgrave Macmillan.

Stetting, Karen. 1989. "Transediting: A New Term for Coping with the Grey Area between Editing and Translating." In *Proceedings from the Fourth Nordic Conference for English Studies*, edited by Graham Caie, Kirsten Haastrup, Arnt Lykke Jakobsen, Jørgen Erik Nielsen, Jørgen Sevaldsen, Henrik Specht, and Arne Zettersten, 371-82. Copenhagen: University of Copenhagen.

Taft, Ronald. 1981. "The Role and Personality of the Mediator." In *The Mediating Person: Bridges between Cultures*, edited by S. Bochner, 53-88. Cambridge: Schenkman.

Thom, René. 1980. *Modèles mathématiques de la morphogenèse*. Paris: Christian Bourgois.

Weissbrod, Rachel. 2004. "From Translation to Transfer." *Across Languages and Cultures* 5 (1): 23-41.

Werner, Michael, and Bénédicte Zimmermann. 2006. "Beyond Comparison: Histoire Croisée and the Challenge of Reflexivity." *History and Theory* 45 (1): 30-50.

Wichter, Sigurd, and Gerd Antos, eds. 2001. *Wissenstransfer zwischen Experten und Laien*. Bern: Peter Lang.

Reclaiming the past

Translations from the Anglo-Saxon for the twenty-first century

Susan Bassnett

Abstract
The revival of interest in classical studies is leading to some exciting and innovative translations from ancient languages. Until recently, however, although this tendency has been apparent in translations from Ancient Greek and Latin, there has not been a similar process involving the translation of Anglo-Saxon literature. This essay suggests that the increased attention now being paid to the history of the period once dismissed as the Dark Ages is fuelling an increase in translations, a trend that has been gathering momentum in the twenty-first century since the publication of Seamus Heaney's best-selling version of Beowulf in 1999. Using Lieven D'hulst's distinction between transfer studies and translation studies it is suggested that the current revival of interest in translating Anglo-Saxon texts is linked to a broader interest, both academic and popular, in the period when those texts were being produced and circulated.

In 2001, two academics, Patrick W. Connor and Stuart D. Lee created an online publication entitled *Dragons in the Sky*, a reference to a sentence in the *Anglo Saxon Chronicle* for the year 793 AD, when "terrible portents appeared in Northumbria, and miserably affected the inhabitants" (Conner and Stuart 2001). The terrible portents were described as exceptional flashes of lightning, while it was claimed that people had seen fiery dragons flying through the air. Connor and Lee say that they used this famous quote to signal the apprehension that was in the air in their own time at the start of a new millennium, and the first essay, by Lee himself, "Whither Old English" (Lee 2001) does indeed strike a somewhat apocalyptic note. Lee's essay is about the campaign of opposition to the study of Anglo-Saxon in Oxford, and later in other British universities, starting with the heated debates of the early 1990s when Valentine Cunningham, among others, argued that neither the language nor the literature had any relevance to what happened later as English began to develop into what we know today. Lee shows how the battle to retain Anglo-Saxon was won at Oxford in 1993, but reopened in 1998, and he endeavors to understand the hostility towards a subject that had formed a fundamental part of most undergraduate degrees in English for decades. Part of the problem, as he saw it, is that so many students had little or no understanding of rules of grammar, often minimal acquaintance with another language and almost no knowledge of early English history. The aim of the *Dragons in the Sky* editors was therefore to promote a new form of popular medievalism and to try and make the Anglo-Saxon period more relevant. It is also significant that they refer to "Old English" rather than "Anglo-Saxon", a shift that is not only linguistic but also ideological.

I was one of the generation of English literature students who also studied Anglo-Saxon/ Old English. I still have my heavily annotated copies of G. L. Brook's *Introduction to Old English*, and Sweet's *Anglo-Saxon Reader*, first published in 1876 and still very much in use nearly a hundred years later. We studied Anglo-Saxon as a second language, learning verb tables and declensions and doing two translations every week. I was lucky, in that I went up to university with seven years of Latin behind me and four years of German, as well as my other Romance languages, but for many of my fellow students who had only minimal acquaintance with French, studying Anglo-Saxon was torture. In contrast, I loved it: Anglo-Saxon helped me to understand more about contemporary English, it taught me how English verse is based on stress patterns, not necessarily on the number of syllables in a line, and it also enabled me to see connections between other Northern European languages. My first Lectureship in a British university was at Lancaster, where I was hired to teach compulsory Old English to second-year students, where I tried (mostly in vain) to convey some of the passion I felt to young people who had no idea about grammatical gender and could not understand what a declension was. My strategy was to try and engage the students with the history and the culture of the Anglo-Saxon world, so we did projects on place names, on surnames, on the history of the period, on Anglo-Saxon stone carving and on the runic alphabet. We also read a lot of translations, since it was pretty clear to me that with two hours a week none of my students was going to learn much about the actual language. Not long after I left Lancaster, compulsory Old English disappeared from the syllabus.

Anglo-Saxon emerged as an area of study, both academic and popular, in the nineteenth century, along with related interest in Old Norse and the Vikings, as well as in the pan-Celtic world. However, much of the interest was on the militarism of those societies, which were perceived as warrior tribes endlessly fighting one another, when not fighting the British tribes, the Scots and the Picts and later the Viking Danes. Francis Palgrave's *History of the*

Anglo Saxons, published in 1876, is a good example of this, being an account of numerous battles between war lords from different tribal groups. Sir Arthur Quiller-Couch, who held the Chair of English Literature at Cambridge from 1912 was contemptuous of the men he saw as supporters of Anglo-Saxon and accused them of lacking sophistication. In his lecture, "On a School of English", published after the Great War in 1920, just a year after the founding of the Cambridge Faculty of English, he describes the Anglo-Saxonists as valiant fighters, but with no sense of proportion: "All their geese were swans, and *Beowulf* a second *Iliad*" (Quiller-Couch 1925, 99). These scholars, in his view, were obsessed with myths of origins of Englishness and turned inwards. Instead of looking outwards to long-established connections with Europe, they "turned aggressively provincial, parted their beards in the Anglo-Saxon fashion" and composed long sentences "painfully innocent of any words not derivable from Anglo-Saxon". He went even further, suggesting that it was impossible to reason with these scholars who had locked themselves into an imaginary world of their own making: "There was no reengaging them in dialectic, an Athenian art which they frankly despised. If you happened to disagree with them, their answer was a sturdy Anglo-Saxon brick" (Quiller-Couch 1925, 101).

Quiller-Couch is being facetious here, but behind the irony was a serious belief in the need for the newly emergent degrees in English to be outward looking, to embrace European classical knowledge and, following Matthew Arnold, to recognize that everywhere there is connection. Moreover, the emphasis on militarism, and the philological interest in pan-Germanic linguistic origins can be seen with hindsight as a first stage on a road that was to lead some towards a far-right ideology. A few years later, W. H. Auden and Louis MacNeice in their *Letters from Iceland* (1937) would write about Nazi tours to Iceland so as to see a society with "genuine" tall, blond and blue-eyed Arians. Anglo-Saxon and Old Norse were perceived as the languages of ancient Proto-Germanic civilization, and although after the Second World War associations of Anglo-Saxon with Nazism were no longer prevalent, nevertheless some felt that studying the language and culture was somehow tainted.

But the wheel of fortune turns and today, despite the disappearance of Old English as a compulsory university subject, there is a renewed interest in re-imagining the Anglo-Saxon world. Dragons are flying again, and this time with millions of television viewers. This shift is due to a number of factors, which have come together in a confluence of related interests. At one end of the scale we can see the impact of J.R.R. Tolkien's works, particularly the film versions of the *Lord of the Rings*, along with the novels of George R.R. Martin which have become the global success of the *Game of Thrones* television series, reaching a whole new generation interested in fantasy and epic story-telling. There are a number of very successful writers who have created a series of novels based on the history of northern Britain, such as Bernard Cornwell's Saxon stories, Matthew Harffy's Bernicia chronicles, Edoardo Albert's Northumbria series, or the popular historian Max Adams' books, including his study of the life of Oswald, one of the most renowned kings of Northumbria. Such is the popular interest in the period today, that a quick internet trawl showed no less than eight fictionalized biographies of Aethelfled, daughter of Alfred the Great who ruled the kingdom of Mercia from 911 until her death in 918, all published since 2015. At the other end of the scale we have a transformation of research interest in what used to be called the Dark Ages: social, economic, military and maritime historians, archaeologists and literary scholars have all started to reexamine the centuries following the decline of the Roman empire and the rise of vernacular European languages.

David Rollinson's *Northumbria, 500-1100. Creation and Destruction of a Kingdom* is a good example of this kind of interdisciplinary scholarship. Rollinson acknowledges the problem of establishing authoritative unprejudiced sources for his study of the great North British kingdom, sources which include not only well-known works such as the *Anglo-Saxon Chronicle* and histories written by Gildas (c.490), the Venerable Bede (c.731) and Nennius (c.830), but also monastic hagiographies, land charters, Welsh and Irish poems, extant illustrated manuscripts such as the *Lindisfarne Gospels* (produced c.715-720), stone carvings, church architecture, coins, place-names, topography, burial sites and other archaeological evidence. Rollinson is just one of a number of historians whose research is transforming our knowledge of the period, not only of the Anglo-Saxons and the Vikings, but also of the Scottish tribes, the Picts and the Celtic tribes of the western British Isles.

In his important essay, "(Re)locating translation history: from assumed translation to assumed transfer", Lieven D'hulst distinguishes between transfer studies and translation studies, drawing attention to similarities and differences. He notes, rightly, that there has been very little attention paid to the historical methodology applied to the field of transfer in literature, but also draws attention to the difficulty that transfer studies poses. Transfer, he suggests, "is an opaque process – partly invisible, partly mental, and therefore only partly observable", unlike translation where there is a firm point of reference, namely the source text (D'hulst 2012, 142). D'hulst takes as his case study the construction of nineteenth-century Belgian literature, but the construction of Anglo-Saxon culture that is currently underway in Britain could represent another significant example. As he points out, transfer is, unlike translation, a continuous process: "a transferred product may itself give way to another produce using a different carrier, then back again (for example the transfer from a book to a movie or vice versa, then to a cartoon, to a game)" (D'hulst 2012, 140).

This is precisely what has been happening with the renewed interest in the Anglo-Saxon world at the present time. What remains to be seen is whether this interest which extends over a range of disciplines and art forms will lead on to more translations of Old English literature, comparable to what has been happening with Ancient Greek, where, although knowledge of the language has declined, the number of often highly creative translations is growing every year. We may therefore ask whether we might see the same process with the important body of Old English literary texts, very few of which are widely known and yet which may be considered as having laid the groundwork for the literature in English which developed in the later Middle Ages and Renaissance.

Not a great deal of Old English poetry has survived, and almost all of what remains is collected in four manuscripts, written somewhere around 1000 AD in late West Saxon dialect. Analysis of the poems shows that they had mostly been composed in very different dialects, much further north, in Mercia or Northumbria, several centuries earlier, so had undergone what can be described as intralingual translation probably by generations of scribes. Almost all are anonymous, with only two short poems identified as by Caedmon (c.654-684) and Bede (672-735) and four longer works by Cynewulf, who lived somewhere around the end of the ninth century. These four poems, *Juliana*, *Elene*, *Ascension* and *Fates of the Apostles* are all religious works, and contain the poet's name incorporated in eight runes, thus presenting an interesting problem for translators.[1]

The best-known Old English poem is *Beowulf*. Since it was first edited and published in 1815 controversy has raged about the exact meaning of certain passages, about the structure, about its performability, about its oral origins, about the balance between Christian and pre-Christian elements, about the accuracy of the historical passages, about the acceptability of the monsters, Grendel and Grendel's mother. The great Anglo-Saxon scholar Dorothy Whitelock in her book, *The Audience of Beowulf* (1951), suggested that the poem had been composed by a Christian poet working with pre-Christian materials from an oral Germanic tradition, a theory now widely accepted.

---

1   In his prose translation of Juliana, R.K. Gordon gives the runes as capital letters in brackets, Charles Kennedy also opts for capital letters but without brackets, as in "Sadly shall depart/ C, Y, and N", while Charles Williamson gives a transliteration of the runes, as in Cen, Yr, Nyd in brackets.

J. R.R. Tolkien in a lecture given in 1936, "*Beowulf:* The Monsters and the Critics" offered a view of the poem as being about an existential struggle between good and evil, arguing that the monsters can be read literally and also symbolically as manifestations of the darkness within human beings. He also suggested that rather than trying to compare *Beowulf* to classical epics, the poem should be seen as "heroic-elegiac", given that in the latter part with the death and funeral of the hero the tone is indeed elegiac. In 1999 the Irish Nobel Laureate, Seamus Heaney published a new translation of *Beowulf* which, remarkably, entered the British best-seller lists and remained there for several weeks. In his preface, Heaney praises Tolkien's essay which he suggests changed the way in which the poem was interpreted and initiated a new era of appreciation for Old English literature:

> Tolkien assumed that the poet had felt his way through the inherited material – the fabulous elements and the traditional accounts of a heroic past – and by a combination of creative intuition and conscious structuring has arrived at a unity of effect and a balanced order (Heaney 1999, xi).

Heaney offers an account of his own relationship with the poem, starting with his early undergraduate studies when he developed "not only a feel for the language, but a fondness for the melancholy and fortitude that characterized the poetry"(Heaney 1999, xxii). He recounts how a publisher asked him to translate *Beowulf* when he was teaching at Harvard in the 1980s, but he found the task impossible. Some thirty five years later he found a way back to the poem, having recognized that in his own poetry, "without any conscious intent on my part" he was affected by the Old English metrics, perhaps unconsciously, from the poetry he had studied years before, perhaps via the sprung rhythm of one of his favorite poets, Gerard Manley Hopkins. The way back into the poem for Heaney was, paradoxically, through his own Northern Irish heritage and understanding the relationship between his own Ulster English and the Old English of the *Beowulf* poet. He explains the break-through moment:

> What happened was that I found in the glossary of C. L. Wrenn's edition of the poem the Old English word meaning 'to suffer', the word *tholian*; and although at first it looked completely strange to me with its *thorn* symbol instead of the familiar *th*, I gradually realized that it was not strange at all, for it was the word that older and less educated people would have used in the country where I grew up. 'They'll just have to learn to thole,' my aunt would say about some family who had suffered un unforeseen bereavement. (Heaney 1999, xxv)

Heaney considers the history of the journeying of the verb *tholian*, from its Anglo-Saxon origins somewhere in Northern England, moving up to Scotland, then across to Ireland with the planters in the seventeenth century, even as far as America where he finds it in a line by John Crowe Ransom. Through that word he came to see that he could indeed start to translate *Beowulf*, a poem in a language that did not only belong to the English but to the world: "What I was experiencing as I kept meeting up with *thole* on its multi-cultural odyssey was the feeling that Osip Mandelstam once defined as 'nostalgia for world culture" (Heaney 1999, xxvi). For Heaney, then, *Beowulf* was a work of world literature, which he approached through his own Irishness, having moved on beyond seeing English and Irish as "adversarial". Mindful of the oral dimension of the poem, he explains how he wanted to create a version of contemporary English that could be spoken by his relatives, plain-speaking Ulstermen who enunciated with "a weighty distinctness", marking phonetic units as separate, with forthrightness. Heaney points out that the first word of the poem, *hwaet* has been variously rendered as 'lo', 'hark', 'behold', 'attend', 'listen', but he chose 'so', as used in Ulster English "because in that idiom 'so' operates as an expression that obliterates all previous discourse and narrative, and at the same time functions as an exclamation calling for immediate attention. So, 'so' it was" (Heaney 1999, xxvii). Heaney's opening lines take up the forthright rhythms of his Ulster culture:

So. The Spear-Danes in days gone by
and the kings who ruled them had courage and greatness.
We have heard of those princes' heroic campaigns (Heaney 1999, 3)

Heaney's conscious choice to use a version of English with echoes of his Northern Irish background marks a shift in attitudes to translating classic Old and Middle English texts, comparable to what has been happening with the translation of Greek and Latin works. In 2007, the now Poet Laureate, Simon Armitage produced a version of *Sir Gawain and the Green Knight*, describing himself as "a northerner who not only recognizes plenty of the poem's dialect but who detects an echo of his own speech rhythms within the original" (Armitage 2007, vii). Armitage, like Heaney, stresses not only the orality of the source text and its continuity to the present day, but also the need for new translations to break from the older tradition of translating into a high register of Standard English.

In the introduction to his edited collection *Living Classics. Greece and Rome in Contemporary Poetry in English*, the Oxford classicist Stephen Harrison notes the paradox that at a time when fewer people than ever before have been able to read Greek and Latin in the original languages, classical texts have achieved a high profile in contemporary Anglophone literature. He attributes this to a number of factors, principally a greater democratization of classical literature away from what can be seen as the traditional canonical and establishment ownership, which has led to more willingness to experiment with translations. There has been a shift from what Harrison terms as a spirit of homage in approaching ancient texts towards a spirit of appropriation, which can be linked to the idea that the meaning of a work of literature is realized (at least partly) at the point of reception. This greater sense of democratization comes also with greater awareness of the extent to which ancient texts have been manipulated over time. Centuries of transcribing, editing, commentary, and other forms of rewriting call into question our understanding of the 'original'. The ancient world, whether Greek, Roman or Anglo-Saxon has to be reconstructed for each generation, since, as the classical translator Josephine Balmer succinctly puts it:

> The problem is not just the meagre biographical information available about a poet's life, often only surviving from sources written centuries after their deaths, but that the cultural context in which they flourished has vanished. Not only are classical authors silent, but their texts come from a silent, long-dead world, a world that must be reconstructed in tatters from the rubble. (Balmer 2009, 45)

However, Balmer argues that these difficulties can serve to empower a translator, and she even proposes that creative solutions found by translators can shed light on aspects of ancient texts that scholars might overlook: "For it is through translation that ancient fragments can revive their dead, silent language, 'blood brought to ghosts', as Pound saw it, awarding them a new voice, a new music, albeit in new notes, carrying them forward in time" (Balmer 2013, 231). Balmer here refers to Ezra Pound, one of the boldest and most contested translators of the early twentieth century, whose appropriations of canonical texts still serve as a model for contemporary translators. Pound only translated one Old English poem, *The Seafarer* (1911), from which he quite deliberately removed all the Christian references.[2] The Old English scholar and translator Michael Alexander describes Pound as a genius, and his translation as "much the most intense impression of an Old English poem available", but he is also wryly critical:

---

2   For a discussion of Pound's translation strategies in *The Seafarer*, see Bassnett 2014, 102-110.

Pound's *Seafarer* is a bravura realisation of the effect of reading the original on a poetic sensibility with great sensitivity to rhythm and language and a mind coloured by American attitudes of a hundred years ago to the early English past. (Alexander 1983, 117)

Alexander dedicated to Pound his own collection of translations of Old English poetry, entitled *The Wanderer: Elegies, Epics, Riddles. Poems from England's Ancient Origins*. First published in 1966, the volume was revised and expanded several times and the latest edition dates from 2013. Significantly, on the cover of this edition is a sticker that reads "Classics that inspired J.R.R Tolkien's *The Hobbit*", obviously an attempt to reach a generation more familiar with Gollum than with Cynewulf. Alexander has been a prolific translator of Anglo-Saxon poetry, including *Beowulf*, and provides notes on his translation strategies. Commenting on his own version of *The Seafarer*, he draws attention to the final elegiac lines:

> This is one of the greatest passages of our literature, and those unsatisfied by my version should look at Ezra Pound's *Seafarer* to see what *le grand translateur* of our age did with it. (...) Translation involves as many decisions as there are words in the original – indeed, many more; however inadequate, it is the best critique one can make. (Alexander 2013, 47)

The Seafarer is one of a small number of Old English poems that deal with the theme of exile and loss, and are generally known as the elegiac poems, the others being *The Wanderer, The Wife's Complaint, The Husband's Message, Deor, The Ruin, Wulf and Eadwacer* and *The Rhyming Poem*, all of which were collected in the Exeter Book, the largest of the four codices of Old English poetry, which is all that has been preserved. The titles are, of course, modern. Anthologies of Old English poetry tend to include the elegies, probably because they appeal more to modern readers' taste than do the more overtly religious poems and the riddle poems. In his 1926 anthology, R. K. Gordon declares that the elegies are the most interesting of extant Old English poems, and declares *The Ruin* to be "one of the greatest of Old English poems" (Gordon 1926, 84).

The first complete translation of the entire Old English body of poetry, over 31.000 lines, some only fragments, was published with the University of Pennsylvania Press in 2017. The translator is Craig Williamson, a distinguished Anglo-Saxon scholar and translator, who provides both notes on his translations and an introductory essay. He points out that he has not followed any single edited text but has consulted a range of editions as well as scholarly commentaries and research by lexicographers and philologists, so that his translations are based on these combined readings. He also provides a list of the prose translations he has used, and then considers some of the stylistic and linguistic problems specific to the translation of Old English poetry. One aspect to which he draws attention is that some of the poetry was translated from the Latin, so that in addition to the oral dimension, there is also the question of texts that have already been recomposed from another linguistic source. Williamson uses the image of the translator as a dancer, carefully measuring steps. He defines translation as mediation, as "a human dance between two minds, two languages, two literary traditions, two cultures" (Williamson 2017, 25). Williamson's collected Old English poems is a great achievement and makes available some of the lesser known works with the fragments. He also provides an appendix with possible solutions to the riddle poems many of which continue to be debated. In his Introduction, he discusses the way in which some texts "seem to defy translation" because of the impossibility of establishing a clear meaning, and gives three examples – the opening lines of *Beowulf*, the great cry of despair in *The Wanderer* and what he terms the mysterious and enigmatic ending of *Wulf and Eadwacer*.

This poem has been the subject of a great deal of debate, and because it was in the Exeter Book just before the riddles, it was at first assumed also to be a riddle poem. Then Henry Bradley, the great lexicographer, argued that the poem is not a riddle but probably part of a dramatic monologue, similar to *The Wife's Lament* and *Deor*. R. K. Gordon notes that parts of the text are so difficult that any translation must be regarded as tentative, while Williamson raises a whole set of questions for a translator. His version of the ending reads:

> Do you hear, Eadwacer, guardian of goods?
> Wulf will bear our sad whelp to the woods.
>
> It's easy to rip an unseen stitch
> Or tear the thread of an untold tale-
> The song of us two together. (Williamson 2017, 524)

In his introductory essay, however, he offers a range of alternatives in a literal translation of the last one and half lines: "One may easily (readily, lightly) tear apart (sever, rend, wound, break open, destroy) what (that which) was never united (joined, assembled, collected, gathered together) / The song (poem, saying, word, speech, proverb, riddle, tale) of us two together (united)" (Williamson 2017, 24). What is it that is easily torn and never really together, is the question, given that the speaker of the poem is a woman lamenting the loss of Wulf (who may be her husband, her lover or even her brother) and challenging Eadwacer (who may be her husband, her lover, her owner, if she is a captive). Williamson expands the line and a half in the Old English to three lines, and opts for the image of stitching something together, drawing on the Anglo-Saxon concept of woman as 'peace-weaver' (*frithwebba*), and with the word "stitch" signaling both sewing and the idea of pain (a stitch in the side). The child is a "sad whelp" and may belong to either of the two men named in the poem.

The English poet Jane Draycott won the Stephen Spender Poetry in Translation Prize in 2010 for her version, entitled *Song for Wulf from the Exeter Book*. Her commentary on the poem explains her strategy:

> I have inserted stanza breaks and additional indentation, and have in several places played with re-sequencing phrases and ideas. The translation also pushes out a little from the original's taut metrics towards a more contemporary kind of lyricism, as a way of creating more interpretative elbow-room. (Draycott 2011, 24)

Draycott interprets the poem as a lament by a woman bound in some way to Eadwacer, separated from Wulf, her lover, sustained by the thought of their child, their wolf-cub, who has gone with Wulf far away. The title stresses the significance of Wulf, as she does not use the standard title with both names. Nor is there any ambiguity in her ending, where the child becomes the song:

> Remember, Eadwacer, warrior: it's easy
> to sever those ties never truly united.
> Remember that Wulf has carried our unhappy wolf-cub
> away with him into the woods-the song
> he and I made together. (Draycott 2010, 14)

R. K. Gordon takes a very different view:

> Dost thou hear Eadwacer? Our cowardly cub
> Wulf shall bear off to the wood.
> They can easily sunder that which was never joined together,
> The song of us two together. (Gordon 1926, 83)

In this reading, the speaker threatens Eadwacer with something that has yet to happen, and the child is not only not Wulf's, it is a "cowardly cub", the assumption being that Eadwacer is its father. Michael Alexander's version is very similar, only he sharpens the ending to emphasize the threat:

> What was never bound is broken easily
> our song together (Alexander 2013, 62)

Writing in the introduction to her translation of *The Wanderer*, the poet Jane Holland argues that there should always be room for experimentation when translating:

> Translators need to respect the essential thrust of the original – otherwise the act of translating is rendered more or less pointless – but not so slavishly that new solutions and interpretations are feared, especially if those solutions provoke vital discussion on the way forward for future translations. (Holland 2008, 7)

By this measure, Draycott's interpretation of *Wulf and Eadwacer* opens up a completely different narrative: Wulf has already taken the child, it is not something that is yet to happen in the future, and the poem ends almost on a celebratory note, as Draycott explains:

> What touched me the most was what lies buried perhaps in that final image: the woman separated irremediably from her lover, sustained by the thought of her child, made out of love, like the song the poet has left us. (Draycott 2010, 14)

Draycott's version offers a differently gendered perspective, as does Holland's translation of *The Wanderer*, where she has changed the sex of the speaker from male to female. Holland also takes out the overtly Christian elements in the poem, arguing that there is no scholarly consensus as to whether these were added by scribes to a poem that had a much older history. Similarly, Pound removed the Christian elements from his version of *The Seafarer*, and given the lack of clarity about the origins of both poems, Holland's interpretation does not look so radical. The gender shift is more contentious; Holland explains it by saying that as a female poet, she felt that a gender change would give her version "greater authenticity". She also argues that contemporary readers might fail to understand the close bond in a warrior society between lord and faithful retainer which "takes on a strongly homoerotic charge when read with a modern sensibility" (Holland 2008, 6). This is an idiosyncratic interpretation of a poem which is a lament by a warrior who has lost his comrades and, most significantly, his lord, and has been driven into exile, now a man without kin and without a country.

Holland also uses language that recalls contemporary warfare – "fell in the line of duty, caught off-guard in the crossfire, blasted to bits at the roadside, picked off by snipers, your president's big push" – but her protagonist is a woman "forced into exile" (Holland 2008, 17), grieving for the loss of her old life and the man she loved. Holland's poem is therefore about a refugee, her protagonist no longer a defeated warrior but an ageing woman, a Hecuba figure. By cutting the last 10 lines which offer a message of Christian hope in an afterlife, Holland offers a much darker vision, but her protagonist comes across as strong even in her desperation:

> The best we can do, not knowing the future,
> is to stay resolute, resisting our grief,
> the terrible grip of its torments, and keep faith
> with ourselves, refuse to forget (Holland 2008, 21)

Both Draycott and Holland have produced woman-centered translations, creating strong female protagonists who confront hardship with defiance, and in this respect they have made what Balmer terms "transgressive translations" (Balmer 2013, 171), for twenty-first century readers. Both have been mindful of the conventions of Old English poetry (Holland's version also has the Old English text on facing pages) and have produced translations that echo elements of that prosody, but both have chosen to reinterpret the poems in a new way. But as Eliot Weinberger says, every translation is a re-imagining of a poem, and every reading of a poem is itself an act of translation. Moreover, "as no individual reader remains the same, each reading becomes a different – not merely another – reading. The same poem cannot be read twice" (Weinberger 2016, 46).

Anglo-Saxon poetry has not, to date, received the attention it deserves from translators, but there are signs that this may be starting to change. The unexpected success of Seamus Heaney's *Beowulf*, combined with the surge of interest by scholars and popular audiences in the age of Anglo-Saxon and Viking culture promises well for the future. Thanks to Craig Williamson's monumental effort there is now a complete corpus of Old English poetry available in a single volume, so perhaps what has been happening with the literature of the Greek and Roman worlds may be starting to happen with the literature of Northern Europe. But it is also important to note that these translations are connected to a much broader interdisciplinary interest in the world in which the texts were first produced, hence the confluence of research in both translation studies and transfer studies.

It is also timely to remember that translation was highly significant for the Anglo-Saxons, so much so that King Alfred (c. 847-899) not only actively promoted translation of key texts, but undertook translations himself. In the preface to his translation of St. Augustine's *Soliloquies*, Alfred describes translation as an act of building. He depicts himself going out into the forest to collect wood for the basic structures he wanted to build, though mindful of the enormity of the task:

> Each time I shouldered the wood home, I wanted the forest, but it was more than I could carry. In each beam I saw something I needed at home. So I urge those who have knowledge and good wagons to go to the woods where I cut my beams and fetch their own beautiful branches so they can weave lovely walls and shape splendid buildings and bright towns and live there joyfully summer and winter as I have not yet been able to do. (Williamson 2017, 26)

Alfred understood that translation means being selective – he could never have the whole forest, but he could gather enough good wood to make something beautiful. He also understood that translation requires effort, hence he encourages those with both good wagons and knowledge to engage with the linguistic building process. This is a strong metaphor and although these days, concrete and plate glass have replaced going out into the forest to cut down trees, the image of the translator as intelligent builder is one that still endures.

References

Alexander, Michael. 1983. *Old English Literature*. London: Macmillan.
Alexander, Michael, trans. 2013. *The Wanderer: Elegies, Epics, Riddles. Poems from England's Ancient Origins*. London: Penguin.
Armitage, Simon. 2007. *Sir Gawain and the Green Knight*. London: Faber.
Balmer, Josephine. 2009. *The Word for Sorrow*. Cambridge: Salt Publishing.
— 2013. *Piecing Together the Fragments. Translating Classical Verse, Creating Contemporary Poetry*. Oxford: Oxford University Press.
Bassnett, Susan. 2014. *Translation Studies*. London: Routledge.
Conner, Patrick W. and D. Lee Stuart. 2001. "Dragons in the Sky: English Speaking Communities at the Close of the Millennia." http://users.ox.ac.uk/~stuart/dits/main.html
D'hulst, Lieven. 2012. "(Re)Locating Translation History: From Assumed Translation to Assumed Transfer." *Translation Studies* 5 (3): 139-155.

Draycott, Jane. 2010. *Song for Wulf from The Exeter Book.* London: Stephen Spender Foundation.
Gordon, Robert K. 1926. *Anglo-Saxon Poetry.* London: Dent.
Harrison, Stephen, ed. 2009. *Living Classics. Greece and Rome in Contemporary Poetry in English.* Oxford: Oxford University Press.
Heaney, Seamus, transl. 1999. *Beowulf.* London: Faber.
Holland, Jane, transl. 2008. *Lament of the Wanderer.* Coventry: Heaven Tree.
Lee, Stuart D. 2001. "Whither Old English?" http://users.ox.ac.uk/~stuart/dits/contents_intro.html
Quiller-Couch, Arthur. 1925. *On the Art of Reading.* Cambridge: Cambridge University Press.
Rollinson, David. 2003. *Northumbria, 500-1100. Creation and Destruction of a Kingdom.* Cambridge: Cambridge University Press.
Weinberger, Eliot. 2016. *19 Ways of Looking at Wang Wei, with more ways.* New York: New Directions.
Whitelock, Dorothy. 1951. *The Audience of Beowulf.* Oxford: Oxford University Press.
Williamson, Craig, transl. 2017. *The Complete Old English Poems.* Philadelphia: University of Pennsylvania Press.

From Britain to Brussels and back again

On the transfer of national images and linguistic interactions in Charlotte Brontë's *The Professor* and its first Dutch and French translations

Dirk Delabastita & Maud Gonne

Abstract

This chapter examines the transfers of cultural images and linguistic interactions staged by Charlotte Brontë in her notoriously unsuccessful novel *The Professor* (published posthumously in 1857), and their back transfers as evidenced by the first French (Paris, 1858, tr. Henriette Loreau) and Dutch (Groningen, 1859, anonymous) translations. Brontë's novel tells the story of a young Englishman leaving Great Britain to work in Brussels as a teacher and ultimately finding professional and romantic happiness after many struggles. It presents numerous critical and often dismissive images of the "Flemish" (meaning 'Belgian') and French people, of the Catholic Church it is associated with, and more generally of the mores and culture of "continentals." With its negative and often hostile representation of (parts of) the receptor culture, it was a sensitive text to translate/transfer (back) into Dutch and French. In addition, the ample use of heterolingualism (French, occasionally Flemish) created several potential practical obstacles to a smooth transfer process. This paper compares two very early translations of *The Professor* against the backdrop of the wider historical pattern of reception of Charlotte Brontë's works, with a special focus on how these translations rendered the original text's heterolingualism and how they transferred its underlying axiological oppositions (British vs continental, Catholic vs Protestant, French vs English, French vs Belgian, Dutch vs Belgian).

1. Introduction

This contribution examines the transfers of national images and linguistic interactions staged by Charlotte Brontë in her lesser-known novel *The Professor* (1857) and their back-transfers as evidenced by its first French (1858) and Dutch

(1859) translations. Brontë's novel tells the story of a young Englishman leaving Britain to work in Brussels as a teacher and ultimately finding romantic and professional fulfillment after many struggles. The novel makes numerous negative comments on the French and Belgian people, on the Catholic Church they are associated with, and more generally on the mores and culture of 'continentals'. Unlike *Villette*, Brontë's later and more successful recycling of a similar theme, the work struggled to convince English publishers, critics, and readers.

With its hostile representation of the target culture, *The Professor* would have been a sensitive text to transfer (back) into Dutch and French; in addition, the ample use of heterolingualism (mainly French) throws up several potential obstacles to a smooth transfer process. This chapter aims to compare these two very early translations and to see if and how transfer techniques (D'hulst 2012) such as selective translation, adaptation and non-translation are used to reduce the original's heterolingualism and/or to blunt the edge of Brontë's polemical attitude with prospective Belgian or Catholic readerships in view.

2. *The Professor*

William Crimsworth is the novel's protagonist and first-person narrator. Growing up as an orphan, he is given a job as a clerk by his wealthy older brother, Edward Crimsworth, who treats him arrogantly and tyrannically. William meets the enigmatic Hunsden Yorke Hunsden, who becomes his mentor. While descending from an old aristocratic family, Hunsden has embraced radical republican, liberal and internationalist views. William decides to quit his job and look for his fortune abroad.

Hunsden's letter of recommendation secures Crimsworth a job as an English teacher in a Brussels boys' school run by the Frenchman M. Pelet. Later on, he takes a second job as an English teacher at the adjacent girls' school run by Mlle[1] Zoraïde Reuter. Crimsworth finds the Belgian girls just as rude and obtuse as the boys. He feels attracted to Mlle Reuter but quickly discovers her flirtatious and manipulative nature. William gives her the cold shoulder and now becomes intrigued by a special new pupil in the girls' class, Frances Evans Henri, a poor, half-Swiss, half-English orphan. The master and pupil start to feel drawn to each other. Out of spite and jealousy, Mlle Reuter fires Frances from her part-time teaching job and maliciously keeps

---

1   *Mlle* is the abbreviation for *mademoiselle* (miss). We will use Brontë's naming conventions.

her address secret from William. William finds Frances back at the Protestant cemetery, where she is mourning her recently deceased aunt.

Feeling shocked by the lies and hypocrisy of Mlle Reuter and M. Pelet, William gives up both his jobs, which leaves him without sufficient means to consider proposing to Frances. Fortunately, with the help of the Dutchman Victor Vandenhuten, William gets a well-paid appointment as an English teacher at a College in Brussels and can now ask Frances to marry him. The couple later start their own school, a lucrative project which attracts pupils from some of the best families in Belgium. After several years, they can afford to retire and move back to England, where they purchase a house close to Hunsden's residence. Leading a comfortable and happy life, they can devote themselves to the care of their only son.

Brontë finished the novel in 1846, making it her first fully completed novel, predating *Jane Eyre* (1847), *Shirley* (1849) and *Villette* (1853). In terms of publication, however, it followed these three novels by a significant margin. *The Professor* had been turned down by publishers time and again. Even the growing success of Charlotte's later books, published under the same pseudonym "Currer Bell", could not entice publishers to take the book on. Charlotte's husband A.B. Nicholls finally decided to publish *The Professor* posthumously, but it has remained the least successful among Charlotte Brontë's novels. The fact that it was published just a few months after Mrs. Gaskell's famous biography *Life of Charlotte Brontë* in 1857 gave it some extra attention, but also narrowed the perspective defining the book's potential interest: not as a great Brontë novel, but as a book whose autobiographical origins could shed some light on the author's life and the Brussels years in particular.

The Professor was unmistakably inspired by the author's stay in Brussels in 1842-1843.[2] In February 1842, Charlotte and Emily Brontë left Haworth for the private school *Pensionnat Heger* in Brussels, where they attended lessons to improve their French and to learn German. Charlotte fell in love with Constantin Heger, the husband of the owner of the school and a part-time teacher there. Being a married man and a devout Catholic, Heger was out of her reach, which doomed Charlotte's devotion to him to end in hopeless frustration. These and other painful experiences found their way into *The Professor*, staging a form of life-into-fiction transfer. The novel also fictionalizes Charlotte's relationship with her Belgian pupils, from whom she felt estranged and socially isolated. Crimsworth has a very dim view of his Belgian pupils.

---

2   The Brussels Brontë Blog (http://brusselsbronte.blogspot.com/) offers splendid further documentation on Brontë's Brussels years.

He finds a general depravity in them, whose origins he traces back to the corrupting influence of Roman Catholicism. Such would have been the understanding of Charlotte Brontë herself, who had been brought up in an orthodox Anglican household.

3. Language transfers in the source text

As suggested by the plot synopsis above, plurilingualism and language learning are key components of *The Professor*. French especially is given great visibility. The most frequently used technique for the rendering of French in *The Professor* is a moderate form of discursive interference (terminology borrowed from Sternberg 1981). This means that, while the text is mainly in English, it incorporates some heterolingual French material (resulting in code-mixing or code-switching) and/or stages instances of interference in order to suggest that the entire speech event is 'really' taking place in French. The following is a typical example. Mlle Reuter is introducing a new pupil (Frances) to William:

> (1) <u>Monsieur Creemsvort</u> (…), that young person who has just entered (…) is not a pupil of the house – she is indeed, in one sense, a teacher, for she gives instruction in lace-mending and in little varieties of ornamental needle-work; she very properly proposes to qualify herself for a higher department of education and has asked permission to attend your lessons (…); of course it is my wish to aid her in an effort so praise-worthy; you will permit her then to benefit by your instruction – <u>n'est ce pas Monsieur</u>? (ST 97)[3]

Mlle Reuter's French speech is essentially rendered in English, but both the beginning ("monsieur") and end ("n'est-ce pas Monsieur") of it remain heterolingually French. The name 'Crimsworth' appears to be something like a shibboleth to Mlle Reuter (as it is to M. Pelet, for that matter). She keeps mispronouncing it *à la française* ("Creemsvort"), showing a typical instance of phonetic interference. The syntax, too, shows a certain French coloring (e.g., the post-position of the adjective in "an effort so praise-worthy"). Along with what we already know about Mlle Reuter's monolingualism, the combination of these features suffices to make it quite clear to the reader that she is expressing

---

3   Since many editions use the convention of italicizing words and phrases in other languages, we shall refrain from using italics for emphasis and use underlining instead.

herself in French – without for a moment jeopardizing comprehension for the English reader and without the need for a metalingual cue.

Metalingual cues and comments on the French language are otherwise found throughout the novel. The following example shows William newly arrived in Brussels, having breakfast at his hotel:

(2) I repaired to the public room (…) and there were two gentlemen seated (…), <u>talking in French</u>; impossible to follow their rapid utterance, or comprehend much of the purport of what they said – yet French, in the mouths of Frenchmen, or Belgians (I was not then sensible of <u>the horrors of the Belgian accent</u>) – was as music to my ears. (ST 48-49)

This example is also illustrative of the narrator's disdain for Belgium and all things Belgian, including its variant of the French language.

In some cases, the heterolingual material that is incorporated moves beyond the word-level to reach sentence length, which potentially poses a greater challenge to understanding for the non-Francophone reader. The following example raises the stakes by presenting the reader with several consecutive sentences rendered in French. William is about to confront Mlle Reuter about the disappearance of Frances:

(3) "I am sure I often wish intensely for liberty to spend a whole month in the country at some little farmhouse, <u>bien gentille, bien propre, tout entourée de champs et de bois; quelle vie charmante que la vie champêtre! N'est-ce pas, monsieur?</u>"
"<u>Cela dépend, Mademoiselle.</u>"
"<u>Que le vent est bon et frais!</u>" continued the directress; and she was right there – for <u>it was a south wind, soft and sweet</u> – I carried my hat in my hand, and this gentle breeze, passing through my hair, soothed my temples like balm. Its refreshing effect, however, penetrated no deeper than the mere surface of the frame, for as I walked by the side of Mdlle. Reuter, my heart was still hot within me, and while I was musing the fire burned, then spake I with my tongue:
"I understand Mdlle. Henri is gone from hence, and will not return?"
(ST 128)

Here too, code-mixing occurs (and it should be repeated that it is the narrator-quoter who is shifting between languages and not the characters being quoted). We also see that Brontë is careful not to push her readers too far. The idyllic description of life in the countryside ("bien gentille [etc.]")

is expendable in terms of plot or characterization. The remark about "le vent" being "bon et frais" is equally of little wider significance, but even so, Brontë arranges for her narrator to provide an English paraphrase ("she was right there (...) a south wind, soft and sweet") to make sure all readers remain on board.

Beyond this point the conversation between Crimsworth and Mlle Reuter continues for another three pages or so, until the end of the chapter (128-132). Brontë uses the convention of using idiomatic English-standing-for-French with the frequently repeated forms of address *Monsieur* and *Mademoiselle* and the odd loan word thrown in to simulate the French-only linguistic set-up of the conversation. Curiously, the following signal (cf. underlined words) is given to give an extra boost to the language illusion:

(4) "[A] change of instructors is often beneficial to the interests of a school (...)."
"Yet when you are tired of a professor or maîtresse, you scruple to dismiss them?"
"No need to have recourse to such extreme measures, I assure you. Allons, Monsieur le professeur – asseyons-nous – je vais vous donner une petite leçon dans votre état d'instituteur." (<u>I wish I might write all she said to me in French – it loses sadly by being translated into English.</u>) We had now reached the garden-chair; the Directress sat down, and signed to me to sit by her (...) (ST 129)

Again, the sentence "Allons, Monsieur (...) d'instituteur" shows the narrator abruptly code-switching from English to French and then back again by way of a reminder. What is different about this instance is the narrator's meta-fictional awareness of the code-switching. No reason is given here (or anywhere else, for that matter) as to *why* the French conversation could not be represented more fully in French by adhering more closely to the norm of vehicular matching (Sternberg 1981). Are we supposed to assume that Crimsworth is being mindful of the comfort of his monolingual readers? Or is he perhaps alluding to the difficulty he would have experienced remembering and reproducing the sophistication of Mlle Reuter's French? Brontë raises our awareness of the difficulty of representing heterolingual discourse, but finally does little more than pique our curiosity.

Crimsworth's remark illustrates the 'lost in translation' trope. He seems to believe that meanings can be so deeply rooted in a language and culture that translation is doomed to flounder. This conviction may also account for Crimsworth's habit of using French loan words in his own narratorial discourse (i.e., when he is speaking in his own name rather than quoting French used by the characters in his tale), as in the following description of M. Pelet:

(5) his features were pleasing and regular, they had a French turn (for M. Pelet was no Fleming, but a Frenchman both by birth and parentage) yet the degree of harshness inseparable from Gallic lineaments was, in his case, softened by a mild blue eye, and a melancholy, almost suffering, expression of countenance; his physiognomy was "fine et spirituelle" – <u>I use two French words because they define better than any English terms the species of intelligence with which his features were imbued</u>. (ST 52)

Our final example illustrates the need for readers to be alert to the representational shifts and modulations that a text like this is likely to present. More specifically, Brontë's use of English in a dialogue can be ambiguous, representing either English or English-standing-for-French. Similarly, the use of interference-ridden English can either signify that the character is "really" using French or that s/he is in effect speaking poor English. The excerpt is from chapter 17, which reports the first lengthy conversation between Crimsworth and Frances:

(6) "Speak English, if you please."
"<u>Mais</u> – "
"English – "
"But" (slowly and with embarrassment) "my parents were not <u>all the two</u> Genevese."
"Say *both*, instead of 'all the two', mademoiselle."
"Not *both* Swiss: my Mother was English."
"Ah! and of English extraction?"
"Yes – her ancestors were all English."
"And your father?"
"He was Swiss."
"What besides? What was his profession?"
"Ecclesiastic – pastor – he had a church."
"Since your Mother is an Englishwoman, why do you not speak English with more facility?"
"<u>Maman est morte – il y a dix ans</u>."
"And you do homage to her memory by forgetting her language? Have the goodness to put French out of your mind so long as I converse with you – keep to English."

> "C'est si difficile, monsieur, quand on n'en a plus l'habitude."
> "You had the habitude formerly, I suppose – ? Now answer me in your mother-tongue."
> "Yes, Sir – I spoke the English more than the French when I was a child." (ST 116)

The allotment of languages here, as in the rest of chapter 17, respects the convention of vehicular matching, alternating between English (predominant), French and *franglais*. As to the two potential ambiguities we mentioned, it is plain to see that there is no heterolingual trickery involved here: Crimsworth's English is decidedly *his* English; both the French and the *franglais* of Frances are unquestionably *hers*. All things considered, it is surprising how easily readers resolve the potential ambiguities that the heterolingualism of a novel such as *The Professor* can bring about. True, in the previously quoted lines there is ample metalingual guidance in the form of the teacher's linguistic corrections and admonishments ("speak English!"), but in many other instances readers have to do a lot more of the interpretive work themselves. It will not do, therefore, to conceive of the reader's 'willing suspension of disbelief' as a passive state of mind, as no more than the acquiescent consent to be taken for a ride in the fictional game of make-believe. If writers show variety and creativity in representing the linguistic otherness of discourses, readers too have to be credited with a set of subtle skills, including familiarity with the representational conventions possibly at play, an alertness to verbal nuance and metalingual cues, and a high responsiveness to context.

Given the novel's setting in Brussels, the recourse to French fulfills an obvious mimetic function, creating an impression of 'realism'. That such rhetorical effects of the text must not be confused with historical accuracy may be illustrated by the novel's very restricted and uncertain representation of Flemish, that is, the variant of Dutch spoken in Belgium (in those days a grouping of unstandardized dialects). While Brontë regularly uses the words 'Flemish' and '*flamand(e)*', she basically treats them as near-synonymous with 'Belgian', including Francophone Belgians.[4] This amalgamation was widespread during this period, which preceded the breakthrough and international recognition of the Flemish Movement and its linguistic claims: 'Flemish' was not primarily used to refer to language, but to origin.

Be that as it may, Brontë's narrator describes the *Flamands* in less than flattering terms. Following the logic of a racially based taxonomy, they are

---

[4] In what follows, we will be using the term 'Flemish' in its usual acceptance, to refer to the people of Flanders and the variant of the Dutch language spoken there.

described as being "inferior" both intellectually and physically. In the following example the crudeness of these perceptions outweighs Brontë's (Crimsworth's) compassionate and humanitarian impulse ("still they were men"):

(7) I fear, however, two poor, hard-worked Belgian ushers in the establishment could not have said as much – to them the director's manner was invariably dry, stern and cool: I believe he perceived once or twice that I was a little shocked at the difference he made between them and me and accounted for it by saying, with a quiet, sarcastic smile: "Ce ne sont que des Flamands – allez!"
And then he took his cigar gently from his lips and spat on the painted floor of the room in which we were sitting. Flamands certainly they were, and both had <u>the true Flamand physiognomy</u>, where <u>intellectual inferiority</u> is marked in lines none can mistake; still they were men and in the main, honest men, and I could not see why their being aboriginals of the flat, dull soil should serve as a pretext for treating them with perpetual severity and contempt. (ST 58)

The ushers referred to here would have been native speakers of Flemish (with some knowledge at least of French), as also suggested by their Flemish names *Kint* and *Vandam*. While French was the language of culture, power and social mobility, the speakers of Flemish in the 1830s-1840s, especially the monolingual ones, mainly belonged to the lower classes in Flanders. The 'Flemish housemaid', clearly of peasant origin, who Crimsworth meets in his Brussels hotel early in the story, may serve as an example:

(8) she had wooden shoes, a short red petticoat, a printed cotton bedgown, her face was broad, her physiognomy eminently stupid; when I spoke to her in French, <u>she answered me in Flemish</u>, with an air the reverse of civil, yet I thought her charming; if she was not pretty or polite, she was, I conceived, very picturesque. (ST 48)

The diglossia which characterized Belgian society remains under the radar of Brontë's linguistic mimetism, apart from a few unspecific observations such as the one just quoted, or the reference to Flemish-sounding names, or to realia such as *koek* (rendered in Frenchified spelling as "couc"):

(9) I stepped into a baker's and refreshed myself on a couc? (it is <u>a Flemish word</u> – I don't know how to spell it) à Corinthe – anglice – a currant bun – and a cup of coffee (ST 138)

Clearly, Brontë's linguistic soundscapes are *less* than truly 'realistic'. And, of course, they simultaneously do far *more* than merely pretending to mimetically describe the world. Deeper layers of meaning are unearthed when we start thinking about how the tension between English and French in the novel correlates with other axiological oppositions that run through its semantic and ideological universe: Protestantism vs. Catholicism, England vs. the Continent, or nationalism vs. cosmopolitanism, to name but those. As Cohen (2017, 171) puts it, "for a variety of historical and cultural reasons, French is highly charged for English speakers, in terms of its political associations with democracy, revolution, and military and colonial rivalry, as well as in terms of its erotic possibilities as a signifier of libertinism, sophistication, and freedom." It is especially the culturally encoded associations of Frenchness with sexual immorality that Brontë taps into. We have earlier suggested that the novel posits an indissoluble link between general depravity and Catholicism. It comes as no surprise, then, that the novel also constructs French as the natural linguistic medium for the alleged lies and empty rituals of this religion (e.g., ST 99).

4. The cultural transfer from England to Belgium and France and back again

When viewed from the perspective of William Crimsworth, the plot rests on a spatially based deep logic that can be modeled in terms of a double transfer:

ENGLAND		BELGIUM		ENGLAND
home	⇒	abroad	⇒	home
Protestant		Catholic		Protestant
English		French		English

Figure 1. The home-and-return plot represented in linear terms

As the diagram shows, the novel exemplifies the typical circular pattern of the 'journey-and-return' plot. This circularity combines with the linearity of two other standard plots that structure the narrative, namely, the 'rags-to-riches' plot (after years of hardship, the two heroes achieve economic independence) and the romantic 'virtue-rewarded' plot (the heroes meet the moral and practical challenges of life and reap the fruits of virtue).

The picture is somewhat more complicated for Frances, the author's other fictionalized alter ego. Frances was born in Geneva (known as one of the hotbeds of European Protestantism!) out of a Francophone Protestant Swiss father and an Anglophone Protestant English mother and came to Brussels with her aunt after being orphaned. While Crimsworth initially finds her proficiency in English to be quite limited, her talent for learning the language far more quickly than her fellow pupils points to an English substratum in her personal history and linguistic identity. This fact, combined with her impeccable Protestant credentials and the pure English ancestry of her mother, prompts the reader to see her trajectory from Switzerland to Brussels and from there to England as a "return" to her true "motherland," which she had never seen before. And yet, as we shall see below, she will never quite completely let go of her continental (Swiss and Francophone) moorings.

The opposition between England and Belgium is clearly central to the novel, especially as several other prominent oppositions are grafted onto it, including a linguistic and a religious one: English and Protestantism are the language and the religion of the author's and the protagonist's 'self'; French (as spoken in Belgium) and Roman Catholicism are very much the inferior language and religion of the 'other'. However, Brontë's use of Belgium as a narrative space should also be understood in the light of the historically fraught relationship between France and England. Frenchness is partly represented by a few female teachers but its main exponent is M. Pelet, the French – not Belgian – director of the boys' school, whose loose sexual morals ("Pelet's bachelor's life had been passed in proper French style with due disregard to moral restraint," ST 156) are compounded by duplicity, arrogance and ferocity. As Longmuir (2009, 167) puts it, the "middle-ground of Belgium epitomizes the conflict between British and French values in Brontë's fiction." Longmuir shows that Belgium was an intermediate space between England and France not only geographically, but also symbolically as a place for British patriotic self-construction, as the site (Waterloo) of Britain's decisive victory over France, and consequently as a popular continental tourist destination for British people. Moreover, Belgium, just like England, was a monarchy (with family ties between their respective monarchs into the bargain) rather than a republic, as well as being a neutral nation, less revolutionary and less sensible to French influence than the United Kingdom of the Netherlands had been. Finally, the Belgian territory, just like Britain, hosted different nations unified by a single language of culture and government. In brief, Belgium appears as a "more manageable" and less threatening version of France (Longmuir 2009, 176), a space where Anglicization and Anglo-French dialogue and reconciliation could be envisaged. In the novel, Belgium is indeed praised for the modesty of its inhabitants in comparison to English pride and French arrogance, and Brussels for its multilingual cosmopolitanism (e.g., ST 49).

When Crimsworth first arrives in Belgium, the country presents itself as an exciting space of promise and opportunity: "This is Belgium, Reader – look! Don't call the picture a flat or a dull one – it was neither flat nor dull to me when I first beheld it" (ST 46). But once the initial excitement has given way to the 'real' confrontation with Belgian people, habits and values, Crimsworth is soon on the path to a definitive reconciliation with his native England, a country that is decidedly superior to Belgium. To earlier examples of the author's contemptuous image of Belgians we could add the following one. The girls in Crimsworth's class include

(10) a band of very vulgar, inferior-looking Flamandes, including two or three examples of that deformity of person and imbecility of intellect whose frequency in the Low Countries would seem to furnish proof that the climate is such as to induce degeneracy of the human mind and body. (ST 84)

This description is part of the narrator's devastating portrait gallery of female pupils sketched in chapter 12, which also includes other nationalities, reflecting the status of Brussels as a cosmopolitan space. For example, Crimsworth also introduces the reader to a "half-breed between German and Russian" who is "deplorably ignorant and ill-informed" (ST 82), and to a pupil "of mixed Belgian and Spanish origin" who "makes noises with her mouth like a horse" (ST 84). Frances left aside, qualities such as cleanliness, "intellectual (...) features," "grave and modest countenances," or "a general air of native propriety and decency" can only be observed together in the "British English" pupils who attend the school (ST 86). Clearly, it is all a matter of English Protestant superiority and continental Catholic inferiority.

There is one character that conspicuously remains outside of this axiology, who indeed rejects it, namely, Hunsden, who calls himself a "universal patriot" (ST 201) and whose very looks and attitudes resist easy classification in the narrator's racial taxonomy of 'national' features:

(11) I know not what it was in Mr. Hunsden that (...) suggested to me, every now and then, the idea of a foreigner. In form and features he might be pronounced English – though even there one caught a dash of something Gallic – but he had no English shyness: he had learnt somewhere – somehow, the art of setting himself quite at his ease, and of allowing no insular timidity to intervene as a barrier between him and his convenience or pleasure. (...) he resembled no one else I had ever seen before. (ST 24)

Hunsden does not refrain from referring to his native England as a "dirty little country" (ST 197). Nations mean nothing to him, much to the annoyance of Frances, who is, among other things, an ardent Swiss patriot: "Mr. Hunsden, (...) you don't acknowledge what really exists; you want to annihilate individual patriotism and national greatness as an Atheist would annihilate God and his own soul, by denying their existence" (ST 200). When the argument between Frances and Hunsden risks becoming a little too spirited, Crimsworth typically intervenes as a conciliatory mediator/translator:

(12) "If Tell [Wilhelm Tell, national hero of the Swiss, DD & MG] was like Wellington, he was an ass."
"Does not *ass* mean *baudet*?" asked Frances turning to me.
"No, no," replied I, "it means an *esprit-fort* and now," I continued, as I saw that fresh occasion of strife was brewing between these two, "it is high time to go." (ST 202)

This illustrates the extent to which an *histoire croisée* or 'entangled history' approach (Werner and Zimmermann 2006) is needed to see beyond the binaries and appreciate the extent to which Crimsworth comes to find his own identity and destiny as an Englishman through multiple contacts with different nationalities and with both pro- and anti-nationalist ideologies. Belgium, located at the crossroads of nations and languages, turns out to be an ideal site for intercultural mediations and transfers which are instrumental in defining what it means to be 'English'.

Predictably perhaps, the outcome of this process of self-discovery is that England and its Protestant values prevail. It is the country where Crimsworth and Frances find their ultimate fulfillment. But, while the supremacy of Protestantism remains beyond doubt throughout the novel, the self-discovery process involves certain other ambiguities which are never entirely resolved. Crimsworth's efforts to linguistically de-gallicize and anglicize his half-continental wife turn out to be fruitless: "Talk French to me she would, and many a punishment she has had for her wilfulness" (ST 211). Her double nationality is epitomized by her hybrid name 'Frances Evans Henri' – 'Evans' is English, 'Frances' is English but semantically evokes Frenchness, 'Henri' is French – and it is simply too deeply ingrained to be erasable. This sits very uneasily with any simplistic nation-based axiology. In a very different but complementary way, the programmatic internationalism of Hunsden further muddles simple, pure notions of Englishness, and it is worth pointing out that Brontë keeps Hunsden center-stage until the end of the book as a neighbor and mentor to Crimsworth and indeed as a disturbingly strong influence on their young son.

None of this alters the fact that the novel abounds with scornful and hateful remarks about Belgium and Roman Catholicism, making one wonder what might happen when a text like this is transferred 'back' to the linguistic medium and cultural context in which the greatest part of the story takes place. Wouldn't translators be tempted to tone down somewhat the novel's crassest anti-Catholic and anti-Belgian sentiments, when writing for a Catholic or Belgian readership? And how would the early translators have dealt with the novel's French heterolingualism, which was potentially a big challenge for both the French translator (how to foreground the otherness of the French passages when the target language itself is French?) and the Dutch one (can the French be kept if it is not necessarily part of the general readers' linguistic repertoire?).

5. The translations and the wider pattern of reception

Despite its lukewarm English reception, *The Professor* was promptly translated into Danish and Russian (1857), into French, Swedish and German (1858), and into Dutch (1859). Before the end of the nineteenth century, Hungarian (1874), Spanish (1884) and Italian (1890) translations were to follow. The way for these translations had been paved by the international success of *Jane Eyre* and Emily Brontë's *Wuthering Heights*. Reflecting a general decline of the literary reputation of Charlotte Brontë in the first half of the twentieth century, interest in *The Professor* was on the wane until WWII, but since then further translations have been published into some twenty other languages, including Chinese (1998), Persian (2013) and Ukrainian (2016). In total, the novel has been translated into 28 different languages. According to the Brussels Brontë Blog,[5] which keeps track of Brontë translations worldwide, *The Professor* occupies the sixth position, behind *Wuthering Heights* (61 languages), *Jane Eyre* (59 languages), *Villette* (31 languages), *The Tenant of Wildfell Hall* (30 languages), and *Shirley* (29 languages).

---

5   Last update on 29 December 2016. Our bibliographical data on the translations are based on this source.

The Dutch translation in our corpus was published anonymously in Groningen by a publisher named de Erven C. M. van Bolhuis Hoitsema, who had earlier brought out the first Dutch translation of *Jane Eyre* (1849). We have not been able to identify the translator, who also remains unnamed in the lengthy book review that appeared in the Dutch literary journal *Vaderlandsche letteroefeningen* in the same year as the novel (Anon. 1859). The reviewer suggests that the novel had deserved a more careful translator and lists a few mistakes to prove his/her point but acknowledges that the translation's overall quality is better than these occasional blunders would suggest (Anon. 1859, 518). The reviewer also comments on the bizarre title that was given to the translation: *Edward Crimsworth. Het leven van een onderwijzer* ('Edward Crimsworth. The life of a teacher'). This choice is indeed hard to comprehend, as Edward Crimsworth – William's brother – all but disappears from the plot from chapter 6 onwards. Would the title have been put in accidentally by someone who had read the first few chapters only?

The French translation was published in Paris and bears the name of Henriette Loreau (1813-1879). Little is known about this translator but an obituary in the *Gazette des Femmes* of 10 September 1879 informs us that she was the wife of a doctor-journalist who had worked for the journal *La Démocratie pacifique* during the French Second Republic, and that she had been awarded the *Langlois* prize for her English-into-French translations of Stanley, Livingstone, Dickens and Mayne-Reid, as well as the *Prix de l'Académie* for her translation work. She is said to have passed away at home in her sixteenth-century chateau de la Chauvinière, situated in the Loire valley. As we can infer from this biographical notice, Henriette Loreau would have belonged to the democratically minded French upper classes (*La Démocratie pacifique* was known as a leftist journal, censured during the Second Empire). Her translation of *The Professor* seems to have been favorably received in France, if we can go by the opinion of reviewer A. Legrelle (1861, 6), who speaks of the "excellente traduction de Mme Loreau." Its inclusion in Hachette's series *Bibliothèque des meilleurs romans étrangers* in the 1860s is further testimony to its good reputation. There have been four later French-language translations of *The Professor*, but these have not stood in the way of frequent later reprints of Loreau's version, which now counts no fewer than 23 editions, the most recent one being from 2016. With more than 160 years on the clock, it stands as the most prominent French version of *The Professor*.

5.1 The rendering of the ST's French heterolingualisms

That the first French and Dutch versions take a very different approach to the translation project may be obvious from their renderings of Example (3).

(3a) Qu'il m'est arrivé souvent de désirer un mois de liberté que je passerais à la campagne, dans une petite ferme proprette, entourée de champs et de bois ! Quelle vie charmante que la vie champêtre! ne trouvez vous pas, monsieur? — Cela dépend, mademoiselle. — Quel bon vent, qu'il fait de bien ! » poursuivit Zoraïde. En ceci elle avait raison ; je tenais mon chapeau à la main, et la brise en passant dans mes cheveux rafraîchissait mes tempes ; néanmoins son effet bienfaisant s'arrêtait à l'épiderme, le sang bouillonnait dans mes veines, et, tandis que je regardais au hasard, un feu intérieur dévorait ma poitrine.
« Si j'ai bien compris, dis-je enfin, Mlle Henri a quitté votre maison pour ne plus y revenir. (TT Fr 172-173)

Ik ben zeker, dat ik dikwijls sterk naar de vrijheid verlang om eene geheele maand op het land door te brengen in eene kleine, aardige, nette boerderij, van alle zijden door velden en bosschen omgeven; welk een kostelijk leven is dat land leven! Is het niet zoo, Monsieur?" "Dat hangt er van af, Mademoiselle." "Dat er een goede en frissche wind is!" vervolgde de kostschoolhouderes; en zij had gelijk, want er woei een zachte, luwe zuidewind. Ik had mijn hoed in de hand en dit liefelijk koeltje, dat door mijn haar heenstreek, gleed als een verzachtende balsem over mijne slapen. Zijne verkwikkende uitwerking drong echter niet verder door dan enkel tot de oppervlakte van mijn voorhoofd; want terwijl ik naast Mdlle Reuter voort-wandelde, gloeide ik nog inwendig en terwijl ik er over mijmerde, dat daar een vuur brandde, sprak mijn mond de woorden: "Ik begrijp, dat Mdlle Henri van hier gegaan is en niet zal terug komen ?" (TT Du 172)

The French version counts 123 words, against 158 for the Dutch version and 146 for the English original, illustrating the effort made by the Dutch translator[6] to stay as close as possible to the wording of the original at the cost even of a certain long-windedness, whereas Henriette Loreau does not shy away from textual cuts in the interest of instant readability.

---

6   We are using the term 'translator' in a comprehensive way which includes other agents (e.g., the publisher) who may have had a hand in producing the translation.

Loreau's domesticating approach also shows in the absence of any effort to preserve the distancing effect of the original's French heterolingual words and sentences. The words, phrases and sentences that Brontë had introduced in French (underlined in Examples (3) and (3a)) merge imperceptibly into the target language and lose their specific function as markers of Frenchness. The translator's concern for readability even leads her to edit Brontë's French. For instance, the original's "Que le vent est bon et frais!" is rewritten for greater idiomaticity as "Quel bon vent, qu'il fait de [sic] bien!"[7] Interestingly, the phrase which Brontë put in the narrator's mouth as an explanatory translational gloss of this French sentence ("for it was a south wind, soft and sweet") is simply left out by the French translator, presumably because it would have struck her as redundant for the French reader. Economy of expression and the removal of traces of the original's French heterolingualism are made to work together to produce clear, transparent, and monolingual French prose.

The Dutch translator follows a different approach with respect to Brontë's heterolingualism. Individual French words are simply left untranslated. Witness the preservation of "Monsieur" and "Mademoiselle" in the example. Various toponyms and other names are similarly kept in French, even where a Dutch equivalent would have been available, as in the following example.

(13) I saw what a fine street was the <u>Rue Royale</u> (...) and I looked down into a narrow back street, which I afterwards learnt was called the <u>Rue d'Isabelle</u>. I well recollect that my eye rested on the green door of a rather large house opposite, where, on a brass plate, was inscribed, "<u>Pensionnat de demoiselles</u>." Pensionnat! (ST 50-51)

ik zag welk eene fraaije straat de <u>rue royale</u> was (...) en naar beneden zag in eene naauwe donkere straat, welke zooals ik later vernam, de <u>rue Isabelle</u> heette. Ik herinner mij goed, dat mijn oog bleef rusten op de groene deur van een vrij groot huis aan de overzijde, prijkende met eene koperen plaat met het opschrift <u>Pensionnat de demoiselles</u>. Kostschool! (TT Du 64)

The reader is thus reminded that the characters' social milieu is predominantly a French-speaking one. Italics are even used here to highlight the linguistic otherness of the street names and the name of the school. That said, the end of Example (13) shows the translator's effort not to push Dutch readers out of their linguistic comfort zone. While the word 'pensionnat' in the original is repeated with an exclamation mark to express the narrator's amazement, in the Dutch version the word is repeated in the translated Dutch form 'kostschool'

---

7   Ironically, the typo ('de' for 'du') quite undoes the effect of the intended stylistic improvement.

to make sure the reader understands what kind of an establishment (a boarding school) Crimsworth is about to discover.

These isolated words and noun phrases have to carry the full weight of the original's French heterolingual dimension. Returning to Example (3a), we can see that all Brontë's French sentences are silently translated into Dutch. In other words, the Dutch translation welcomes heterolingual French material but below the sentence level only. Brontë's French sentences and speech turns in Examples (3) and (6) above have likewise all been rendered into Dutch. The set phrase "Honi soit qui mal y pense" (ST 77; TT Du 99) is the only full French sentence to be found in the Dutch version.

Similar findings apply to French-English interference phenomena in the text. In Example (1) we saw how French characters tend to mispronounce 'Crimsworth' as 'Creemsvort'. All six instances of this are carefully reproduced in the Dutch version, whereas the French translator systematically 'corrects' the name, quite in line with her general policy of domestication.[8] The renderings of Example (6) show the same norms at work. The French version avoids the heterolingual complications by cutting the *franglais* of Frances and the linguistic corrections it triggers in the original, reducing the dialogue from 167 words to a mere 112 words (TT Fr 156-157) in what becomes a grammatically faultless monolingual exchange which merely sums up Frances's family history. The Dutch version with its 170 words is more complete. While it silently homogenizes Frances's full French sentences into Dutch, at least some of the linguistic interference that colors her *franglais* is conveyed by means of grammatically imperfect Dutch. Here is a brief sample taken from the exchange:

(6a)   — Ma mère était Anglaise.   "Maar" (langzaam en verlegen), "mijne ouders waren niet alle *twee* van Genève."
— Et votre père?   "Zeg *beide*, in plaats van 'alle twee', Mademoiselle."
— Il était Suisse.   "Niet *beide* Zwitsers; mijne moeder was eene Engelsche."
(TT Fr 156)   "Ah! en van Engelsche afkomst?"
"Ja, al hare voorouders waren Engelschen."
"En uw vader ?"
"Hij was een Zwitser." (TT Du 155-156)

Turning to English now, the novel's source language becomes an "other" language in both translations. Has some of it been preserved for heterolingual

---

8   Correspondingly, and not surprisingly, the English name 'Edward (Crimsworth)' is maintained in the Dutch version but is systematically Frenchified into 'Edouard' by Henriette Loreau.

effect? The Dutch version maintains references to the narrator's English background, as in the following example:

(14) she would be happy to see me to take my "goûter" (a meal which answers to our English "Tea") with her in the dining-room (ST 60) | Mme Pelet me priait de venir goûter avec elle dans son cabinet particulier (TT Fr 75) | Mad. Pelet (...), die zich gelukkig zoude rekenen, als ik mijn _goûter_ (vesperbrood, een maal dat gelijk staat met het Engelsche _tea_) bij haar in de eetzaal wilde komen gebruiken (TT Du 76)

The Dutch translator fully renders the narrator's gloss ("a meal which answers to our English 'Tea'"), but two interesting micro-shifts occur. First, the inclusive first-person 'our' in "our English 'Tea'" is replaced by the neutral definite article *het* (the), shifting the deictic position of the narrator to the more external position of the Dutch translator. Second, the translator adds the extra Dutch gloss *vesperbrood* (evening bread) to make doubly sure the reader understands the French *goûter*. Other than that, the Dutch version scrupulously tries to follow the original as much as possible, unlike the French one, in which the word *goûter* is copied, albeit as a verb and, more crucially, without any heterolingual effect and thus without any need for the explanatory gloss into which the English reference to 'tea' was embedded. With all these heterolingual corners cut, Loreau provides a straightforward monolingual gist rendering of the original's basic meaning. In more standard situations, however, Loreau does preserve forms of address (e.g., "sir," "gentleman") and names (e.g., a street name such as "Grove Street") in English, endowing her text with a very modest degree of English heterolingualism in references to English characters and places.

As to the few Flemish names and the one single example of Flemish heterolingualism *couc* (Example (9) above), these have been preserved in both translations. It is surprising that the Dutch translator makes nothing of the fact that *couc* is really the Flemish (and Dutch) word *koek*. S/he presumably wanted to recreate the narrator's sense of interlingual alienation.

(9a) j'entrai chez un boulanger afin de me restaurer d'un *couc* (mot flamand dont j'ignore l'orthographe ; à Corinthe, *anglice*), d'une tarte aux groseilles et d'une tasse de café (TT Fr 185) | in een bakkerswinkel binnentrad en mij op een *couc* (?) (het is een Vlaamsch woord, dat ik niet weet hoe het gespeld moet worden) *à Corinthe*, d.i. een krentebroodje, en een kop koffij onthaalde (TT Du 185)

The French translator's parenthesis and the fact that she has Crimsworth buy three items from the bakery rather than two show that she failed to understand *anglice* (meaning "in English"). Her *tarte aux groseilles* (redcurrant pie) is a mistranslation for 'currant bun', which Brontë had introduced in the original as an explanatory English near-equivalent for *couc à Corinthe* and not to treat the hungry narrator to an extra pastry. But Loreau's effort to maintain the metalingual comment on the Flemish word is duly noted.

Most of Brontë's metalingual comments are translated in the Dutch and French versions. By way of example, Table 1 lists the number of occurrences of the most elementary metalingual way to identify the language spoken in the fictional world:

Table 1. Language identification accompanying quotation verbs

ST	TT Fr	TT Du
"in French": 10	"en français": 6	"in het Fransch": 7
"in English": 18	"en anglais": 11	"in het Engelsch": 18

The numbers match up roughly but with the Dutch version again staying closer to the original. The use of such metalingual identifications enables the translator to maintain a semblance of heterolingualism while linguistically homogenizing the dialogues and narrative discourse *themselves*. As we have seen, this is exactly what both translators do in various degrees with respect to French, the original's main 'other' language.

The Dutch translator is happy to transfer Brontë's French but below the sentence level only. He or she was clearly not writing with fully bilingual Dutch/French readers in mind. More specifically, his or her intended readership would appear to have been Dutch rather than Belgian, which is consistent with the fact that the translation came out from a Dutch (Groningen-based) publisher. While the translator stays as close as possible to the original in other respects, the significant shift away from Brontë's occasionally audacious recourse to vehicular matching towards a linguistically far more homogeneous text in Dutch appears to bespeak a concern with the readability and marketability of the translation, to be achieved by lowering the threshold of multilingual skills expected in the reader. In Dutch society around the 1850s-1860s French was well-known in educated circles and among social elites, but to a lesser extent in the middle classes; the translator may have been reaching out to the latter and to potential readers who had only attended elementary forms of education. The average Dutch-speaking Belgian general reader in the same period, on the other hand, being more fluent in French, would not have been bothered by more extensive French heterolingualism.

As to the French translator, she simply dissolves *all* of Brontë's heterolingual French into a target-language discourse that is homogeneously, seamlessly and elegantly French, not hesitating even to edit the original's French where needed. The disappearance of othered and othering French is here part of an overall strategy of translational domestication.

5.2 The rendering of the STs axiological oppositions

In addition to serving to identify the language in which utterances are produced, metalingual observations may also describe *how* the language is being used, for instance, how well or how inadequately according to certain norms. As already suggested, Brontë was appalled by the "horrors" of the Belgian-French accent and the two translators clearly show no shyness in taking over her contemptuous comments:

(15) | "How do you like Belgium, Monsieur?" asked she in an accent of the broadest Bruxellois – I could now well distinguish the difference between the fine and pure Parisian utterance of M. Pelet, for instance, and the guttural enunciation of the Flamands (ST 61) | — Comment trouvez-vous la Belgique, monsieur? Vous y plaisez-vous » ? me demanda-t-elle avec un accent du plus franc bruxellois ; je sentais maintenant toute la défférence [sic] qui existait entre la prononciation élégante et pure de M. Pelet, par exemple, et le parler guttural et traînard des Flamands (TT Fr 77) | Hoe vindt gij België, Monsieur?" vroeg zij met het platste Brusselsch accent. Ik konde nu zeer goed het verschil opmerken bij voorbeeld tusschen de beschaafde en zuivere Parijsche uitspraak van Mons. Pelet en het keel- en neusgeluid van de Vlamingen (TT Du 77)

The three versions agree that the linguistic norms for correct French usage are defined and upheld in Paris and that the French spoken by Belgians is a woefully deficient derivative of it. For the French translator this sociolinguistic reality was apparently so obvious that the word 'Parisian' wasn't even worth translating because of its pleonastic nature as a localizing qualifier of Pelet's "elegant and pure" French. While Brontë's narrator describes Belgian French as having an unbecoming "guttural" pronunciation, the French translator adds that the Belgians also speak it in a *traînard* manner (drawling, sluggish, slow), which is arguably suggestive of intellectual backwardness. The Dutch translator, too, goes one step further than Brontë by giving spoken Belgian French a nasal ("neus") as well as a guttural ("keel") ring and by lowering its semiotic status from the level of an imperfect "enunciation" to that of mere noises ("geluid"), just this side of animal communication.

Example (10) above illustrates Brontë's hostile portrait of the Belgian girls. The Belgian boys are nothing better: they are said to have feeble brains and strong physical appetites; they are dull, stubborn and lazy, occasionally reminding one of "desperate swine" (ST 56); teachers hoping to receive any form of gratitude from them will have to lower themselves to the depth of their "imbecility," and the pupils' gratitude will then express itself through unwelcome "showers of Brabant saliva and handfuls of Low-Country mud" (ibid.). Those assuming that this class of boys perhaps make up a non-representative sample of Belgians are told to think again: "Pelet's school was (...) an epitome of the Belgian Nation" (ST 57). Both translators convey these and dozens of other dismissive comments on Belgium without attenuating their polemical force.

Such comments were bound to cause offence to Belgian readers, and they did. In a review of Loreau's translation[9] published in the Belgian newspaper *Le Soir* (14 January 1890), journalist René Gange rebukes Brontë for her unfair portrait of the Belgians, using a strong-worded comparison which ironically displays a startling level of racial prejudice itself by shifting the opprobrium of inferiority from the Belgians to the people who inhabit Belgium's African colony: "Mais, là, vraiment, ne croirait-on pas lire la description morale de quelque peuplade sauvage du Congo?" ("wouldn't you believe, really, that you were reading the moral description of some savage Congolese tribe?"). Why was it then that the translators did not tone down Brontë's anti-Belgian sentiments? The answer to this is complex but must include the consideration that neither translation was primarily produced for a Belgian readership.

Flemish readers would not have been foremost in the mind of the Dutch translator. Flemish culture, and Belgium more generally, were seen as being peripheral to Dutch culture and lacking in prestige. In political terms, Belgium had seceded from the United Kingdom of the Netherlands in 1830 and the international community did not formally recognize it until 1839, barely twenty years before the publication of the translation. Belgium in the 1850s was a young and small state; its Catholicism and exclusive recourse to French as

---

9   We have not been able to find any contemporary Flemish (Dutch-speaking) review of *The Professor*.

an official language alienated it from the Netherlands; as a language, Flemish (Dutch) wasn't even officially acknowledged by Belgium's own institutions and French-speaking bourgeoisie. In other words, Brontë's critique of Belgium and its Flemish inhabitants would not have upset the Dutch translator, his/her publisher, or the majority of his/her readers, inasmuch as Flemings and Belgians were very much 'others' to the Dutch. It is crucial in this respect that Brontë's novel very clearly makes the distinction between the Netherlands and Flanders/Belgium. Intriguingly, the Dutch translator remains on the alert to clarify things where the possibility of ambiguity arises regarding the target of Brontë's hostility. In Example (10), Brontë's phrase "in the Low Countries" is normally understood as covering both Belgium and Holland. As seen in Example (10a), this is, indeed, exactly how the French translator renders it: "en Belgique et en Hollande." The Dutch translator must have spotted the danger of any such interpretation and narrowed down the geographical range of the phrase to "in België."

(10a)   deux rangées de Flamandes vulgaires, parmi lesquelles se faisaient remarquer deux ou trois exemples de cette difformité et physique morale que l'on rencontre si fréquemment <u>en Belgique et en Hollande</u>, et qui semble prouver que le climat y est assez insalubre pour amener la dégénérescence de l'esprit et du corps. (TT Fr 112)

een troep zeer gewone Vlaamsche meisjes van ondergeschikten aard, waaronder twee of drie voorbeelden van die mismaaktheid van persoon en zwakheid van geest, welke men zoo menigvuldig <u>in België</u> aantreft, hetgeen een bewijs zoude schijnen op te leveren, dat het klimaat er eene ontaarding van den menschelijken geest en hel ligchaam medebrengt (TT Du 109)

As the Dutch translator saw it, the climate-induced "degeneracy of the human mind and body" may well have afflicted people south of the Dutch-Belgian border but surely not north of it!

The Dutch-Belgian border was construed not only as a national and a linguistic border but also, importantly, as a religious one, separating the predominantly Protestant Dutch from the predominantly Catholic Belgians. This helps us understand not only why the Dutch translator would not have minded, and may well have relished, Brontë's virulent anti-Catholic and anti-Belgian feelings, but also why his/her translation promptly received a glowing and lengthy review in *Vaderlandsche Letteroefeningen*, one of Holland's leading literary and cultural magazines (Anon. 1859). Among other things, the reviewer praises the freshness and psychological realism of the novel, but Brontë is lauded above all else for her moral fibre and for the "levendig gevoel voor waarheid, regt en pligt" ("lively sense of truth, rightfulness and duty") (Anon. 1859, 521) that pervades the novel. The Dutch reader would have been pleased to find that the novel contains a Dutch character of high moral caliber, Victor Vandenhuten, who plays a limited but crucial part in the story by putting Crimsworth on the professional track that will lead him to financial independence and marriage. As with Frances, Brontë lets one Protestant help another to lift himself out of the morass of Catholic ineptitude and corruption.

If the Dutch translator made no effort to tailor the text to Flemish readers, we can likewise say that Francophone Belgians would not have been central to Loreau's intended readership. The French tended to see Belgium as a small nation of little significance. If anything, Loreau's faithful translation of Brontë's negative depiction of Belgium would have chimed with common perceptions in France.

This leaves us with the problem that France was also predominantly a Catholic country in the nineteenth century and that Brontë's contempt for this religion would by extension also have been offensive to many of Loreau's readers. The translator does little to accommodate such sensibilities. In the following example, we see that she deletes Brontë's praise for the merits of an "honest *protestant* education," but this remains an isolated example, while the original's strong views on the pernicious influence of Catholicism are copied wholesale:

| (16) | these poor girls had never known the advantages of settled homes, decorous example, or <u>honest protestant education</u>; resident a few months now in one <u>Catholic</u> school, now in another as their parents wandered from land to land (…) they had picked up (…) many bad habits, losing every notion even of the first elements of <u>religion</u> and morals, and acquiring an imbecile indifference to every sentiment that can elevate humanity (ST 86) | pauvres enfants n'ayant jamais eu d'intérieur régulier ni de bons principes, encore moins de bons exemples; partageant la vie errante de leurs pères, allant (…) de pension en pension <u>catholique</u>, où elles ramassaient (…) beaucoup de mauvaises habitudes, où elles perdaient les premières notions de morale et d'instruction <u>religieuse</u> qu'elles avaient pu recevoir, et les remplaçaient par une stupide indifférence pour tous les sentiments qui élèvent l'humanité (TT Fr 114) |

The negative image of the M. Pelet presents a comparable problem, as it was obvious to English and French readers alike that he was being portrayed as a typical Frenchman. As a one reviewer (Legrelle 1861, 6) put it, "M. Pelet, notre compatriote fixé en Belgique, a été pour l'auteur, je le crains, l'occasion de dessiner non pas uniquement une silhouette de Français, mais bien la silhouette des Français" ("I fear that M. Pelet, our fellow countryman living in Belgium, has for the author been an occasion to sketch a portrait not just of a Frenchman but of the French"). It is possible to find the odd instance of Pelet's image being retouched, as in Example (5a).

(5a) des traits réguliers, une figure agréable, <u>fine et spirituelle, qui attestait son origine, car il était né de parents français</u> ; mais dont le caractère gaulois, toujours <u>un peu</u> dur, était modifié par des yeux bleus d'une <u>grande</u> douceur et par une certaine expression de mélancolie. (TT Fr 66)

The positive personality traits "fine" and "spirituelle," along with the regularity of Pelet's features and the agreeable aspect of his figure are associated more directly and in a more explicitly approving manner to his French ancestry. Brontë's phrase "the degree of harshness inseparable from Gallic lineaments" is softened by the use of "un peu" ("a little"). But then, such corrections of Brontë's anti-French position remain few and far between. As Example (17) shows, Loreau does not hesitate to render Brontë's equation of Frenchness with sexual immorality.

(17) Pelet's bachelor's life had been passed <u>in proper French style with due disregard to moral restraint</u> – and I thought his married life promised to be very French also. (ST 156)

M. Pelet avait mené la vie de garçon <u>d'après la méthode française, c'est-à-dire sans égard pour les mœurs</u>; et je pensai que la période matrimoniale de son existence rentrerait dans le même système. (TT Fr 208)

In stylistic terms, Loreau adopts a domesticating approach, but apparently she set herself a fairly strict limit as to how far she could go in modifying the original's semantic and ideological positions.

The translator's reluctance to improve the image of Catholicism and of M. Pelet is possibly related to the post-1789 French self-image as a secular republic with an ideal of universal liberty, including religious freedom and indeed a tradition of libertinism. Other factors that may have played a part include the considerable symbolic capital that the Brontë sisters had built up in France through the massive successes of *Wuthering Heights* and *Jane Eyre* (O'Neil-Henry 2013). On that basis, the French translator, publisher and readers may have been willing to entitle these quintessentially English novelists to the bizarre opinions one should be ready to expect from the English. It is worth recalling that *The Professor* was often read through an autobiographical lens and that the national and religious biases expressed in the novel could thus by ascribed to and excused by the naivety of Charlotte Brontë in the 1840s, a young woman from the Yorkshire countryside who would have been quite unprepared for the different customs of the continentals she was to discover. Such is the view expressed by reviewer W.G. in *La Revue critique des livres nouveaux* (April 1858, 166): "là, cette Anglaise pur-sang avait été assez effarouchée de certaines coutumes continentales, et l'on voit dans son livre des traces de sa naïve stupéfaction" ("there [in Brussels], this thoroughbred English woman [Charlotte Brontë] had been quite dismayed by certain continental customs, and in the book we see the traces of her naive astonishment").

Other critics, including Selden (1863), were less forgiving and pointed out that Brontë was the uncritical mouthpiece for a dismal collection of old English prejudices ("tous les vieux préjugés conservés en Angleterre"):

> Vive l'Angleterre, l'histoire et les héros ! A bas la France, la fiction et les faquins ! (...) Ils croient que nous n'avons point d'empire sur nous-même (...) et pour eux, la plus simple marque de cette infériorité morale, c'est la persistance avec laquelle nous nous en tenons à la religion. On devine bien que Miss Brontë, à cet égard, est bonne protestante (...) Elle est bien vraiment anglaise de religion, d'instinct, d'antipathies, de préférences, et on la reconnait pour telle dans l'opposition de ses héros et de ses coquins. On la reconnait plus visiblement encore dans le contraste patriotique qu'elle établit entre les gens du continent et ses chers anglais. (Selden 1863, 263-264)

> (Long live England, its history and heroes! Down with France, its fiction and its scoundrels! (...) They think that we have no control over ourselves (...) and for them, the most obvious sign of this moral inferiority is the persistence with which we stand by our religion. It is easy to guess that Miss Brontë in this respect is a good protestant (...) She is truly English in terms of religion, instinct, antipathies, preferences; one easily recognizes her as such in the opposition between her heroes and her villains, and, more easily even, in the patriotic contrast between the people of the continent and her dear English.)

The transfer of Brontë's hostile representation of aspects of the target culture in these two translation projects took place in a complex field of forces. All in all, however, selective translation, adaptation and non-translation were used far less than might have been expected to make Brontë's polemical attitudes more palatable to her prospective Belgian, French, Dutch or Catholic readerships. Possibly, this helps to account for the fact that, like *The Professor* in English, these translations remained in the shadow of the great Brontë novels that had catapulted Charlotte and her sisters to international fame.

6. Concluding remarks

In 2012, Lieven D'hulst responded to Even-Zohar's (1990) call to integrate the study of translation into the wider field of transfer studies. Working with the Toury-inspired concept of 'assumed transfer' and entering into an interdisciplinary dialogue with existing Franco-German literary and historical research programs operationalizing the notions of *histoire croisée* (Werner and Zimmermann 2006) and *transferts culturels* (Espagne and Werner 1987), D'hulst wanted, from a strictly historical perspective, to do justice to the interrelations between transfer practices (be they verbal or not), including translations, to the reciprocity of cultural exchanges, and to their intercultural mediators. The case of *The Professor* and its early Dutch and French translations surely demonstrates the relevance of this research program.

On the one hand, the English novel as such displays an array of multidirectional transfer processes and techniques at different levels (text genesis, plot, cultural images, languages). At first sight, it might be tempting to model these in terms of a straightforward model England ⇨ Belgium ⇨ England, as visualized above in Figure 1. However, a more careful reading reveals a multiplication of interactions and mutual perceptions, with Dutch, French and Swiss characters and viewpoints adding depth, complexity and indeed a degree of unresolved ambiguity to the novel. This complex *histoire croisée* finds linguistic expression in a novel that displays various forms and degrees of linguistic interference and heterolingualism, staging many bilingual and translation scenes. Its focus is mainly, but not exclusively, on the transfers between French and English – a confrontation whose significance can only be grasped in a wider historical context of international interactions, and onto which a set of cultural images and axiological oppositions are grafted.

On the other hand, being itself a site for multiple transfers, *The Professor* has turned out to constitute a challenge for 'back' transfers into Dutch and French, that is, Belgium's two main languages. Here too, a wider international constellation of interacting cultural agents, images and values needs to be considered, making it impossible to model the French and Dutch translations in the straightforward linear terms of a novel finally 'coming home' to the linguistic and cultural setting in which most of the story unfolds – something like [England ⇨ Belgium ⇨ England] ⇨ Belgium. Neither of the translations were published in Belgium or were primarily intended for a Belgian readership. Rather, they came from France and Holland, with Catholic Belgium belonging to the overlapping peripheries of these two receptor systems, making it easier for Brontë's negative images of Belgium to be kept intact in both translations.

Acknowledgments

Parts of the presentation of Charlotte Brontë's novel are inspired by Delabastita (2019); we thank the Presses Universitaires de Louvain for permission to reprint the relevant passages. Thanks are also due to our Namur colleagues Laurence Mettewie and Elisabeth Leijnse for their help and encouragement.

References

Anon. 1859. Review of *Edward Crimsworth, of het leven van een Onderwijzer*, by Currer Bell. *Vaderlandsche Letteroefeningen*, April 1859: 518-524. https://www.dbnl.org/tekst/_vad003185901_01/_vad003185901_01_0167.php

Brontë, Charlotte. (1857) 1991. *The Professor*, edited by Margaret Smith and Herbert Rosengarten. Oxford: Oxford University Press.

— 1858. *Le professeur par Currer Bell, auteur de "Jane Eyre, Shirley, Villette," etc. Roman anglais, traduit avec l'autorisation de l'éditeur par Mme Henriette Loreau*. Paris: L. Hachette.

— 1859. *Edward Crimsworth, het leven van een onderwijzer. Een verhaal door Currer Bell, schrijfster van Jane Eyre, Shirley, Villette, enz*. Groningen: De Erven C.M. van Bolhuis Hoitsema.

Brussels Brontë Blog. 2006. http://brusselsbronte.blogspot.com/. Accessed November 5, 2019.

Cohen, William A. 2017. "Why Is There So Much French in *Villette*?" *ELH* 84 (1): 171-194.

Delabastita, Dirk. 2019. "The Master, The Professor." In *Sparks and Lustrous Words. Literary Walks, Cultural Pilgrimages: Essays in Honour of Guido Latré*, edited by Paul Arblaster, Ingrid Bertrand, Véronique Bragard, and Dirk Delabastita, 309-326. Louvain-la-Neuve: Presses Universitaires de Louvain.

D'hulst, Lieven. 2012. "(Re)Locating Translation History: From Assumed Translation To Assumed Transfer." *Translation Studies* 5 (2): 139-155.

Espagne, Michel, and Michael Werner. 1987. "La construction d'une référence culturelle allemande en France : genèse et histoire (1750-1914)." *Annales. Économies, Sociétés, Civilisations* 42 (4): 969-992.

Even-Zohar, Itamar. 1990. *Polysystem Studies*, special issue of *Poetics Today* 11 (1). Tel Aviv: Porter Institute for Poetics and Semiotics.

Gange, René. 1890. "Une Anglaise à Bruxelles." *Le Soir*, January 15, 1890.

Gaskell, Elizabeth. 1857. *The Life of Charlotte Brontë*. London: Smith, Elder & co.

Legrelle, A. 1861. Review of Currer Bell's *The Professor*. *Revue de l'instruction publique en France et dans les pays étrangers* (April 1861): 5-6.

Longmuir, Anne. 2009. "'Reader, Perhaps You Were Never in Belgium?' Negotiating British Identity in Charlotte Brontë's *The Professor* and *Villette*." *Nineteenth-Century Literature* 64 (2): 163-188.

O'Neil-Henry, Anne. 2013. "Domestic Fiction Abroad. *Jane Eyre*'s Reception in post-1848 France." In *Aller(s)-Retour(s): Nineteenth-Century France in Motion*, edited by Loic Guyon and Andrew Watts, 111-124. Newcastle upon Tyne: Cambridge Scholars Publishing.

Selden, Camille. 1863. "Charlotte Brontë et la vie morale en Angleterre." *La Revue nationale et étrangère* (14): 250-279.

Sternberg, Meir. 1981. "Polylingualism as Reality and Translation as Mimesis." *Poetics Today* 2 (4): 221-239.

Werner, Michael, and Bénédicte Zimmermann. 2006. "Beyond Comparison: Histoire Croisée and the Challenge of Reflexivity." *History and Theory* 45 (1): 30-50.

W.G. 1858. Review of *Jane Eyre* and *Le Professeur*, by Currer Bell. *La Revue critique des livres nouveaux*, April 1858: 165-168.

The figure of the translator in two Francophone African classics

Jean-Marc Moura

Abstract

In 2015, in "The figure of the translator revisited: a theoretical overview and a case study", Lieven D'hulst examined a new branch in translation studies: translator studies, which focuses primarily on the agents involved in translation. In his theoretical overview of the figure of the translator, he observed that recent research on this topic follows two separate paths: 1. The study of the way the translator is represented within fictional or autobiographical works, either as a narrator, or as a character; 2. The analysis of the discursive forms and functions of translational enunciations in translations, as they appear in their two main discursive spaces: the paratext (prologues, prefaces, postfaces, footnotes) and the translated text. This chapter examines these two paths by studying two Francophone novels that became African classics: *L'étrange Destin de Wangrin* (*The Fortunes of Wangrin*) by Amadou Hampâté Bâ, which includes a representation of the interpreter in a colonial context, and *Une vie de Boy* (*Houseboy*) by Ferdinand Oyono, which has been translated into fourteen languages, in particular into English, Dutch, Portuguese, Arabic and Chinese. Because of the specificities of the political and social histories of these countries, the translations inevitably evoked different associations among their readers. By examining the way translation is represented in these two works of fiction, this study will allow us to better grasp the complexities of translating and the translator.

1. Introduction

In a 2015 paper, following Andrew Chesterman's suggestion, Lieven D'hulst examined a new branch in translation studies: translator studies (D'hulst 2015, 1). The main object of this new subfield would be to assemble all kinds of "research which focuses primarily and explicitly on the agents involved in translation, for instance on their activities or attitudes, their interaction with their social and technical environment, or their history and influence"

(Chesterman 2009, 20). In his theoretical overview of the works on the translator category, D'hulst observed that current research on this topic follows two separate paths: "the first one looks at the way the translator is represented within fictional or autobiographical works", while the second path "focuses on the discursive forms and functions taken by translational enunciation in translations by occupying their two main discursive spaces, i.e., the paratext (prologues, prefaces, postfaces, footnotes, etc.) and the translated text." (D'hulst 2015, 1). This chapter examines these two paths, taking the example of two Francophone African novels: *L'étrange Destin de Wangrin* by Ahmadou Hampâté Bâ and *Une vie de Boy* by Ferdinand Oyono, that both include a representation of the interpreter in a colonial context. Thus, the complexities of translating and the translator in a postcolonial context, and, in particular, the transfer from orality to writing, may be grasped, as may be exemplified by these two works.

Postcolonial literature can be understood as a form of translation, whereby the language of imperialism is bent, twisted or plied to capture and convey the sociocultural reality or the *Weltanschauung* of a dominated culture. Writing about the experiences of formerly colonized societies in the language of the colonizer is thus likened to translation as a metaphor for the representation of Otherness (Bandia 2010). Empirical studies have enhanced the equation of postcolonial literatures with translation, when they describe postcolonial fictionalization in terms of translation strategies (Bandia 2008; Tymoczko 1999; Zabus 1991). The rationale for these studies is grounded in what Bandia has referred to as the orality/writing interface:

> the representation of cultures of orality in colonial language writing is viewed as a double transposition process involving translating oral narrative cultures into written form and translating between distant or alien language cultures (Bandia 2010, 265)

Therefore, postcolonial literatures often involve the practice of polylingualism and literary heteroglossia: the hybridization and multilayering of languages (Mehrez 1992; Ashcroft 1989). They also frequently focus on a familiar figure in colonial and postcolonial contexts: the interpreter and/or the translator, who appears in our two African classics.

2. L'étrange Destin de Wangrin

L'étrange Destin de Wangrin was translated into English as *The Fortunes of Wangrin*. The novel, published in 1973 by the Malian scholar Ahmadou Hampâté Bâ (1900-1991), deals with the story of Wangrin, a Bambara interpreter and tradesman, who lived under French colonial rule. The general argument of the book is commonplace: Wangrin told his life to Bâ, who merely transcribed the tale in a slightly disconcerting narrative form – a kind of biography with picaresque echoes. Wangrin's life fits a classical ternary structure: initiation, struggles and victories, fall. During his childhood, Wangrin received a double education: his native Bambara education and the French colonial school education. Thanks to his many talents, he became an interpreter and a rich tradesman able to deal both with French colonizers and with his people. But in the end, he forgot his native customs, sunk into debauchery and alcoholism, and died miserably.

The plot could belong to a novel cast in a realistic aesthetic. When Bâ insists on the truth of his story and on his personal acquaintance with the subject, he respects a standard feature of realistic novels. However, Wangrin did really exist and Bâ did not romanticize his life: Wangrin's real name was Samba Traoré and he belonged to a noble Bambara family (Heckmann 1993, 517). The book is in fact part of Bâ's long-lived project: the import of elements of his native oral culture into writing.

Bâ was renowned for his work on Fulani oral traditions. Through his education, both Fulani and Bambara, he received a Muslim and a traditional training. He was a prolific writer and he has published extensively on these traditions.[1] He intended to get Western readers to know and recognize his Fulani oral culture (and, generally, Sub-Saharan Africa) when he worked for UNESCO objecting to the dominant and colonialist definition of his culture. For more than 40 years, through various types of works (ethnography, history, poetry, theology, philosophy, autobiography), he was an interpreter of African cultures to Western readers; first, to French readers, then to a much wider

---

1   Alain Ricard (1995, 160-161) has given a classification of these works:
- books concerning history or theology: *L'Empire peul du Macina* (1955) or the first edition of *Tierno Bokar* (1957);
- various transcriptions of Pular oral texts with a French translation: *Koumen* (1961), *Kaydara* (1969), *L'Eclat de la grande étoile* (1974);
- a "narrative" written in French: *L'étrange Destin de Wangrin* (1973), and his autobiography, *Amkoullel, l'enfant peul* (1991), *Oui mon commandant !* (1993);
- various books written from former lectures: *Aspects de la civilisation africaine* (1972), *Jésus vu par un musulman* (1976);
- a historical and theological book published with M. Cardaire: *Vie et enseignement de Tierno Bokar* (1980).

audience, when he was appointed as a member of the UNESCO executive council, working on African oral tradition, from 1962 to 1970.

For Bâ, as an interpreter, orality is one of the foundational elements of his tradition, a mode of knowledge:

> La tradition orale, c'est la grande école de la vie ; elle traite de la religion, des sciences de la nature comme de la connaissance des minerais, de la pharmacopée et de la médecine, de l'initiation professionnelle, de l'histoire, des jeux et des loisirs, de l'amour et de la mort. Liée au comportement concret de l'homme en société, la connaissance dans les sociétés africaines orales n'est donc pas abstraite et autonome par rapport à la vie. Elle est liée à la vie actuelle et à l'origine de toute connaissance, par la parole divine. (Aggarwal 1990, 206)
> (Oral tradition is the great school of life; it deals with religion, with natural sciences as well as with the knowledge of minerals, of pharmacopeia and medicine, of professional initiation, of history, of games and leisure, of love and death. Knowledge, in African oral societies, is concerned with the practical behavior of man in his group. It is not abstract and cut off from life. It is bound to the present life and to the origin of all knowledge, through the word of God.)

As such, orality requires a technique to facilitate its entry into Western print culture. Before Bâ, the Fulani language (including many dialects spoken by millions of persons) had been recorded in manuscripts. But every writer used specific written forms, each marabout had his own alphabetic form for certain phonemes. The result was that a composer or a writer who did not have a thorough knowledge of his text could not read over his manuscript after six months. The lack of a standard of reference prevented the texts from spreading (Ricard 1995, 160). Bâ insists on this difficulty when he presents the teaching of his Sufi spiritual guide, Tierno Bokar:

> Une Parole toute vibrante de vie et d'amour comme celle qu'a entendue Bandiagara, ce n'est pas un livre qui peut la restituer dans toute sa force. Mais c'est pourtant notre devoir, à nous, qui avons hérité d'une tradition orale, que d'essayer d'en transmettre ce que nous pouvons avant que le temps et l'oubli ne la fassent disparaître de la mémoire des hommes.
> Une difficulté particulière a résidé dans le passage du peul au français, du fait des différences de structure qui caractérisent ces deux langues. (Bâ 1957, 128)
> (A book cannot restore the whole strength of the speech, vibrant with life and love, that was heard in Bandiagara. It is, however, our duty. We have

inherited an oral tradition and we must try to pass on whatever we can before it vanishes into the mists of time and oblivion. A peculiar difficulty lay in the passage from Fulani to French, because of the structural differences of the languages.)

For Bâ, the difficult transfer from oral to writing is the source of a historical process of domination. African knowledge has been relegated to a subaltern position by colonialism as well as by "the literacy bias of modernity based on the privileging of writing over orality" (Bandia 2011, 109), and it is maintained in that position because its specificities prevent him from entering into written archives. Therefore, through the collection of oral tales, Bâ wanted to develop an African perspective on African cultures, which would be accessible to Western scholars:

> Il appartient en effet aux Africains de parler de l'Afrique aux étrangers, et non aux étrangers, si savants soient-ils, de parler de l'Afrique aux Africains. (Bâ 1972, 31)
> (It is indeed up to Africans to speak of Africa to foreigners, and not to foreigners, learned though they may be, to speak of Africa to Africans.)

Moreover, Bâ confronted this problem in French: a language that he first considered as a kind of metalanguage, necessary only to record his knowledge. French became only gradually his second language, a medium through which a vision of the world affected by colonial experience could be expressed.

L'étrange Destin de Wangrin belongs to Bâ's undertaking to record Fulani oral treasure. Only, in this case, he has not chosen a documentary or a scientific presentation, but a narrative that seems close to fiction. In the book, he shows that in a colonial society, orality has been used as a means of domination. During Wangrin's life, ethnographers collected oral narratives in order to uncover a hidden, introspective dimension of Africa, a dimension that would help colonial officers to control the natives if they had access to it.

The character, Wangrin, and the author, Bâ, belonged to the same culture and were friends (Bâ 1973, 7). Their lives could be compared: in spite of important differences (concerning, in particular, religion and religious practice), both men have been interpreters and, at the end of his life, Wangrin was regarded as a wise man and became a storyteller, a situation Bâ could identify with. Readers have even asked Bâ whether he had drawn on his own life to write *L'étrange Destin de Wangrin* (Heckmann 1993, 511). The intimacy between Bâ and Wangrin had two advantages for the author. First, it allowed him to meditate on his own career while speaking of someone else. When he wrote Wangrin's life, he also described important elements of his own life and of his work as an interpreter (D'hulst 2014, 245-47). He did not only tell the extraordinary course of Wangrin's life, he made his readers acquainted with the society in which he, Bâ, was educated, with the conditions of education and initiation that made his career possible, and, ultimately, with the enunciative situation of his first books. From a sociological point of view, *L'étrange Destin de Wangrin* is a description of the socio-cultural context in which Bâ acquired his ability to become an interpreter and a mediator between the cultures. It depicts Bâ's context of education (an explanation of his career as an interpreter) and is at the same time an example of what a good piece of 'ethnographic research' should be. As such, the book can be considered as a meditation on the relationship of orality to writing, a topic underpinning a lot of research in translation studies (Ong 1992; Finnegan 2014; Bandia 2011). It demonstrates the efficiency of the transcription (and interpretation) of orality when this transcription does not favor technical mastery but empathy and 'inner' knowledge of its subject.

3. *Une vie de boy*

Une vie de boy allows us to examine the second path evoked by D'hulst, focusing on the discursive forms and functions taken by translational enunciation.

In 1956, Ferdinand Oyono (1929-2010) published two short novels: *Une vie de boy* and *Le vieux Nègre et la médaille*, in the publishing house of René Julliard, in the series "Les Lettres nouvelles", edited by Maurice Nadeau. *Une vie de boy* could be regarded as a kind of *Bildungsroman*. It pretends to be the found diary of a young Cameroonian who becomes a domestic servant first to a European Catholic priest and then to the French commandant of the district town. In this diary, the young Joseph Toundi Ondoua, known as Toundi, reports on his life. Initially, he becomes a houseboy for Father Gilbert, the local priest, who teaches him how to write and keep a journal, but when Father Gilbert dies in an accident, Toundi becomes 'le boy' of the district commandant. When the commandant's wife, whom he calls "Madame", arrives from France, she has an affair with the local prison director, Moreau. As a houseboy, Toundi is aware of everything, but he continues to serve Madame naïvely. Soon, the whole town knows of the affair, except the husband. When the commandant finds out, knowing that he has lost his colonial authority, he lashes out at Toundi who must have seen it all and who did not inform him. 'Le boy' is sent to prison on vague grounds, where he is whipped to the brink of death.

A prime example of translator studies, focusing on the second path mentioned by D'hulst, is to be found in David Chioni Moore's project "An African Classic in Fourteen Translations: Ferdinand Oyono's *Une vie de boy* on the World Literary Stage" (Chioni Moore 2013, 101), presenting eleven essays exploring the translation of Oyono's classic into Arabic, Chinese, Danish, Dutch, English, German, Nynorsk Norwegian, Portuguese, Russian, Slovene, Swahili, Swedish, and Vietnamese. The critic explores the novel's vexed 1966 translation into English (even the title, with the French African word *boy*, is not easily translated); surveys other translations, over four decades, into twelve additional languages; and discusses the research methodology that was necessary to confront so many different interpretations.

Chioni Moore shows that John Reed's English version of *Une vie de boy*, *Houseboy* (the most widely circulated of the novel's translations, published in 1966 as the twenty-ninth installment of the Heinemann Writers Series), systematically, even ideologically, blunts the offensive language that Oyono's narrator diarist Toundi pervasively uses to diminish his own people and elevate the French (Chioni Moore 2013, 105). To elaborate on this point, it is important to remember that *Une vie de boy* tells of a young Cameroonian who initially has no sense of self other than that given to him by the French. Young Toundi presents himself as a colonized mind: "Je dois ce que je suis devenu au père Gilbert. Je l'aime beaucoup, mon bienfaiteur... [L]orsque j'étais petit, [il] me considérait comme un petit animal familier... Il me présente à tous les Blancs... comme son chef d'œuvre" (24; "I owe what I have become to Father Gilbert, he is my benefactor and I am very fond of him...[W]hen I was small he treated me like a little pet animal... He presents me to all the Whites... as his masterpiece").

A key marker of Toundi's colonized mind is the register of names he uses for Africans. Toundi (or rather, his translator from Ewondo) principally uses *nègres* or *indigènes* for his people and less frequently *compatriotes* or *Noirs*. Reed translates the terms as 'Africans' and only once as 'Negro' (p. 53). In 1956, the term *nègre* is rather pejorative. The movement of *Négritude*, that reappraised the word, is not yet widely known. *Cahier d'un retour au pays natal*, a key poem of this movement, has just been published in its final version by Aimé Césaire. As for *indigène*, the term is definitely colonialist.

Reed's alterations probably flowed from the 1960s expectations of (or desires for) African equality on the global stage: a colonial-to-postcolonial shift, in an era when it became imperative for well-meaning Europeans to upgrade the terms used for the ex-colonized, and when the ex-colonized likewise demanded more respectful terms (Chioni Moore 2013, 107). As a consequence, an important aspect of the novel was ignored in Reed's translation: "the fact that self-directed racism was Oyono's point got lost in his translation." (Chioni Moore 2013, 107).

Another interesting example from this project lies in the comparison between the Flemish-Belgian and the Dutch interpretations of the novel, by Jeroen Dewulf. The novel was translated as *De huisjongen* by today's best-selling author Herman Koch and was published in 1980 by Kosmos, in Amsterdam. Compared to Dutch readers, Flemish readers tended to have a stronger familiarity with the Franco-Cameroonian world described by Oyono. Dewulf speculates that if the translator had been Flemish and not Dutch, the word *boy* would not have been removed from the title, since the term is still familiar in Flemish society today (Dewulf 2013, 115). Because of the specificities of the colonial and social histories of Belgium and the Netherlands, the same Dutch translation inevitably evoked different associations among Flemish and Dutch readers, for instance: "While it is likely that Dutch readers found a confirmation of their worldview in the scenes of torture in the novel's final chapters, many Flemish readers might have focused on Toundi's cunning resistance against an enemy they shared with him." (Dewulf 2013, 117).

Many more aspects of this multischolar project could be mentioned. All reflect the unexpected trajectories that world literary studies take when examining an African text which has been translated from its own tradition into others. Chioni Moore's article and the various associated essays examine the discursive forms and functions taken by transnational enunciation. Let us here focus on the novel's relation to language and translation.

As David Chioni Moore observed, several generations of critics have explored many themes in Oyono's classic: the novel's pervasive eye motif (the natives see everything that happens in the colonial quarter while the Europeans are blind to everything that goes on in the native quarter); the text's mobilization of a child narrator lending credence to the descriptions of French immorality and colonial injustice; the sexual dimension of the tale (white men's African mistresses and white women's licentiousness, contrasted with Toundi's threatless asexuality). But Chioni Moore insists rightly on the novel's engagement with languages:

> This begins at the outset, as the frame narrator notes (while in Spanish Guinea) that Toundi kept his diary not in French but in Ewondo, "une des langues les plus parlées au Cameroun" ("one of the most widely spoken languages in Cameroon") (…) Thus, *Une vie de boy* in French, it seems, is already a translation. (Chioni Moore 2013, 103)

Like Wangrin, Toundi notices that one of the first attractions of the colonists for him is their poor knowledge of the local tongues. His first employer, the Catholic priest Father Gilbert, "connaissait quelques mots Ndjem, mais il les prononçait si mal qu'il leur donnait un sens obscène. Cela amusait tout le monde, ce qui lui assurait un certain succès" ("knew a few words of Ndjem, but he pronounced them so badly that they all had obscene meanings. This amused everyone, so his success was assured", 16).

The text often alerts its readers to the linguistic gap that suffuse colonial relations. While touring the district with the commandant, Toundi describes "un étrange baragouin que les villageois prenaient pour du français et les Français pour la langue indigène" ("a weird gibberish that the villagers supposed was French and the French supposed was the native tongue", 63). When the boy accompanies Madame to the market, she is greeted by comments in the local language, which evaluate her figure, hair and buttocks. She asks Toundi to translate, he replies, embarrassed: "Ils...ils... vous trouvent très... très belle." ("They... they... think you're very... very pretty.", 86). Oyono did not include a glossary of African words and expressions in his book as Bâ did. One finds very few footnotes explaining African words (a note explains 'drill' ("une toile blanche"), 27); another explains *Bekôn* ('prison' or *cimetière des prisonniers*, 121, 184), but the problem of translation is a major theme of the novel.

The issue of translation from Ndjem and Ewondo to French figures in one of the most dramatic moments, when the commandant confronts his wife with her affair. He is furious not just because he has been cuckolded but also because the whole native population knew about it first. He shouts at her:

> Pour eux, je n'étais plus que le 'Ngovina ya ngal a ves zut bisalak a be metua' ! Sais-tu ce que cela veut dire ? Bien sûr que non ! Tu as toujours méprisé les dialectes indigènes... Eh bien, partout où je passe, je ne suis plus que le commandant dont la femme écarte les jambes dans les rigoles et dans les voitures. (149-150)
> (For them, I was nothing more than 'Ngovina ya ngal a ves zut bisalak a be metua'! Do you know what that means? Of course you don't! You've always despised the native dialects... Well, everywhere I go I am nothing but the commandant whose wife opens her legs in ditches and in cars.)

As in *L'étrange Destin de Wangrin*, the question of translation is embedded in the colonial asymmetrical relation of power, and, in both texts, the interpreter, the bridge between two cultures, trying to link the Europeans and the natives, is punished and dies miserably. Both texts are clearly anti-colonial, but Bâ's narrative allows him to consider his own career as an interpreter, whereas Oyono's novel insists on the tragic lack of understanding between the two poles of colonial society.

Apart from widening the contexts of translation beyond the simplistic notion of transfer between languages, translation studies has recognized the importance of translating for postcolonial literatures (Bandia 2010). Lawrence Venuti has considered that "translation is uniquely revealing of the asymmetries that have structured international affairs for centuries" and especially now (Venuti 1998, 158). Studies of the novels by Bâ and Oyono show precisely how the treatment of the very character associated with translation and cultural transfer, the interpreter, is revealing of the deep violence of the colonial situation. Thus, in the two paths surveyed by D'hulst, translator studies allow a methodological expansion of literary research. They concentrate on the textual encapsulation of orality, which is a crucial issue for postcolonial literatures, and they help to diversify the world-literature canon, that was often notoriously Eurocentric, only spiced by few (and ancient) texts from other continents, before the 1980s. Studies of the Francophone (as well as Anglophone or Lusophone) African fiction (usually published in Europe or in the United States) and of its many translations fully globalize literary scholarship, and help avoiding our long-lasting Eurocentric perspective.

References

Aggarwal, Kusum. 1990. *Amadou Hampâté Bâ et l'africanisme*. Paris: L'Harmattan.
Ashcroft, Bill, Griffiths, Gareth, and Helen Tiffin. 1989. *The Empire Writes Back. Theory and Practice in Post-Colonial Literatures*. London: Routledge.
Bâ, Amadou Hampâté. 1957. *Vie et enseignement de Tierno Bokar, le sage de Bandiagara*. Paris. Présence Africaine.
— 1972. *Aspects de la civilisation africaine*. Paris: Présence Africaine.
— 1973. *L'étrange Destin de Wangrin*. Paris: 10/18.
— 1993. *Oui mon commandant !* Paris: Actes Sud.
Bandia, Paul F. 2008. *Translation as Reparation: Writing and Translation in Postcolonial Africa*. Manchester: St. Jerome.
— 2010. "Post-colonial Literatures and Translation." In *Handbook of Translation Studies*, vol. 1, edited by Yves Gambier and Luc van Doorslaer, 264-269. Amsterdam: John Benjamins.
— 2011. "Orality and Translation." in *Handbook of Translation Studies*, vol. 2, edited by Yves Gambier and Luc van Doorslaer, 108-112. Amsterdam: John Benjamins.

Chesterman, Andrew. 2009. "The Name and Nature of Translator Studies." *Hermes – Journal of Language and Communication Studies* 42: 13-22.

Chioni Moore, David. 2013. "An African Classic in Fourteen Translations: Ferdinand Oyono's *Une vie de boy* on the World Literary Stage." *PMLA* 128 (1): 101-118.

D'hulst, Lieven. 2014. *Essais d'histoire de la traduction. Avatars de Janus*. Paris: Classiques Garnier.

— 2015. "The Figure of the Translator Revisited: A Theoretical Overview and a Case Study." *Convergences francophones* 2 (2): 1-11.

Dewulf, Jeroen. 2013. "When Oyono's 'Boy' Speaks Dutch: Two Readings in One Language." *PMLA* 128 (1): 112-118.

Finnegan, Ruth. 2014. *Literacy and Orality*. Milton Keynes: Callender Press.

Heckmann, Hélène. 1993. "Annexe à Bâ, A.H. *Oui mon commandant !*" Paris: Actes Sud.

Mehrez, Samia. 1992. "Translation and the Postcolonial Experience: The Francophone North African Text." In *Rethinking Translation*, edited by Lawrence Venuti, 120-138. London: Routledge.

Ong, Walter. 1992. *Orality and Literacy: The Technologizing of the World*. New York: Methuen.

Oyono, Ferdinand. 2016. *Une vie de boy* [1956]. Paris: René Julliard, "Pocket".

Ricard, Alain. 1995. *Littératures d'Afrique noire*. Paris: CNRS/Karthala.

Tymoczko, Maria. 1999. "Post-colonial Writing and Literary Translation." In *Postcolonial Translation. Theory and Practice*, edited by Susan Basnett and Harish Trivedi, 19-40. London: Routledge.

Venuti, Lawrence. 1998. *The Scandals of Translation: Towards an Ethics of Difference*. London: Routledge.

Zabus, Chantal. 1991. *The African Palimpsest. Indigenization of Language in the West African Europhone Novel*. Amsterdam: Rodopi.

Short remarks about titles

Translation, transfer… and trade

Yves Chevrel & Isabelle Nières-Chevrel

Abstract

As with any translated work, a title is subject to encounters and clashes, both formal and cultural, which are increased by the brevity of its formulation, by the author's personal intentions (which may, in turn, run up against the expectations of the publishing house and its managers), and by the cultural roots of receivers. A translated title is also subject to adaptations which, since the end of the nineteenth century, often start with the transfer of the work into other media (cinema, television), thus offering an 'other' product that tends to replace the translated work and, beyond that, the original work. This chapter studies these phenomena on the following bases. First, a corpus that is not limited to literary works alone (this includes children's literature), but that also draws on works from the humanities. Second, a historical background based on the nineteenth and twentieth century volumes of the *Histoire des traductions en langue française*, published by Verdier. After a brief introduction that takes stock of current research in translation studies (which focuses mainly on literary works), we will analyze the status of the translated title (in particular: who owns the title and can act on it? What legal protection is there for the translated title?) and the cultural stakes of the translated title (themes/thematic titles; respect for the reader; respect for the original title; losses and gains; new meanings; cultural compromises). In the last part, we will analyze translated titles in literature and mass culture.

1. Introduction

At the beginning of his work, *Seuils* (1987), Gérard Genette devotes about forty pages to titles, while adding a note on a "petite discipline, à ce jour la plus active de toutes celles (…) qui s'appliquent à l'étude du paratexte" (Genette 1987, 54) ("little discipline, which to date is the most active of all the disciplines (…) concerned with studying the paratexte"); Genette calls it 'titrologie'. He lists approximately fifteen studies, including those of Leo H.

Hoek, whom he regards as one of the "fondateurs de la titrologie moderne", in particular his work, *La Marque du titre: dispositifs sémiotiques d'une pratique textuelle* (Mouton 1981). More than thirty years later, this "little discipline" has continued to develop, all the while remaining confined to the study of literary works and ignoring other possible fields of application. To what extent, then, could it be said to inscribe itself in this, also recent, discipline, namely translation studies? The bibliography on *paratext* has increased considerably since 1987, as is shown in Kathrin Batchelor's recent book *Translation and Paratexts* (2018), a very valuable attempt to provide an overview of numerous postgenettian studies.

A title can, first of all, be defined as an invitation to readers: a label that provides information about a product placed on the market, or that informs us, at least, of its presence there. But the title is not the product itself, which consists of the *work*. What happens when the message the title sends is translated and presented to the market of another country?

The approximately forty translated titles on which this chapter is based (see Appendix) are taken from about ten European languages and encompass not only literary works (with a special emphasis on children's literature), but also philosophical, historical and religious works. This rather unusual gathering of literary and nonliterary works is rooted in a larger research project that was carried out in *Histoire des traductions en langue française*. First, we will examine what happens to a translated title: whom does it belong to? We will then see how translated titles can reveal cultural gaps in the field of human and social sciences, before devoting the third part of this study to literary works (examples will be largely drawn from the 'canon' of Western literature). A fourth and final part, based on the particular position of children's literature, will deal with aspects specific to contemporary societies: the development of a 'mass culture', marked, in the twentieth century in particular, by the overwhelming presence of film adaptations.[1]

2. Title, intellectual property and copyright

A volume, an article, is indicated by a title; this is the case, at least in modern Europe, where the development of printing has accelerated the use of this mode of identification of a work. However, in classical antiquity, Pliny the Elder already pretended to marvel at how "wonderfully happy" the Greeks

---

[1] This study is largely based on the documentation gathered in the four volumes of the *Histoire des traductions en langue française*, co-edited by Yves Chevrel and Jean-Yves Masson.

were in their choice of titles, and went on to quote some of them, before commenting: "But when you enter upon the works, O ye Gods and Goddesses! how full of emptiness!" (Pliny 1855, § 18 and 19). He adds that he, himself, would be happy to settle only for "this or that person was doing this", (ibid. § 20) following the example of the painter Apelles or the sculptor Polycleitus: for Pliny, it suffices to know who the author is.

Genetic studies, a rapidly developing field of studies in recent years, highlights the importance that authors attach to the choice of a title. However, they hardly make it possible to identify norms in the motivations and behaviors of authors: the scope of options is very wide, ranging from titles as the starting point for writing (e.g., Giono, who states, with regards to *Deux cavaliers de l'orage*, 1965: "Il faut un titre, parce que le titre est cette sorte de drapeau vers lequel on se dirige ; le but qu'il faut atteindre, c'est expliquer le titre." quoted in Duchet 1973, 53. "You need a title, because the title functions as a sort of flag you're heading towards; the goal is to explain the title") – to titles that are provided on commission – or even titles that are only found once the work is finished, sometimes after many attempts (e.g., Zola, churning out 133 possible titles while writing, before deciding on *La Bête humaine*, 1890). Whatever the case, a manuscript is generally transmitted to a publisher with a title; in the case of unfinished posthumous works, the heirs or successors often title or even re-title, as Max Brod did when confronted with the texts left by Kafka. As long as the manuscript has not become a *work*, modifications can be made.

The case of *La Nausée* is famous. Sartre presented Gallimard with a manuscript entitled 'Melancholia'. Gaston Gallimard asked him "to change this title, which does not seem very favorable to the launch of the book." After the author suggested 'Les Aventures extraordinaires d'Antoine Roquentin' – which was not retained – it was Gallimard who, in the end, proposed what would become the definitive title, which Sartre commented on in the blurb written for the 1938 original edition (on this episode, consult the file compiled by Contat and Rybalka 1981, 1686-1694).

While it was the publisher's intervention which was decisive in this case, the reading community can also play a role. The definitive title given by Jean-Jacques Rousseau to his novel, *Julie ou la nouvelle Héloïse*, which was the title given to all editions published during the author's lifetime, was quickly reduced to *La Nouvelle Héloïse*, which is sometimes even used for university editions of the novel. Goethe, on the other hand, accepted to release a short title, *Werther*, instead of *Die Leiden des jungen Werther*, for his famous text. It is not necessary to multiply examples to demonstrate that, in practice, a title easily escapes its author; therefore, a translator, or an editor, may also feel authorized to choose the expression that would appear most appropriate.

Translations can even reflect back on the original title. Here are two examples taken from outside a strictly literary field. In 1909, James George Frazer published *Psyche's Task: A Discourse concerning the Influence of Superstition on the Growth of Institutions*, which was translated into French in 1914, under the title, *L'Avocat du diable ou la tâche de Psyché* (The Devil's Advocate or the Task of Psyche). Does that title explain why, on the occasion of a new edition in 1927, Frazer changed the original title into *The Devil's Advocate: A Plea for Superstition*? In a note of the foreword, he explains that: "[T]he ambiguous title of *Psyche's Task* has been changed for one which, it is hoped, will convey the general scope of the work more clearly to English readers unfamiliar with the beautiful creations of Greek mythology" (Frazer 1927, ii). In 1956, Samuel Noah Kramer published a highly acclaimed book in the United States, with a somewhat enigmatic subtitle: *From the Tablets of Sumer: Twenty-Five Firsts in Man's Recorded History*. The following year, the French publishing house Arthaud published an edition with a more concise title, in the form of an aphorism: *L'Histoire commence à Sumer*. This title, then, was taken up in other languages as well: in German, *Die Geschichte beginnt mit Sumer* (1979), Spanish, *La historia empieza en Sumer* (1985) and, finally, even made its way back into the English title: *History Begins at Sumer: Thirty-Nine "Firsts" in Recorded History* (1988).

These two examples remind us that authors have the right to repent, and that they can exercise this right on titles as well as on texts. However, under the current French Intellectual Property Code, a translator is also considered an author: in the case of a new original translation, is a new translator then allowed to use the title of an earlier translation? In most cases, for famous works of *Weltliteratur*, the reworking of a title does not pose a problem.[2] However, there are cases where a translated title is so original that it can be considered as a new creation. The title of Emily Brontë's novel, *Wuthering Heights* (1847), has given rise, in several languages, to multiple and varied translations: approximately ten in German, and some fifteen in French. One of them has become established in French: *Les Hauts de Hurle-Vent* (1925, translated by Frédéric Delebecque). The lucky find *Hurle-Vent* (also written *Hurlevent*) was protected by French courts on the grounds that "the term *Hurlevent* deserves protection in itself", because it "constitutes the essential and attractive element of the title *Les Hauts de Hurlevent*" (Paris Court of

---

[2] Goethe's bestseller *Die Leiden des jungen Werther* was most often translated and re-translated into English under the title *The Sorrows of Young Werther*. An arguably more literal translation, *The Sufferings of Young Werther*, did not take hold, and when a translation of *Die neuen Leiden des jungen W.* (1973) from Ulrich Plenzdorf appeared, the English translator opted for the title *The New Sorrows of Young W.*

Appeal, 25 Oct. 1995).³ Because a publisher is liable, he must always ensure the originality of the titles of the works he intends to publish: he has the copyright on the book.

3. Translation / Transfer: non-literary examples

In "Le paradigme de la traduction", a text originally published in *Esprit* (No. 853, June 1999), Ricœur distinguishes two points of view on the act of translation: either, in the strict sense, "transfert d'un message verbal d'une langue dans une autre" ("the transfer of a verbal message from one language to another"), or, in the broad sense, "interprétation de tout ensemble signifiant à l'intérieur de la même communauté linguistique" ("the interpretation of a meaningful whole within the same linguistic community") (Ricœur 2004, 21).

According to this distinction, many translated titles belong to the first category, particularly most scientific, historical and philosophical works – that is to say, those works which require great rigor and where the transfer is, at least in appearance, adequate, term per term. Literary titles, however, give rise to a different set of problems (s. Part 4). Whatever the case, a title may, in the first place, pose a problem to translation because an equivalent, or even a closely related term does not exist in the target language. From the presentation put forward by B. Cassin in the monumental *Vocabulaire européen des philosophies. Dictionnaire des intraduisibles*, it emerges that her enterprise, based on a "réflexion sur la difficulté de traduire en philosophie" ("reflection on the difficulty of translating philosophy"), requires "penser la philosophie en langues, traiter les philosophies comme elles se disent, et voir ce que cela change dans nos manières de philosopher" ("thinking philosophy in terms of language, treating philosophies as they are expressed, and seeing how this changes our way of philosophizing") (Cassin 2004, XVII). This does not mean that translators of philosophical works (who are almost always philosophers themselves) have never considered that question, quite the contrary, nor that solutions have not been found in the past (e.g., neologisms, giving new meaning to old terms).⁴ The precision of the concepts is, however, clearly essential. In June 1813, in a lecture at the Royal Academy of Sciences in Berlin on "different methods of translation", Schleiermacher insisted on the specific

---

3   Maurel-Indart provides details on two cases concerning the use, considered unlawful, of the term 'Hurle-Vent' (2019, 162-163).
4   See, among others, Thomas 2014, in particular the pages dedicated to Locke and his French translator, Pierre Coste.

particularities of each language and on the polysemy of their terms. While first appearing to exclude two concepts (*Begriffe*) which he thinks are universal, namely, a primitive noun (*Urhauptwort*), which designates the divinity, and a primitive verb (*Urzeitwort*), which expresses Being, he nonetheless believes it necessary to add the following reservation: "even the absolutely universal, although it is outside the domain of particularity, is illuminated and colored by language" (Schleiermacher 1838, 239).[5] In fact, while all European languages have a term to express the concept of divinity, this may be not the case in non-European languages: this situation led missionaries to invent this notion by introducing the loan word 'Deus' (Cassin 2004, 320b). This solution is, in fact, frequent when it comes to reconstructing a new 'technical' term: 'theodicy' (Leibniz, *Essais de théodicée*, 1710), and 'aesthetic' (Baumgarten, *Aesthetica*, 1750) have entered into European languages in this way. In other cases, it is advisable to take into account the semantic evolutions of a term: a title such as *Theologia summi boni* appears to encourage an *ad verbum* translation (Theology of the Supreme Good), but Jean Jolivet gave Pierre Abélard's treatise two different titles: *Du bien suprême* (On the Supreme Good) (1978), and *De l'unité et de la Trinité divines* (2001) (On Divine Unity and Trinity), avoiding, in both cases, the use of the term 'theology' (Agard and Zanfi 2019, 1358).

In a relatively new discipline, such as psychoanalysis – a term that first appeared in 1896 in a French text by Freud in the form of 'psycho-analyse' – the definition of concepts, which remains under discussion, raises problems that are highlighted by the translation of titles (Giboux 2019). It suffices to recall the case of the essay "Das Unheimliche" (published in the journal *Imago*, V, 1919), in which Freud asserts that this German concept does not have an exact equivalent in any of the languages in which he conducted research. The title chosen for the first French translation by Marie Bonaparte and Mrs. Édouard Marty (in *Essais de psychanalyse appliquée*, 1933), was *L'inquiétante étrangeté*: this choice, often considered questionable, has nevertheless imposed itself in the language of French psychoanalysis (Giboux 2019, 1620).

Since the nineteenth century, historians have relied on an increasingly rigorous methodology. While no historical work is immune to the ideology of its author, the search for objectivity remains an essential element of any historical work. Regardless of the attention devoted to the text of the original work, some titles, however, undergo curious changes in translation, which evidently cannot be imputed to the translator (Baisez and Lanfranchi 2019). An almost caricatural example is the translation of *Before France and Germany: The Creation*

---

5   German: "auch das schlechtin allgemeine, wiewol ausserhalb des Gebietes der Eigentümlichkeit liegend, ist doch von ihr beleuchtet und gefärbt."

and Transformation of the Merovingian World, by Patrick Geary (Oxford U.P., 1988), which, in French, became *Le Monde mérovingien. Naissance de la France* (Flammarion, 1989), and even (in a re-edition from 2011), *Naissance de la France. Le monde mérovingien*... It is clear that certain interpretative frameworks remain persistent, especially when they are taught in school curricula. For example, since Victor Duruy, French historiography has favored expressions such as *grandes invasions* (great invasions), and *invasion (des) barbares* (invasions by the barbarians) to refer to the upheavals in the Roman Empire from the third to the fifth century, while, in German, *Völkerwanderung* (migration of peoples) was the established term. It is therefore not surprising that *Die Völkerwanderung* by Hans-Joachim Diesner (1976) was translated by Robert Simon as *Les Grandes Invasions* (1977) (The Great Invasions). Just as telling is the fact that the general catalogue of the National Library of France (BnF), consulted on the 21st of July 2019, only mentions one work in French which contains the expression *Migration des peuples*. Moreover, that expression appears in a *Catalogue de (...) monnaies de l'époque de la migration des peuples*, published in Amsterdam in 1931. In German, *Invasion der Barbaren* (2011) is used to translate Peter Heather's work *Empires and Barbarians: The Fall of Rome and the Birth of Europe* (2010), but its use remains exceptional. In contrast, an adaptation of Jean d'Izieu's novel, *Baldur de la forêt* (1957) – a novel for adolescents whose hero is a 15-year-old Franc – is published in German under the title *Die Waldläufer* (The Runners of the Wood), and followed by a subtitle which is absent from the original: *Eine Erzählung aus der Zeit der Völkerwanderung* (A Story from the Time of the Migration of Peoples) (1959). Here, the subtitle of this adventure novel is integrated into a German historical perspective.

4. Translation / Transfer: literary examples

The previous example is situated at the frontier of history and literature. Translations of literary titles, indeed, offer the widest range of cases, leading to transpositions of various types. Recent directives, which are increasingly applied, require publishers to mention the original title of the translated text, but it has long been difficult to identify the original title of a novel, starting from its translation. In her study, "A la recherche du titre perdu" (2006), Marie-Françoise Cachin examines the titles of a corpus of approximately 100 English-language novels published after the Second World War: she adopts an approach that is "ni stylistique ni linguistique, mais essentiellement culturelle" ("neither stylistic nor linguistic, but essentially cultural") (Cachin 2006, § 4), which is in line with the second approach envisaged by Ricœur (see above).

Suffice it to mention that the most straightforward way to introduce a translated book is by simply taking over its original title. *Manhattan Transfer* (Dos Passos), *Berlin Alexanderplatz* (Döblin), *Peterburg* (Belyi), also transcribed as *Petersburg* or *Pétersbourg*, are urban places easily identifiable, which, in turn, have become familiar places, in part because of these titles. We find a somewhat similar example in cases where the title is written in a language that is both foreign and recognizable to many readers: the global bestseller *Quo vadis?* (1896), by Pole Sienkiewicz, retained its Latin title in most European languages.

Many titles can be translated word for word, but the ease with which a title can be transferred into another language does not mean, however, that any title that is translatable *ad verbum* is automatically easy to understand. *Le Rouge et le Noir* and *Vojna i mir* (*War and Peace*) are worldwide bestsellers: in most European languages, both couples of words are translated literally and in the same order each time. This does not prevent the fact that questions are persistently raised about the meaning of the title chosen by Stendhal.[6]

Umberto Eco states that in a novel "a title is unfortunately already a key to interpretation" and suggests that "[t]he titles that are most respectful of the reader are those which are reduced to the name of the eponymous hero" (Eco 1983, 507).[7] Indeed, many European novels (and it seems, even more theater plays) bear the name of their hero or heroine, which is then eventually adapted to the target language (John/Johann/ János/Jos, etc.). Eco's suggestion finds application: recourse to such a solution is common when, for one reason or another, the original title may cause problems in the source language: Ibsen's play *Et dukkehjem* (1879) first appeared in German, in the same year, and in English the following year, under the title, *Nora*, which was taken over in many languages, before a more equivalent title (*A Doll's House, Ein Puppenheim*) imposed itself in the twentieth century. However, *Heimat* (1893) by H. Sudermann, easily translated into Swedish as *Hemmet* (1893), was rendered in French as *Magda*, after the name of the play's heroine, a title which was subsequently taken up for other translations, such as the English version from 1895. The German term covers the meanings 'home', 'fatherland', 'homeland'. Was this polysemy too difficult to convey?

In many cases, especially in literature 'for the general public', titles are adapted in translation in view of the target culture. The reasons for these

---

6   Bokobza has devoted a book to this question (Bokobza 1986). The question of translations of the title is not addressed.

7   "un titolo è purtroppo già una chiave interpretativa", "I titoli più rispettosi del lettore sono quelli che si riducono al nome dell'eroe eponimo."

changes are not always clear, but it appears that many of them are made not by the author, but by the publisher, who is aware of the 'appealing' function of a title. Sometimes it may simply be a matter of avoiding a problematic confusion, as in the case of Zadie Smith's novel, *White Teeth* (2000). Marie-Françoise Cachin points out that a verbatim translation in French "aurait pu évoquer (...) un célèbre slogan publicitaire des années 1950" ("could have evoked a famous advertising slogan of the 1950s") (Cachin 2006, § 17). It was subsequently translated as *Sourires de loup* (Wolf Smiles) (2001). There are other transposition effects that appear to be explainable. For example, there have been several modulations to the title of the novel, *The Watch* (2012) by the Indian author Joydeep Roy-Bhattacharya. For an English-speaking reader, the polysemy of the title becomes clear from the start of the book. The Italian translation, *L'Attesa* (2016), and the Spanish one, *La Guardia* (2017), however, dispel any ambiguity by foregrounding the dominant motif of the novel. The Dutch translation, first published in 2014, was given the title, *De zoon van mijn moeder* (My Mother's Son), whereas the French translation, which dates from 2016, was *Une Antigone à Kandahar*. These two titles refer more or less explicitly to Sophocles' tragedy; the Dutch choice is rather subtle since the expression 'my mother's son' is said by Sophocles' heroine who refers to her brother Polynices in verses 466-467. Sophocles' tragedy is, indeed, evoked in counterpoint in this novel, which is built around the story of a young girl claiming her brother's corpse at an American military base.

In some cases, the translator is confronted with a title that is so culturally rooted that any transfer is – or would be – a veritable *tour de force*. Thomas Hardy's novel, *Far from the Madding Crowd* (1874), the heroine of which is called Bathsheba, is simply titled *Barbara* in the first French translation (1901). The translator thus glosses over two cultural references: that of the original title, which is a verse from Thomas Gray's famous poem, *Elegy Written in a Country Churchyard*, and that of the protagonist's first name. 'Barbara' is, indeed, phonetically close to the name of the original text's main character, but it has no connection to the name of the woman coveted by King David. From 1980 onwards, re-editions of the same translation were reprinted under the literal title, *Loin de la foule déchaînée*, which was used again for a new translation published in 2011. In contrast, a Spanish translator, Federigo Climent Guerrero, while keeping the name Bathsheba, also borrowed two words of an "Oda a la vida retirada" from Fray Luis de León, and translated Hardy's novel as *Lejos del mundanal ruido* (1969) (Far from the Noise of the World).

These kinds of problems can be dealt with by looking for what we could call 'literary modulations'. Some translators tried to be creative (as was demonstrated in the case of *Wuthering Heights* – s. Part 1) and found equivalents.

In German, *L'Éducation sentimentale* has given rise to several translations. One translator chose the title *Lehrjahre des Gefühls* (1951), while another opted for *Lehrjahre des Herzens* (1957). Such references to Goethe's *Wilhelm Meisters Lehrjahre* distinctly inscribe Flaubert's novel in the tradition of the 'Bildungsroman'. The Shakespearean title, *Brave New World* (1932), became *Le Meilleur des mondes* (1933) in French, thus clearly referring to Voltaire's *Candide* (1759), a parody on the famous phrase from Leibniz's *Theodicy*: "the best of all possible worlds." Conversely, Scott Moncrieff borrowed a verse from Shakespeare's 30th sonnet to turn *À la recherche du temps perdu* into *Remembrance of Things Past* (1924).

Such literary modulations can be quite subtle at times. One of them is exemplified by the title of the Serbo-Croat novel *Na Drini ćuprija* (1945), by Ivo Andrić. This title has a rather unusual sentence structure, which literally reads '[on (the) Drina (a) bridge]' and uses a rare word, *ćuprija*, to design a bridge, while the more habitual term would be *most*. Andrić had earlier written a short story, *Most na Žepi* (1925), where he used a more common structure: [(a) bridge on (the) Žepa]. English and German translations of the novel are simply: *The Bridge on the Drina, Die Brücke über die Drina*, as well as a recent French one: *Le Pont sur la Drina* (1994). However, the first French translator, Georges Luciani, alluded to the 'legendary' touch of the original title by proposing the title, *Il est un pont sur la Drina* (1956).

All those attempts give testimony to the creative effort of translators who use the appealing function of titles to facilitate the reception of a title that has no connection with the target culture. In such cases literary modulations offer what could be called 'literary transfers'; some translators who are concerned with the effects of literary transfer, nonetheless face obstacles that are beyond their control. M.-E. Coindreau refers, in his *Mémoires d'un traducteur*, to the translation of John Steinbeck's *The Grapes of Wrath* (1939) which he had undertaken before the beginning of the Second World War. He had meditated on the title, which combines a textual reference to the *The Battle Hymn of the Republic* with a reference to the Book of Revelation, and had thought up "Le ciel en sa fureur" (Heaven in its Fury), using a quote from La Fontaine's well-known fable, "Les animaux malades de la peste" (The Animals Sick of the Plague). For reasons of financial gain, however, the final title, chosen in collaboration with a new translator, Marcel Duhamel, simply became, *Les Raisins de la colère* (1947) (Coindreau 1992, 60-61).

It is not always easy to understand the reasons (other than commercial ones) behind the re-translation of certain literary titles, sometimes years later. A possible explanation could be that a deeper knowledge of the text of the original work leads to the realization that more attention ought to be paid to the polysemy of its title. The title of Kafka's short story, *Die Verwandlung*, was first translated into Spanish as *La Metamorfosis* (1925) and into French as *La Métamorphose* (1928), before a first English translation proposed the title, *The Transformation* (1933). The term 'transformation' (and its equivalent in various languages of translation), did not impose itself, not even in English: the 1933 translation was reissued in 1936 under the title *Metamorphosis*. It was only later that new translations would take up this term again: *The Transformation* re-appeared in English in 1992, followed by *La Transformación* in Spanish in 2005. This comeback may have been chosen to avoid the mythological connotations of the originally Greek term *metamorphosis*, which the German word *Verwandlung* does not necessarily imply.

Finally, a new trend in translation practice seems to be emerging in France, where some translators are not only creating new translations of 'classics' but are also re-titling them, thus underlining – twice – the vigor of their translation choices. An example in case is that of the translator Frédéric Boyer: he replaced the traditional French title of Augustine's work *Les Confessions* (*Confessiones*), with *Les Aveux* (2007), and he re-titled *Le souci de la terre* (Care of Earth) (2019), Virgil's famous poem and agricultural treaty *Georgica*, known as *Géorgiques*; Boyer thus aligns new translations with new titles. Other well-known examples are Henri Meschonnic's attempts in the field of Bible translations: *Gloires* (2001) for the Psalms, *Et il a appelé* (2005) for Leviticus, *Dans le désert* (2008) for the Book of Numbers, and *Les Noms* (2009) for Exodus.

Sometimes the power of the original title may still impose itself after a long series of trials. Because of problems due to title copyright, and after a long translation journey riddled with pitfalls (including legal ones), the solution that Gallimard chose in 2002 for Volume 2 of the collected works of the Brontë siblings in the 'Bibliothèque de la Pléiade' was *Wuthering Heights et autres romans (1847-1848)*.

5. Children's literature and mass culture

The commercial power of titles did not escape the attention of nineteenth-century publishers. Their economic potential, however, becomes even more obvious in the twentieth century when we look at examples that are situated at the frontier of the strictly literary domain, such as cinematographic adaptations or children's and young people's literature. This domain, wherein the status of text and title is often weak, offers a particularly favorable ground to illustrate the market function of titles in the mass culture of the second half of the twentieth century.

Indeed, it appears that the original titles of books for children and young people are more vulnerable than those that belong to a more 'general literature'. The first translation of *Brieven aan niemand anders* (Letters to No One Else) (1996), a children's book from the Dutch writer Toon Tellegen, was translated into French in 2000 under the title, *Lettres de l'écureuil à la fourmi* (Letters of the Squirrel to the Ant). This collection of very short stories was soon translated into Danish under the title *Breve med vinden* (Letters to Friends) (2001), and into Swedish under the title, *Riktigt goda vänner* (Really Good Friends) (2001). Curiously enough, it was the title of the 2000 French translation that served as the model for the titles of the German (*Briefe vom Eichhorn an die Ameise*, 2001) and Italian (*Lettere dello scoiattolo alla formica*, 2001) translations, and which inspired the Catalan (*Cartes de l'esquirol, de la formiga, de l'elefant, de l'ós...*, 2001) and Castilian titles (*Cartas de la ardilla, de la hormiga, del elefante, del oso...*, 2001) (Letters from the Squirrel, the Ant, the Elephant, the Bear...). It is possible that the different publishers discovered Toon Tellegen's book at the French Montreuil Youth Book Fair (close to Paris) in December 2000. However, the English translation of the book, published in 2009, is titled *Letters to Anyone and Everyone*.

Children's books frequently introduce a first name into their titles to install an initial complicity with their future readers. To recreate the familiarity effect of the original title, some translators consider it necessary to 'naturalize' the first name, in particular when it may appear strange to future readers, or may not even be identified as a first name. When the English children's picture book, *Time to get out of the Bath, Shirley* (1978), was translated, Shirley became Marcelle in French (1978) and Eva in German (1980). In the Norwegian picture book *Farvel, Rune* by Marit Kaldhol (1986), the first name was kept in Danish, German and English, but became Valentin (1990) in French. In addition, sometimes a name in the title can create ambiguity in the target culture. Hence, it was to avoid any association with the verb *to pee 'faire pipi'* that Astrid Lindgren's *Pippi Långstrump* (1945) became *Fifi Brindacier* (1951) (Steelstrand Fifi) in French.

The first French translation of *Eight Cousins, or the Aunt-Hill* (1875) by Louisa May Alcott was published in Switzerland in 1876, under the lapidary title *Sept cousins!* The second French translation, published in Paris by Hetzel in 1887, has a whole list of characters as its title: *La Petite Rose, ses six tantes et ses sept cousins* (Little Rose, her Six Aunts and Seven Cousins). Of course, this difference is brought about by the fact that French must make a distinction between *cousins* (for boys) and *cousines* (for girls), whereas both are covered by the word 'cousins' in English. It is clear, nonetheless, that the 1887 French title is much more attractive for young readers than the 1876 Swiss one.

The titles of children's and young people's literature can also, like those of general literature, inscribe themselves in literary genres or even refer to other literary traditions. Not surprisingly, French makes use of the term *conte* (tale) when referring to children's literature, which suggests that there is an oral dimension to these texts. Under the title, *Les Contes du chat perché* (1934) (Tales by the Perched Cat), Marcel Aymé brings together a set of stories that had previously been published in the press. He forges a title that combines the name of a schoolyard game with the storytelling genre. On the contrary, the English translation, entitled *The Wonderful Farm* (UK, 1939; USA, 1951), emphasizes an aesthetic of fantasy. In the German translation, *Kater Titus erzählt* (1964) (Titus, the Cat, Tells Stories), the Czech translation, *Co vyprávěla kočka na jabloňove vetvi* (1939) (What the Cat Said when Seated on the Apple Branch) and the Polish translation, *Bajki Kota na plocie* (1983) (Cat Stories on the Fence), the cat is put forward as being the storyteller of the work. Those last two titles also foreground the rural universe in which the stories take place.

Writers, even for children, can playfully suggest the literary genre of a text in their titles. In English, 'books of manners' or, to use an even older expression, 'books of etiquette', refer to what the French call *livres de civilité*. Maurice Sendak, for example, illustrated two pastiches of books of manners, written by Sesyle Joslin, entitled *What do you say, Dear?* (1958) and *What do you do, Dear?* (1961). In 1979, the publishing house *École des loisirs* published a French translation of the two picture books under the respective titles, *Que dites-vous, cher ami?* et *Que faites-vous, cher ami?* The translation of those two titles suggests that the translator misjudged the importance of the allusion to this forgotten genre. She translated '*Que dites-vous, cher ami?*', where she should have chosen '*Qu'est-ce qu'on dit, mon chéri?*' and make use of the *on* that is used in French to indicate that a particular form of conduct is in conformity with the social norm. It so happens that a French translation of the first of these two manuals was published in the United States in 1966 under the perfectly satisfactory title, *Qu'est ce qu'on dit, Mon Petit?*[8] This example shows how important it is, even when translating a simple title, to be familiar with the literary genre to which the translated work belongs.

Johanna Spyri aspires to write a fully literary work when she titles her first children's novel, *Heidi's Lehr- und Wanderjahre* (1880) (Years of Learning and Traveling). The allusion to the two titles by Goethe's famous *Bildungsromane* disappears in its first translation, a French one, published in Switzerland in

---

8 Young Scott Books, 1966, New York. This translation, which is accompanied by a "Glossary of French words and phrases", is in line with the American image of 'French courtesy'.

1882 under the title *Heidi. Une histoire pour les enfants et ceux qui les aiment* (Heidi. A Story for Children and Those who Love Them). The translator, a friend of Spyri, probably felt that the reference was inaccessible to young French-speaking readers. The reference was thus lost forever in French culture. The first American translation, however, respects the original title and reads *Heidi: Her Years of Wandering and Learning* (1884). The American translation places Spyri's novel on the side of 'literature', whereas the French translation clearly puts it in the category of children's literature alone. Half a century later, the French publisher Flammarion put an anonymous translation of Spyri's novel on the market in two parts, titled *Heidi, la Merveilleuse histoire d'une fille de la montagne* (1933) (Heidi, the Wonderful Story of a Mountain Girl) and *Heidi grandit* (1934) (Heidi Grows Up) with an open ending that allows him to publish three following novels of his own invention: *Heidi, jeune fille, suite inédite du traducteur* (1936) (Heidi Becomes a Young Girl, unpublished sequel by the translator), *Heidi et ses enfants* (1939) (Heidi's Children) et *Heidi grand'mère* (1946) (Heidi is a Grandmother).[9]

All seven titles of J. K. Rowling's Harry Potter adventures published over a period of ten years (1997-2007) open with the name of her novels' hero. The translation of her first title, *Harry Potter and the Philosopher's Stone* (1997), offers a double surprise. The title became *Harry Potter and the Sorcerer's Stone* (September 1998) in the USA,[10] while the French publisher Gallimard made a mix of both titles by creating the title *Harry Potter à l'école des sorciers* (October 1998) (Harry Potter at the Sorcerers' School), thus indicating where the action was taking place. All the other translations, however, all over the world, took over the English title of Rowling's first novel. We find *Harry Potter y la piedra filosofal* in Spanish (1999), *Harry Potter e la pietra filosofale* in Italian (2001), *Garri Potter i filosofskii kamen* in Russian (2002). The Hindi translation, *Hăirī Pâtara aura pāratthara* (2003), strives to give a phonetic transposition that is as close as possible to the original name of the hero. This effect of international equivalence 'for the ear' – whether the translation is made into Slovenian, Hebrew, Japanese or Turkish – suggests that the English first name and surname of the hero, far from being an obstacle, may be an asset in the context of an international Anglo-Saxon culture.

Beyond the retention of readers through the creation of a collection or editorial series, it is the film industry – a major producer of titles – which may

---

9   With regards to the translations of Johanna Spyri's novels worldwide, see Nières-Chevrel 2017.
10 J. K Rowling later recognized that she should have refused to allow the title to be changed, but that she was not in a powerful enough position to do so at the time.

have become one of the most powerful assets of the book market in the field of children and youth literature. The first translation of *Moby Dick; or, the Whale* was an abridged translation (256 p.), published in September 1928 by the publishing house Gedalge, in a collection for young people, under the title *Le Cachalot blanc* (The White Sperm Whale). Marguerite Gay titles her translation on Melville's subtitle alone, which emphasizes the theme of a maritime adventure. She points out, in her preface, that this is the first French translation of Melville's novel, while adding: "We hope that our young readers will welcome this adaptation as warmly as they applauded *Jim le Harponneur*, the beautiful film that was created from *Moby Dick* and successfully shown in Paris." (Melville 1928, 6).

This cinematographic allusion may hold a valuable clue. It could explain why Gedalge, which until then had not translated any English or American novel, suddenly turned to its only translator, Marguerite Gay, who had so far only translated from Swedish and Danish (eight titles from 1924 to 1928), to translate Melville's novel. Moreover, this would remain the only translation from an American author published by Gedalge. The free film adaptation of Melville's novel was released in the United States on January 15, 1926, under the title, *The Sea Beast*. The French version of the film, titled *Jim le Harponneur*, arrived in France in October 1926. The film was still available in movie theaters when Marguerite Gay's translation, *Le Cachalot blanc*, was released in bookstores in November 1928. The Gedalge house, which initially published only school books, was looking to diversify at that time. Could this publisher have caught wind of the filming of *The Sea Beast* or its release in the United States, and envisioned a translation-adaptation of Melville's novel for the French market? Could it be thanks to American cinema and youth literature that *Moby Dick* made its entry into French culture?

A second, more recent, example confirms the temptation that a publishing house may experience to take advantage of the distribution of a film. *Five Children and It* (1902), a children's novel by the British writer Edith Nesbit, was translated into French under the title, *La Fée des sables* (The Sand Fairy) in 1906. It was reprinted in 1911 and subsequently completely forgotten. Nesbit's work was rediscovered in France in the 1980s, with the publication of about ten titles by various publishers, including two titles by Gallimard. We can trace the beginnings of an American-French-English film adaptation of *Five Children and It* back to June 2003. Could it be in that very summer that Gallimard began to envision having Edith Nesbit's novel re-translated? The translation was released in bookstores in February 2004 under the title, *Une drôle de fée* (A Strange Fairy), but the film adaptation was not released in France until seven months later (October 20, 2004), unfortunately under the title, *Cinq enfants et moi* (Five Children and Me). Gallimard would reissue the 2004 translation in 2007, but this time under the title *Cinq enfants et moi*: two titles for one and the same translation. It is obvious that Gallimard had known, since 2003, that a film adaptation of the English novel was in the making. However, everything points towards the conclusion that the coordination between producer and publisher left much to be desired.

Walt Disney Studios, a major provider of cartoons and children's books, has proven to be more effective. It directed three medium-length films, *Winnie-the-Pooh and the Honey Tree* (1966), *Winnie-the-Pooh and the Blustery Day* (1968), and *Winnie-the-Pooh and Tigger Too* (1974), based on two childhood classics, *Winnie-the-Pooh* (1926) and *The House at Pooh Corner* (1928), by the English writer, Alan Alexander Milne. The distribution in France of these three cartoons was accompanied by the publication of several small books entitled *Winnie l'ourson et l'anniversaire de Bourriquet* (1966) (Winnie the Bear Cub and Little Donkey's Birthday), *Winnie l'ourson* (1967) (Winnie the Bear Cub), *Winnie l'ourson et l'arbre à miel* (1967) (Winnie the Bear Cub and the Honey Tree), *L'Ourson dans le vent* (1976) (The Bear Cub in the Wind), *L'Ourson et l'alerte au feu* (The Bear Cub and the Fire Alert) and *L'Ourson et le gâteau d'anniversaire* (1978) (The Bear Cub and the Birthday Cake) and so on. What is more, the work and name of the author have disappeared in favor of the Walt Disney Company, which imposed its own titles. This is the way titles proliferate in mass culture: two book titles, then three cartoon titles, followed by six new book titles and so on.

The children's market is riddled with works adapted into films that are themselves, in return, readapted into books. Titles thereby end up designating only one of the many possible variants of the same commodity. The economic value of titles in children's publishing is all the greater because, in the minds of parents and children, names of collections or series end up supplanting the name of the author, who is sometimes forgotten, and more often just ignored.

However, this does not mean that there is not an overwhelming power of market at work in all types of children's books' translations as well. Mathilde Lévêque underlines a growing legitimacy, since the 1970s, of children's books translators, whose names are becoming more and more known. Moreover, several famous classics have been translated anew (2019, 1045-1046). As was mentioned at the end of part three of this chapter, new translations are at times marked by new titles. It seems that this renewal applies to children's culture as well. In 1979, Luc de Goustine and Alain Huriot made a new translation (at last) of *Heidis Lehr-und Wanderjahre* under the title *Heidi. Monts et merveilles* (Heidi. Mountains and Wonders). Heinrich Hoffmann's picture book, *Der Struwwelpeter oder Lustige Geschichten und drollige Bilder für Kinder von 3-6 Jahren* (1847) (The Struwwelpeter, or, Pretty Stories and Funny Pictures for Children from 3 to 6), was first translated by Louis Ratisbonne in 1860. It became *the* French, and only, translation of this famous German picture book for more than a century. Ratisbonne's translation, under the title *Pierre l'ébouriffé, joyeuses histoires et images drolatiques pour les enfants de 3 à 5 ans* (Shockheaded Peter, Happy Stories and Funny Pictures for Children from 3 to 5 years old), had become part of the public domain when Cavanna published a fundamentally new and playful translation in 1979, written in Knittelvers, with mocking and humorous plays on different language registers. Instead of retaining the name *Pierre l'ébouriffé*, which for more than a century had been used to refer to this major European classic, Cavanna created a new nickname and thus marked the distinctiveness of his translation with a brand new title, *Crasse-Tignasse ou Histoires cocasses et drôles d'images* (Dirty Mop of Hair or Funny Stories and Comical Pictures).

6. Conclusion

In this chapter, we did not intend to produce a 'theory' of title translation. Indeed, it is important to note that many of the quoted titles are part of a set, or subset, of a much larger corpus, in various languages, from which a number of important questions can be derived.

The first question is: is a title a fragile, perhaps even the most fragile, aspect of a book when translated? It offers publishers the opportunity to interfere, and to turn the title into a purely commercial object. It also offers translators the opportunity to act as true authors, especially in the case of original titles which themselves have a real literary quality. Between those two extremes, many other modulations are possible. To use Genette's terminology, the title of a work is part of the *peritext*, which is always constitutive of the *paratext*. In a translated work, the title assumes the same *peritextual* function with regards to the translated book as a whole. Could it be possible, in cases where the title, for evident reasons (some of which have been mentioned in this study), cannot be attributed to the translator, to distinguish an *epitextual* function, that is, a message that is situated "anywhere outside of the book" (*sic*, Genette 1987, 316)? This could lead to a reconsideration of discussions on translations viewed as *paratexts* (s. overview in Batchelor 2018, 28-31).

This raises a second question: how do translated titles relate themselves to other transfer phenomena? A title brings together, in a concentrated form, a set of processes that translation scholars strive to connect. Lieven D'hulst (2014, 85) has highlighted the complexity of the notion of *transfer*, which has been widely used in recent decades, and has suggested "utiliser un concept englobant couvrant notamment un plus grand nombre de produits, de médiateurs, de techniques ou de véhicules" ("using an encompassing concept covering a large number of products, mediators, techniques or vehicles"), which he proposed to call 'transfer supposé' ('assumed transfer'). For her part, Weber Henking (2019, 293) points out that

> une traduction n'est plus un simple transfert d'un texte entre deux langues et deux cultures, mais fait partie d'un contexte de pouvoirs et d'influences dont elle peut même être le révélateur. Le travail d'un traducteur se lit donc dans sa corrélation complexe, entre réaction et action, avec les forces d'un champ littéraire particulier.
> (a translation is no longer the simple transfer of a text between two languages and two cultures, but is part of a context of powers and influences of which it can even be a revealing factor. A translator's work is therefore revealed in the complex correlation, somewhere between reaction and action, with the forces of a particular literary field)

When translators try to reinvent new titles for literary works which are already well known under another title, we are possibly confronted with a newly emerging trend that marks a break in the translation tradition. These new titles, then, also function as an indication that the translator wanted to create, not just another translation, but an innovative one.

Translation studies conducted within a corpus established in the same target-language culture generally focusses on the diachronic axis. This essentially means: a history of the rhetoric of titles, a focus on the effects of information and seduction, and on the effects of appropriation by successive generations of readers, through the deletion of a subtitle, the reduction of a title, the elucidation or increase of its meaning through cover illustrations, and so on. Enlarging a comparative approach to titles by bringing the diversity of languages into a shared space-time would highlight the multiplication and dispersion of titles, as well as reveal the dynamics of cultural exchanges, the role played by literary prizes, book fairs and exhibitions, films, and sometimes even major theater tours. It would be desirable to be able to confirm these hypotheses through access to the archives of publishing houses, and in particular their correspondence.[11] A titanic enterprise? Maybe so, but

---

11 The Institut Mémoires de l'édition contemporaine (IMEC), located in Caen (France), holds an important private archives collection concerning the twentieth and twenty-first centuries, as well as part of the nineteenth century (thanks to the Hachette collection, which also includes the collections of the publishing houses absorbed by Hachette).

focusing on the problem of title translation, attempting to cross-reference linguistic constraints, the chronology of translations, the compatibility or discrepancies in cultural expectations, and the modes of economic circulation and book-market conditions on an international scale, would allow us to open up new perspectives in the field of translation studies.

Appendix: List of translated titles examined

Abélard, Pierre, *Theologia summi boni*
Alcott, Louisa May, *Eight cousins, or the Aunt-Hill*
Andrić, Ivo, *Na Drini ćuprija*
Augustin, *Confessiones*
Aymé, Marcel, *Les Contes du chat perché*
Baumgarten, Alexander Gottlieb, *Aesthetica*
Belyi, Andrej, *Peterburg*
Brontë, Emily, *Wuthering Heights*
Burningham, John, *Time to get out of the bath, Shirley*
Diesner, Hans-Joachim *Die Völkerwanderung*
Döblin, Alfred, *Berlin Alexanderplatz*
Dos Passos, John, *Manhattan Transfer*
Flaubert, Gustave, *L'Éducation sentimentale*
Frazer, James George, *Psyche's Task, a Discourse concerning the influence of Superstition on the growth of institutions*
Freud, Sigmund, "Das Unheimliche"
Geary, Patrick, *Before France and Germany: The Creation and Transformation of the Merovingian World*
Goethe, Johann Wolfgang von, *Die Leiden des jungen Werther*
Hardy, Thomas, *Far from the Madding Crowd*
Heather, Pieter, *Empires and Barbarians: The Fall of Rome and the Birth of Europe*
Hoffmann, Heinrich, *Der Struwwelpeter*
Huxley, Aldous, *Brave New World*
Ibsen, Henrik, *Et dukkehjem*
Izieu, Jean d', *Baldur de la Forêt*
Joslin, Sesyle, *What do you say, Dear?* and *What do you do, Dear?*
Kafka, Franz, *Die Verwandlung*
Kaldhol, Marit, *Farvel, Rune*
Kramer, Samuel Noah, *From the Tablets of Sumer. Twenty-Five Firsts in Man's Recorded History*
Leibniz, Gottfried Wilhelm, *Théodicée*

Lindgren, Astrid, *Pippi Långstrump*
Melville, Herman, *Moby Dick; or, the Whale*
Milne, Allan Alexander, *Winnie-the-Pooh* and *The House at Pooh Corner*
Nesbit, Edith, *Five Children and It*
Proust, Marcel, *À la recherche du temps perdu*
Rowling, J. K., *Harry Potter*, a series
Roy-Bhattacharya, Joydeep, *The Watch*
Smith, Zadie, *White Teeths*
Spyri, Johanna, *Heidi's Lehr- und Wanderjahre*
Steinbeck, John, *The Grapes of Wrath*
Sudermann, Hermann, *Heimat*
Tellegen, Toon, *Brieven aan niemand anders*
Virgil, *Georgica*

References

Agard, Olivier, and Catarina Zanfi. 2019. "Philosophie." In *Histoire des traductions en langue française : XXe siècle : 1914-2000*, edited by Yves Chevrel, Bernard Banoun, and Isabelle Poulin, 1349-1426. Lagrasse: Verdier.

Baisez, Olivier, and Thibaud Lanfranchi. 2019. "Histoire." In *Histoire des traductions en langue française : XXe siècle : 1914-2000*, edited by Yves Chevrel, Bernard Banoun, and Isabelle Poulin, 1427-1484. Lagrasse: Verdier.

Batchelor, Kathryn. 2018. *Translation and Paratexts.* (coll. Translation theories explored) London: Routledge.

Bokobza, Serge. 1986. *Contribution à la titrologie romanesque. Variations sur le titre «Le Rouge et le Noir».* Paris: Droz.

Cachin, Marie-Françoise. 2006. "À la recherche du titre perdu." *Palimpsestes*, Hors série 2006, published online 1 September 2008. URL: http://journals.openedition.org/palimpsestes/410; DOI: 10.4000/palimpsestes.410.

Cassin, Barbara, ed. 2004. *Vocabulaire européen des philosophies : dictionnaire des Intraduisibles.* Paris: Seuil / le Robert.

Chevrel, Yves, and Jean-Yves Masson, eds. 2012-2019. *Histoire des traductions en langue française.* 4 vol. Lagrasse: Verdier.

Coindreau, Maurice-Edgar. 1992. *Mémoires d'un traducteur. Entretiens avec Christian Giudicelli.* Paris: Gallimard.

Contat, Michel, and Michel Rybalka. 1981. *Œuvres romanesques de Sartre.* Paris: Gallimard.

D'hulst, Lieven. 2014. *Essais d'histoire de la traduction. Avatars de Janus.* Paris: Garnier.

Duchet, Claude. 1973. "La 'Fille abandonnée' et 'La Bête humaine'. Éléments de titrologie romanesque." *Littérature* 12, 49-73.

Eco, Umberto. 1983. *Postille al Nome della rosa*. Milan: Bompiani.

Frazer, James George. 1927. *The Devil's Advocate, a Plea for Superstition*. 2nd edition, revised and enlarged of *Psyche's task*. London: Macmillan.

Genette, Gérard. 1987. *Seuils*. Paris: Seuil.

Giboux, Audrey. 2019. «Psychanalyse et psychologie.» In *Histoire des traductions en langue française : XXe siècle : 1914-2000*, edited by Yves Chevrel, Bernard Banoun, and Isabelle Poulin, 1613-1686. Lagrasse: Verdier.

Hoek, Leo H. 1981. *La Marque du titre : dispositifs sémiotiques d'une pratique textuelle*. The Hague: Mouton.

Lévêque, Mathilde. 2019. "Littérature de jeunesse." In *Histoire des traductions en langue française : XXe siècle : 1914-2000*, edited by Yves Chevrel, Bernard Banoun, and Isabelle Poulin, 981-1052. Lagrasse : Verdier.

Maurel-Indart, Hélène. 2019. "Traduction, plagiat et d'autres formes d'atteinte au droit d'auteur." In *Histoire des traductions en langue française : XXe siècle : 1914-2000*, edited by Yves Chevrel, Bernard Banoun, and Isabelle Poulin, 159-176. Lagrasse: Verdier.

Melville, Herman. 1928. *Le Cachalot blanc*. Translated by Marguerite Gay. Paris: Gedalge.

Nières-Chevrel, Isabelle. 2017. "Heidi et ses langues: de Zurich à Tokyo." In *Les Routes de la traduction. Babel à Genève*, edited by Barbara Cassin and Nicolas Decimetière, 281-297. Gallimard / Fondation Martin Bodmer.

Pliny the Elder. 1855. *Naturalis Historia. Liber I*. Translated by John Bostock and Henry Thomas Riley. http://data.perseus.org/citations/urn:cts:latinLit:phi0978.phi001.perseus-eng1:1.dedication

Ricœur, Paul. 2004. *Sur la traduction*. Paris: Bayard.

Schleiermacher, Friedrich. 1838. "Ueber die verschiedenen Methoden des Uebersetzens." In *F. S. Sämmtliche Werke*, III. Berlin: Reimer.

Thomas, François. 2014. «Philosophie.» In *Histoire des traductions en langue française: XVIIe et XVIIIe siècles : 1610-1815*, edited by Yves Chevrel, Annie Cointre, and Yen-Maï Tran-Gervat, 511-594. Lagrasse: Verdier.

Weber Henking, Irene. 2019. "La traductologie (à partir de 1960)." In *Histoire des traductions en langue française : XXe siècle : 1914-2000*, edited by Yves Chevrel, Bernard Banoun, and Isabelle Poulin, 277-324. Lagrasse: Verdier.

Transfer in news translation

Christina Schäffner

Abstract

Metaphors of movement and transfer have played a prominent role in traditional translation studies. The labels source text and target text indicate origin and destination of a movement, and definitions of translation as meaning transfer explicitly connect translation and transfer. The notion of transfer in such a narrow sense has been replaced by now as more attention has been paid to the socio-cultural settings in which translation (as a process) is performed and translations (as products) function. Research into different types of translation, into a variety of genres, and into different contexts and settings has led to a rethinking of traditional concepts. One such context is journalism. In particular, newsrooms of global and transnational agencies have to deal with processing multilingual information. A growing body of research in this area has illustrated that translation is an integral part of journalistic text production, but that the journalists themselves do not consider their work to be translation (e.g. Bielsa and Bassnett 2009, Valdeón 2015). Guided by values of journalism, especially speed and reader orientation, international journalists edit and transform the information they have available, a practice for which the term 'transediting', coined by Stetting (1989), is often used. Research into news translation, or into journalistic translation more widely, is faced with the challenge that the traditional labels source text and target text hardly ever apply. This in turn poses challenges for the concept of transfer. Since international journalists do perform mediation activities which cross linguistic and cultural boundaries this chapter will reflect on the extent to which the concept of transfer can be employed in news translation research.

1. Introduction

Metaphors of movement and transfer have played a prominent role in traditional translation studies. The labels 'source text' and 'target text' indicate origin and destination of a movement, and definitions of translation as meaning transfer explicitly connect translation and transfer. The notion of transfer in such a narrow sense has been replaced by now, as more attention has been paid to the socio-cultural settings in which translation (as a process) is performed and translations (as products) function. Research into different types of translation, into a variety of genres, and into different contexts and settings has led to a rethinking of traditional concepts. One such context is journalism. In particular, newsrooms of global and transnational agencies have to deal with processing multilingual information. A growing body of research in this area has illustrated that translation is an integral part of journalistic text production, but that the journalists themselves do not consider their work to be translation (see e.g., Bielsa and Bassnett 2009, Valdeón 2015). Guided by values of journalism, especially speed and reader orientation, international journalists edit and transform the information they have available. Research into news translation, or into journalistic translation more widely, is faced with the challenge that the traditional labels 'source text' and 'target text' hardly ever apply. This in turn poses challenges for the concept of transfer. Since international journalists do perform mediation activities which cross linguistic and cultural boundaries, this chapter will reflect on the extent to which the concept of transfer can be employed in news translation research.

2. Translation and transfer

The two concepts 'translation' and 'transfer' have often been connected in conceptualizing translation. In fact, both the English words 'translation' and 'transfer' derive from the Latin roots *trans-* meaning across, and *ferre* meaning to bear, or to carry. In linguistics-based translation studies, translation has been understood as meaning transfer, which can be illustrated with the following definition of translation as an "interlinguistic transfer procedure comprising the interpretation of the sense of a source text and the production of a target text with the intent of establishing a relationship of equivalence between the two texts" (Delisle, Lee-Jahnke and Cormier 1999, 188).

This definition also confirms Göpferich's (2010, 374) argument that translation is frequently "seen as a more constrained mode of transfer associated with equivalence or invariance requirements." A similar argument is put forward by Venuti (2019, 7):

> Since antiquity, around the world, thinking about translation has been dominated by an instrumental model: translation is understood as the reproduction or transfer of an invariant, contained in or caused by the source text, an invariant form, meaning, or effect.

Tymoczko (2007) argues that the view of translation as 'carrying across' is a particularly Western view, as can be seen in the words of Western European languages for translation (e.g., *traducción* in Spanish, *traduction* in French, or *Übersetzung* in German, all of which etymologically relate to the Latin *transferre*). Tymoczko highlights that "[a]ll these words privilege transfer as the basic mode of translation" (Tymoczko 2007, 6). This metaphorical view of translation as transfer entails movement, a carrying over, not only from one language to another, but also from one context to another, a transfer across linguistic and cultural boundaries. The focus on equivalence reflects an expectation that the carrying over will not be combined with any loss or change of content. The transfer metaphor thus involves transportation and preservation, an understanding, however, which has been problematized.

As Tymoczko argues, viewing transfer as an attribute of translation "contains hidden presuppositions: that transfer of a particular sort (namely transfer of the content and semantic transfer) is *ipso facto* the primary attribute of the category of translation and that transfer is a self-evident process" (Tymoczko 2007, 129). This argument is echoed by Guldin when he says that "[t]he core of the problem is the transference metaphor, which postulates translatability thanks to the transportability of an extractable, stable meaning" (Guldin 2016, 53). A similar argument is put forward by D'hulst (2018, 141):

> A well-known criticism against the use of the concept of transfer is the shadow it carries of a seemingly unilateral and mechanistic move and thus of an encounter between active and passive participants, whereas cultures, as we know, interact in both directions, and with more participants.

In Tymoczko's opinion, such a view of translation as transfer is "radically inadequate as a theoretical approach to the transtemporal, transcultural concept" of translation (Tymoczko 2007, 129). She therefore argues in favor of enlarging the concept of translation by considering conceptualizations from various geographical areas, thus including a greater internationalization to the field of translation studies.

Within the discipline of translation studies, we have indeed witnessed an enlargement of the notion of translation from a purely linguistic to a cultural, social and political understanding. This development has largely been influenced by postmodern and sociological approaches to translation which define translation as a cultural-political practice (see e.g., Venuti 1995), or as a socially regulated activity (see e.g., Wolf 2002), respectively. Research has investigated the socio-historical contexts in which translations are produced, disseminated, and received as well as the role of the social agents in these processes. Various relevant aspects of translation have been revealed which the transfer metaphor hides. Above all, it has been shown that the relationship between source text and target text cannot be reduced to one of equivalence, and that indeed change is a key feature in any act of translation. Translation is thus fundamentally a transformative and creative act, informed not only (or exclusively) by considerations of characteristic features of the systems of the source and target language, but by the purpose a translation is to fulfill (its *skopos*, Vermeer 1996), recipients' expectations, socio-cultural constraints or norms (Toury 1995 and 2012), and/or ideological or institutional practices and beliefs (see e.g., Koskinen 2008).

In view of such developments, one can ask whether the concept of transfer is still of any relevance to translation studies. Göpferich (2007, 2010) compares translation studies to transfer studies, a transdisciplinary science, a "field of research which investigates access to knowledge in the broadest sense of the term" (Göpferich 2007, 28). She argues that in transfer studies the transfer concept includes "transformations of texts and other media" (Göpferich 2010, 374). Referring to the work by Antos (2001), she characterizes the objective of transfer studies as investigating "the conditions, principles, forms and strategies as well as problems and chances of creating meta-knowledge about knowledge for the purpose of making (specialized) knowledge available in an unrestricted manner to all people who might be interested in it" (Göpferich 2007, 28). Key questions addressed in transfer studies are then comprehensibility, text optimization and popularization, which are related to function- and audience-specific transformations. Based on a functionalist approach to translation (Vermeer 1996, Holz-Mänttäri 1984), Göpferich argues that since the scope of translation studies has widened and that its object is "any mediated transformation of offers of information performed to fulfil specific functions and meet the needs of specific audiences" (Göpferich 2007, 34), thus also incorporating adaptations, intralingual and intersemiotic translation, it "becomes interesting for the wider scope of Transfer Studies" (Göpferich 2007, 30). Since translation too provides access to knowledge and with transformation conceived as an integral part of translation, Göpferich sees the two disciplines as congruent.

D'hulst (2018, 135) agrees that because of its wider scope, transfer studies "may help to design a broader theoretical framework for the study of both cultural processes and techniques." He lists transmitting, crossing, changing and adapting as cultural processes which are realized by concrete verbal techniques. He makes a distinction between two major sets of transfer modes: institutional transfer, which "applies mainly to categories such as agency (authors, translators, editors, publishers) and organizations (associations, conferences, research departments, disciplines)" (D'hulst 2018, 136), and discursive transfer, which includes techniques such as tropes (comparison, metaphor and metonymy), copying, reproduction, translation, selection and transmission of catch-phrases or memes, paraphrase and summary (D'hulst 2018, 139 ff.). D'hulst is interested in investigating the "role of transfer techniques in the history of translation knowledge" (D'hulst 2018, 135), in establishing which techniques "are applied to concepts, ideas, theories and methods in order to enable or facilitate their travelling" in the domain of translation reflection (D'hulst 2018, 139). He too argues that during such movements, the content of concepts and theories changes to a varying extent, and since he sees translation as a discursive transfer technique, change and transformation are inherent elements.

The enlargement of the concept of translation and thus the widening of the scope of the discipline of translation studies has also been the result of scholars' engagement with areas in which translatorial activities occur which traditionally had not been part of the core of the discipline. One such area is journalistic text production. Newsrooms of global and transnational agencies have to deal with processing multilingual information, and also national or local media refer to texts which originated outside their own context for their reporting. Journalists do perform mediation activities which cross linguistic and cultural boundaries, and thus translation does play a role in these processes. In the next section, I will present some issues related to the concept of translation in news production and then reflect on the extent to which the concept of transfer can be employed in news translation research.

3. News translation

Within the discipline of translation studies, the unique role translation plays in the production and dissemination of international news has been addressed more systematically since about 2005 (e.g., in the journal *Language & Intercultural Communication* 2005). Following a first key monograph on the topic (Bielsa and Bassnett 2009), a number of special issues of journals devoted to news translation have been published (most recently *Perspectives: Studies in Translatology* 2015 and *Across Languages and Cultures* 2018), as well as overview articles (see e.g., van Doorslaer 2010; Holland 2012; Valdeón 2015; Schäffner 2018; Davier 2019).

Research on news translation is concerned with the nature of translation in the media and has investigated the influence of translation on information flows, the translation strategies used and their effects, the practices in specific media settings, and the attitudes to translation prevalent among the agents in the world of news reporting. In this respect, 'news translation' is often used as a cover term for a variety of journalistic genres, such as short news items, news reports, and press releases. Some scholars therefore prefer to speak of 'press translation' (see e.g., Bani 2006) or 'journalistic translation' (Valdeón 2015). Researchers have often combined fieldwork in news organizations, in particular ethnographic observations and interviews with journalists, with a comparative analysis of texts. Studies into the practices and working conditions in media institutions have revealed a diversity of processes in respect of news production. Some media institutions aim at a wider audience and make their texts available in several languages (e.g., *Euronews, Le Monde Diplomatique*). Some magazines operate at an international level and therefore exist in several languages (e.g., *National Geographic, Cosmopolitan*). Also, national newspapers frequently include translated texts which were initially published by media in other countries. Some media institutions employ professional translators, who, however, often work away from the editorial office. The translations they turn in then undergo a complex editing process, with different persons checking the target text against the source text, proofreading the text, and finally deciding how (e.g. regarding omissions) and where the translation will be placed inside the newspaper. These practices are illustrated, for example, by the Italian weekly magazine *Internazionale* (Bani 2006) and the Korean edition *Newsweek Hankuk Pan* (Kang 2007).

Very often, however, it is the journalists themselves whose text production process includes translation. That is, journalists regularly use a variety of sources, including texts originally produced in another language, as input for writing their reports. This can be illustrated with an example from the daily newspaper *The Guardian* of October 22, 2019. A news report of 1.116 words in total on the agreement reached between the Turkish president Erdoğan and the Russian president Putin on a proposed Turkish safe zone in Syria, includes direct and indirect quotes of various politicians:

> (...) Erdoğan hailed the deal as "a historic agreement" while addressing reporters alongside Putin.
> "According to this agreement, Turkey and Russia will not allow any separatist agenda on Syrian territory," he said. (...)
> Russian military police and Syrian border guards controlled by the president, Bashar al-Assad, will from Wednesday at noon facilitate the removal of Kurdish fighters and weaponry to the depth of 18 miles from their positions on the border, the Turkish foreign minister, Mevlüt Çavuşoğlu, and his

Russian counterpart, Sergei Lavrov, said after their respective presidents announced the agreement to reporters. (...)
Assad himself has repeatedly vowed to reunite his entire country under Damascus's rule. In a symbolic visit to southern Idlib on Tuesday – territory the regime now occupies for the first time in years – he called Erdoğan "a thief" and said he was ready to support any popular resistance against Turkey's invasion.
"We are in the middle of a battle and the right thing to do is to rally efforts to lessen the damages from the invasion and to expel the invader sooner or later," he told troops, (...) (McKernan and Borger 2019)

Nowhere in the report is there a reference to the languages in which the statements were originally made, and readers therefore will not know at which stage translation was involved. Moreover, we cannot know whether the English versions of the statements by Erdoğan and Assad, originally in all probability in Turkish and Arabic respectively, were translated directly from the source language by the authors of this report or whether they referred themselves to English versions already prepared by news agencies or the government. The authors could also have attended the Erdoğan – Putin press conference and followed simultaneous interpreting into English. The 2011 News and Media Editorial Code of *The Guardian* states that direct quotations "should not be changed to alter their context or meaning,"[1] but there is no reference to direct quotes which originate from another language. The authors of the article are named as Bethan McKernan in Istanbul and Julian Borger in Washington. The article includes some information about these two journalists, but all we read is that "Bethan McKernan is the Turkey and Middle East correspondent for the Guardian" and that "Julian Borger is the Guardian's world affairs editor. He was previously a correspondent in the US, the Middle East, eastern Europe and the Balkans." There is no explicit information about their own competence in languages such as Turkish or Arabic, although it is usually the case that journalists posted to other countries are multilingual, at least to some extent.

Professional journalists with language competence thus work across language frontiers and act as translators and intercultural mediators, although they have little or no training in translation as such. Their news production process is guided by their own professional standards and ethics, such as speed of production, readability of the texts, factual accuracy, and news worthiness. As a result, reorganization of information, deletion, addition,

---

1   https://www.theguardian.com/info/2015/aug/05/the-guardians-editorial-code

and substitution have been identified as major linguistic operations, or as translation strategies. As Bassnett and Bielsa (2009, 2) argue: "Information that passes between cultures through news agencies is not only 'translated' in the interlingual sense, it is reshaped, edited, synthesized and transformed for the consumption of a new set of readers." Adapting texts to suit the target audience and/or the ideological position of the newspaper can result in an altered point of view and a different conceptualization of social reality for the target readers, as illustrated, for example, by Gumul (2010) with Polish translations of English-language press articles and by Ethelb (2019) with Arabic translations of English texts produced by Aljazeera and Al-Arabiya. Or more generally, "news submitted to translation undergo a reframing process, entailing a reconstruction of a constructed reality" (Gambier 2006, 12).

Translation is an integral but often hidden part of interlingual news writing, and thus not perceived as a separate activity by the journalists (Bielsa 2007, 151). Since journalists consider their work as journalistic writing and not as translation, they prefer terms such 'international journalist', or 'bilingual journalist'. Some scholars in translation studies too have opted for labels such as 'journalators' (van Doorslaer 2012) or 'journalist-translators' (Hernández Guerrero 2010; Matsushita 2019). Moreover, the amount and the nature of the transformations involved in news translation have made researchers reflect on the applicability of the label 'translation'. The term most often used is 'transediting' (see e.g., Hursti 2001; van Doorslaer 2009; Chen 2011), which was originally introduced by Stetting (1989) to account for the fuzzy borderline between translating and editing. For Stetting, journalists drawing on material in other languages for writing their own texts is one of five cases where transediting is practiced (Stetting 1989, 373-374). Stetting herself acknowledged, however, that a "certain amount of editing has always been included in the translation task" (Stetting 1989, 371). With changes and transformations thus recognized as essential features of translation, as already illustrated above, we can ask whether we indeed need a separate term to capture the specifics of news translation or journalistic translation more widely (for a critical reflection on 'transediting' in comparison to 'translation' see Schäffner 2012). Such conceptual issues were also addressed during panels at congresses of the European Society for Translation Studies (EST). The panel theme in 2013 was "News Translation: Subverting the Discipline?" Since research into news translation has been pushing the boundaries of the very concept of 'translation' and of the discipline of translation studies, scholars have argued in favor of a broader definition of the term 'translation' to include the context of media news production (see e.g., van Doorslaer 2010; Schäffner 2012; Davier 2015).

This is in line with the general enlargement of the concept of translation in translation studies mentioned above.

The main challenges which news translation research poses can be summarized as follows: since news texts are often based on multiple (written and/or oral) sources (including multiple languages and genres), one specific source text with one specific author cannot easily be identified. There are no complete texts to use as comparable items. It is therefore difficult, if not impossible, to establish a clear relationship between these texts. Moreover, the translated text in its published form is rarely the product of one person. Texts are volatile, as it happens quite frequently with texts made available online that they are replaced by an updated or more accurate version. The selection of information and sources, as well as their presentation, that is, the transformations which occur in the news production process, are governed by values of journalism (speed, readability, audience sensitivity, cultural and ideological acceptability and desirability). The traditional concepts of translation studies, 'source text', 'target text', 'author', 'equivalence', 'faithfulness', thus hardly ever apply. What about the concept of 'transfer' then? Does it have to be questioned too or does it have a place in news translation research? This question will be addressed in the following section.

4. News translation as transfer?

If we agree that news translation is a type of translation, and that translation is a type of transfer, then we can say that the concept of transfer is indeed relevant to researching news translation, or journalistic translation more widely. The notion of transfer has frequently been used by scholars in commenting about news translation, albeit in different ways. For example, Palmer (2009) states that in the news production process, translation can occur as a part of news gathering, as part of the news writing stage, and in the dissemination process, "when reports are transferred between different news organisations" (Palmer 2009, 187). In presenting the different agents and practices in a South Korean media institution, Kang (2007, 238) argues that the published texts result from "the collaborative work of people assuming different roles and engaged in language transfer, cultural adaptation, proofreading, revising, naturalizing, editing and other textual processes that are carried out repeatedly and cyclically." In reflecting on the applicability of the concept of translation, Davier (2012, 79) claims that "[c]lassical translation studies theories are not equipped to ascertain whether or not these different kinds of interlingual transfers can be considered as 'translations'." And in commenting on the challenges of investigating the multilingual and translational character of news flows, Davier, Schäffner and van Doorslaer (2018, 156) say that "the researcher's eye does not only notice the translational character, but almost simultaneously also the immanent difficulties in tracing it down, in exactly pinpointing the various instances of interlingual, let alone intralingual transfer." We see that Palmer seems to focus on the material movement of texts across institutions, whereas the other authors reserve 'transfer' for the change of language involved in translation, including transformations within the same language in the case of intralingual translation.

Research methodologies and interdisciplinarity were the focus of a panel on "News Translation Challenging Adaptation, Transfer and Translation Studies" during the 2016 EST congress, held in Aarhus (Denmark). Selected papers of this panel were subsequently published in a special issue of the journal *Across Languages and Cultures* (2018). Since there is widespread agreement that the label 'translation' is broad enough to include the specifics of news translation, we can investigate possible exchanges among transfer studies and translation studies, and also adaptation studies (see e.g., van Doorslaer and Raw 2016). That is, disciplinary borderlines do not need to be established and preserved once and for all, but we can explore ways of exporting and importing methods and concepts between disciplines. In respect of transfer, we can ask to what extent this concept can be useful in addressing the theoretical and methodological challenges in researching the phenomena of news translation.

In international news flows, information gets selected and transferred, both in a material and a discursive way. For example, news agencies produce texts, predominantly news reports, which are then sold to other media organizations, such as newspapers, radio and TV stations. Material texts then get transferred. It may be the case that a newspaper publishes the text in exactly the same shape and language as produced by the news agency. In this case, the news agency is usually explicitly referenced as the source. In other instances, however, individual newspapers use the text received from a news agency as one piece of input in combination with others so that the finally published text is the result of information selection and transformation, even if all the input texts are in the same language. In more recent news translation research, such processes have been analyzed as intralingual translation (e.g., by Gagnon, Boulanger and Kalantari 2018 who examine intralingual translations in the form of popularizing discourse for financial news in Canadian media). If the transfer involves crossing language boundaries, the discursive transfer process is even more complex due to the involvement of interlingual translation. As has been shown in previous research, there are relatively few complete translations of clearly identifiable source texts which are also explicitly acknowledged.

More often, we are faced with unclear source text – target text situations, as illustrated above with the news report from *The Guardian*.

Product-oriented studies in news translation have compared different language versions of the same text, as far as it was possible to identify them, and the discovery of shifts, or translation strategies, was then based on such comparisons. Product-oriented comparative analyses have a long tradition in descriptive translation studies. Toury (1995, 33ff.) formulated three main postulates to guide the researcher in investigating translations as products: the source text postulate, the transfer postulate, and the relationship postulate. The source text postulate states that if there is a translation, the existence of a source text is assumed. The transfer postulate states that the translation production process must have involved transfer of something. What precisely has been transferred is to be discovered by the researcher. The relationship postulate states that there is some relationship between source text and target text, the exact nature of which, however, has to be identified in each individual case. A translation is thus tied to another text in another language and culture "from which it was presumably derived by transfer operations (…) by a set of relationships based on shared features" (Toury 2012, 31). For Toury, then, there is no specific criterion or type of relationship which has to hold between source text and target text, transfer for him is understood in a wider sense, and not restricted to meaning transfer or fidelity to the author's intention.

In his reflections on transfer techniques in the history of translation knowledge, D'hulst comments on the difficulties which arise when reconstructing past transfer. He says,

> (…) given that, in contrast with translation relationships which link translation to at least one specific and commonly identifiable source text, transfer relationships are more complex to reconstruct since they vary more considerably in shape and content, but also because most of them keep a looser bond with their source. (D'hulst 2018, 141)

This difficulty applies to the discovery of transfer operations in news translation as well, in particular in cases where a news report is tied to several other texts in other languages. As previous research has established, multiple sources are typical of translation in journalistic environments, which complicates the reconstruction of the exact text production process, let alone the moments of translation. This phenomenon poses challenges for data collection and analysis. Research cannot rely on parallel or comparable corpora which would allow to align the news reports in a straightforward way. Davier and van Doorslaer (2018) address this specific problem of the total or partial absence of a traceable source text from a methodological point of view. They suggest that scholars can build multilingual comparable corpora "according to comparability criteria and then engage in detective work to put together approximate pairs of similar reports" (Davier and van Doorslaer 2018, 249). Using this method, Davier (2017) conducted a comparison between an English and a French news report published by *Agence France-Presse* (AFP) on 3 May 2007. Her 'detective work' led her to discover a press release which both reports had quoted, thus being able to identify which parts in the English text had been translated from French. Davier and van Doorslaer (2018, 250) argue, however, that a "purely textual analysis of potentially translated texts in a comparable corpus produces plausible hypotheses in the best case", that such hypotheses "can be solved if textual data are triangulated with data from the field (e.g., interviews and observations)" (Davier and van Doorslaer 2018, 253), and that "[m]edia artefacts need to be studied along with their production process and/or their socio-historical context" (Davier and van Doorslaer 2018, 254).

This plea for a context analysis ties in with Göpferich's (2007) position on the object of translation studies. Following her definition of translation studies as a field of research whose object is any mediated transformation of offers of information, she argues that "[t]his implies, of course, that social, political and ethical conditions, norms, problems and changes involved in this process have to be taken into account since they represent the context in which any transfer has to be seen" (Göpferich 2007, 34). The transfer we see in news translation is one which is selective and transformative to a larger extent than in, for example, literary or technical translation. Journalists as translators decide which information gets selected to be incorporated in a news report, whose voices will be heard and how. Journalists thus also have a gatekeeping function in the news flows (Vuorinen 1995). Journalists are not primarily concerned with exact meaning transfer or with the 'real' intention of original authors. Rather, they intend to produce readable texts and to pass on, or transfer, newsworthy information to their readers. As Valdeón (2009, 79) states, news translation is "translation of information, rather than (...) translation of texts."

One further advantage of going beyond a more narrow analysis of shifts between one presumed source text and one presumed target text is the inclusion of different language versions of news reports covering the same topic. A product-oriented analysis can reveal differences in the information chosen for transfer as well as its refocusing or reperspectivization, in line with the target audience aimed at and/or the ideological position of the newspaper (illustrated in, for example, Schäffner 2008). Fieldwork in the various media institutions could, again, provide more insights into the motivations behind these processes, although it is difficult to conduct such fieldwork retrospectively, let alone by an individual scholar. Moreover, news reports, including the translational elements they contain, often undergo additional movements and transfer. This is to say, quotes from a text are often taken up by other media and inserted in their own news articles. In such transfer processes, new translations may occur. This can be illustrated by the recent controversial debates following the award of the Nobel Prize in Literature to the Austrian writer Peter Handke. Various media reported that Handke had been indifferent to the victims of the war in ex-Yugoslavia in the 1990s and that he had defended Slobodan Milošević, the former President of Yugoslavia, who was accused of war crimes at the International Criminal Tribunal. The sentence "You can stick your corpses up your arse", supposedly said by Handke, was repeated again and again in recent media reports. In an article, the German news magazine *Der Spiegel* (19 October 2019, 116) reports on its detective work to trace the origin of this sentence. They discovered that it appeared for the first time in an English version of an article in *The Irish Times* of April 3, 1999 in the following extract:

> In the course of his attack on Western coverage of the Balkan conflict, Handke accuses the Bosnians of staging market massacres in Sarajevo and casts doubt on the murder of Muslims at Srebrenica. When critics pointed out that the victims' corpses provided evidence of Serb atrocities, the writer replied: "You can stick your corpses up your arse."

Since no other English-language sources from that time were identified, and since the context of the article refers to the German language area, *Der Spiegel* concludes that Handke must have been speaking in German, and that the quote that appeared in *The Irish Times* was thus a translation. As *Der Spiegel* argues, German texts that quoted this sentence were published later than the text in *The Irish Times* and sometimes explicitly referred to it as their source. Further research then revealed a discussion evening in Vienna in 1996 as the event at which Handke had actually criticized a journalist by saying that he should stick his concerns about Bosnia up his ass. Another article, by Alexandar Hemon, published in *The New York Times* on October 15, 2019, also quotes this sentence, albeit in a corrected version:

> As for Mr. Handke, when a journalist asked him if he was concerned about the suffering in Bosnia, he retorted, "Stick your concerns up your ass!"

The correction, dated October 23, 2019, can be found at the bottom of the article and reads as follows:

> An earlier version of this article included a mistranslation, via *The Irish Times*, of a comment by Peter Handke. When asked whether he was concerned about Serb atrocities, Mr. Handke replied, in German, "You can stick your concerns up your ass," not "corpses up your ass."

What is noteworthy in this correction is the reference to a mistranslation and to *The Irish Times*, which was not provided in the previous version. It would be interesting to investigate whether the correction was the result of *The New York Times'* own subsequent research or of reactions to accusations of other media. Whatever the case may be, the wrong quote had already created its own reality, as argued by *Der Spiegel*. With ongoing re-uses of the same quote, the transfer process, too, can create a cycle of its own. Although linked to the history of translation knowledge, D'hulst's argument that "[t]ransfer techniques indeed shape translation knowledge in ways that may significantly condition the latter's afterlife, spread and impact, including oblivion" (D'hulst 2018, 135) is thus appropriate to news translation as well.

5. Conclusion

In this chapter, I have reflected on scope and limitations in using the concepts of 'translation' and 'transfer' for news translation. Although traditional views of translation as meaning transfer from one source text to one target text do not apply in this context, it is argued that a broader view of translation as a type of transfer is an appropriate conceptualization. It is also interesting to see that the metaphor of translation has found its way into the metalanguage of other disciplines. In his comparison of metaphors which are used to describe translation and the use of the metaphor of translation in the humanities and natural sciences, Guldin (2016, 69) states that the notion of translation "has become *the* metaphor for all kinds of processes of transformation, rewriting, encoding and decoding." Guldin gives as examples, among others, anthropology, ethnography, psychoanalysis, medicine and genetics. In such metaphorical uses in other disciplines, the concept of transfer is also present. For example, in medicine and pharmacy, scholars speak of translational research for the application and transfer of theoretical knowledge and findings of basic scientific research into practical applications such as new therapies, new medical procedures or new tools. The use of theoretical knowledge for innovation and growth of businesses is also the key element of the Knowledge Transfer Partnership (KTP) program in the United Kingdom, which the UK government characterizes as "enable(ing) a business to bring in new skills and the latest academic thinking to deliver a specific, strategic innovation project through a knowledge-based partnership" (UK Government 2020).

In this context, knowledge transfer refers to the dissemination of knowledge from one organization to another, or from one unit of an organization to another one. Knowledge can also be transferred between organizations which are based in different countries. From the perspective of organizational studies and business studies, Ciuk and James (2015, 566) complain about a "lack of studies exploring empirically the role of language and more particularly interlingual translation in the travel of ideas and practices across organisational contexts." They studied the relevance of interlingual translation to processes of knowledge transfer within a pharmaceutical multinational enterprise and present the findings of their analysis "of an attempt by a group of managers in a Polish subsidiary of a US company to translate centrally promulgated corporate values into the local language and context" (Ciuk and James 2015, 566). They illustrate how the engagement in the translation, performed by local managers, "prompted discussions around the meaning of the corporate values and stimulated dialogue around the preferred local meanings" (Ciuk and James 2015, 571), with these preferred meanings then triggering reflections around local identity and relationships with the parent company. The authors acknowledge that they built on insights from translation studies, in particular the notion of translation as a situated practice as put forward by Risku (2002).

Such interdisciplinary research can also be of value for news translation. Although news cannot be fully equated with knowledge, insights gained by Ciuk and James on the role of interlingual translation for the transfer of value-infused practices do apply to news translation as well. They concern the importance of structural and institutional factors which exert a significant influence on how information and ideas are potentially transformed when they are recontextualized as a result of a transfer process. Information, including information which is transferred in news reports, is not an invariant substance but rather socially embedded and constructed, and transfer is not a mechanistic and unidirectional carrying over of an invariant substance to another time and space but information is constructed and shaped in this very act of transfer.

In her reflections on the relationship between translation studies and transfer studies, Göpferich argues:

> All forms of transfer have in common that documents are transformed for specific purposes. It is interesting to investigate not only (a) what types

of transformations (or shifts) occur in this process, (b) what streams of transfer can be observed and why and (c) what their objectives and systemic implications are, but also (d) whether the objectives are met, i.e., whether the product fulfils its function in an ideal way. (Göpferich 2010, 376)

News translation research so far has mainly been concerned with points (a), (b), and (c) and has come up with valuable insights. There is thus scope for studies to investigate the reception of and attitude to translated news, for which interdisciplinary cooperation would be beneficial.

References

Across Languages and Cultures. 2018. "Methods in News Translation." Special issue, volume 19, number 2, guest-edited by Lucile Davier, Christina Schäffner, and Luc van Doorslaer.
Antos, Gerd. 2001. "Transferwissenschaft. Chancen und Barrieren des Zugangs zu Wissen in Zeiten der Informationsflut und der Wissensexplosion." In *Wissenstransfer zwischen Experten und Laien. Umriss einer Transferwissenschaft*, edited by Sigurd Wichter and Gerd Antos, 3-33. Frankfurt am Main: Peter Lang.
Bani, Sara. 2006. "An Analysis of Press Translation Process." In *Translation in Global News. Proceedings of the Conference held at the University of Warwick 23 June 2006*, edited by Kyle Conway and Susan Bassnett, 35-45. Coventry: University of Warwick.
Bielsa, Esperanca. 2007. "Translation in Global News Agencies." *Target* 19 (1): 135-55.
—, and Susan Bassnett. 2009. *Translation in Global News*. London: Routledge.
Chen, Yamei. 2011. "The Translator's Subjectivity and its Constraints in News Transediting: A Perspective of Reception Aesthetics." *Meta* 56 (1): 119-44.
Ciuk, Sylwia, and Philip James. 2015. "Interlingual Translation and the Transfer of Value-infused Practices: An in-depth Qualitative Exploration." *Management Learning* 46 (5): 565-81. https://doi.org/10.1177/1350507614560304
D'hulst, Lieven. 2018. "Transfer Modes." In *A History of Modern Translation Knowledge*, edited by Lieven D'hulst and Yves Gambier, 135-42. Amsterdam: John Benjamins.
Davier, Lucile. 2012. "Légitimé ou illégitimité de la traduction dans les agences de presse?" *Forum* 10 (1): 79-114.
— 2015. "Cultural Translation' in News Agencies? A Plea to Broaden the Definition of Translation." *Perspectives: Studies in Translatology* 23 (4): 536-51.
— 2017. *Les Enjeux de la Traduction dans les Agences de Presse*. Lille: Presses universitaires du Septentrion.

— 2019. "The Moving Boundaries of News Translation." *Slovo.ru: baltijskij accent* 10 (1): 69-86. https://doi.org/10.5922/2225-5346-2019-1-5

—, and Luc van Doorslaer. 2018. "Translation without a Source Text: Methodological Issues in News Translation." *Across Languages and Cultures* 19 (2): 241-57.

—, Christina Schäffner, and Luc van Doorslaer. 2018. "The Methodological Remainder in News Translation Research: Outlining the Background." *Across Languages and Cultures* 19 (2): 155-64.

Delisle, Jean, Hannelore Lee-Jahnke, and Monique Cormier. 1999. *Terminologie de la Traduction / Translation Terminology/ Terminología de la Traducción / Terminologie der Übersetzung.* Amsterdam: John Benjamins.

Ethelb, Hamza. 2019. "The Translator as Journalist: Getting Across the Ideological Intricacies of Translating News." *Dirāsāt fī al-tarǧama* 5 (1): 25-64.

Gagnon, Chantal, Pier-Pascale Boulanger, and Esmaeil Kalantari. 2018. "How to Approach Translation in a Financial News Corpus." *Across Languages and Cultures* 19 (2): 221-40.

Gambier, Yves. 2006. "Transformations in International News." In *Translation in Global News. Proceedings of the Conference held at the University of Warwick 23 June 2006*, edited by Kyle Conway and Susan Bassnett, 9-21. Coventry: University of Warwick.

Göpferich, Susanne. 2007. "Translation Studies and Transfer Studies: A Plea for Widening the Scope of Translation Studies." In *Doubts and Directions in Translation Studies*, edited by Yves Gambier, Miriam Shlesinger, and Radegundis Stolze, 27-39. Amsterdam: John Benjamins.

— 2010. "Transfer and Transfer Studies." In *Handbook of Translation Studies*, vol. 1, edited by Yves Gambier and Luc van Doorslaer, 374-77. Amsterdam: John Benjamins.

Guldin, Rainer. 2016. *Translation as Metaphor.* Abingdon: Routledge.

Gumul, Ewa. 2010. "Explicitating Political Discourse." In *Political Discourse, Media and Translation*, edited by Christina Schäffner and Susan Bassnett, 94-116. London: Cambridge Scholars Publishing.

Hemon, Aleksandar. 2019. "The Bob Dylan of Genocide Apologists." *The New York Times*, October 15, 2019. https://www.nytimes.com/2019/10/15/opinion/peter-handke-nobel-bosnia-genocide.html

Hernández Guerrero, María José. 2010. "Las Noticias Traducidas en el Diario *El Mundo*: el Trasvase Transcultural de la Información." In *Translating Information*, edited by Roberto A. Valdeón, 51-86. Oviedo: Universidad de Oviedo.

Holland, Robert. 2012. "News Translation." In *The Routledge Handbook of Translation Studies*, edited by Carmen Millán and Francesca Bartrina, 333-46. London: Routledge.

Holz-Mänttäri, Justa. 1984. *Translatorisches Handeln: Theorie und Methode*. Helsinki: Suomalainen Tiedeakatemia.

Hursti, Kristian. 2001. "An Insider's View on Transformation and Transfer in International News Communication: An English-Finnish Perspective." *The Electronic Journal of the Department of English at the University of Helsinki* 1: 1-8.

Language & Intercultural Communication. 2005. "Global News Translation." Special issue, volume 5, number 2, guest-edited by Susan Bassnett.

Kang, Ji-Hae. 2007. "Recontextualization of News Discourse: A Case Study of Translation of News Discourse on North Korea." *The Translator* 13 (2): 219-42.

Koskinen, Kaisa. 2008. *Translating Institutions. An Ethnographic Study of EU Translation*. Manchester: St Jerome.

Matsushita, Kayo. 2019. *When News Travels East. Translation Practices by Japanese Newspapers*. Leuven: Leuven University Press.

McKernan, Bethan, and Julian Borger. 2019. "Turkey and Russia agree on deal over buffer zone in northern Syria." *The Guardian*, October 19, 2019. https://www.theguardian.com/world/2019/oct/22/turkey-and-russia-agree-deal-over-buffer-zone-in-northern-syria

n.a. 1999. "Serbia's eloquent ally." *The Irish Times*, April 3, 1999. https://www.irishtimes.com/news/serbia-s-eloquent-ally-1.170173.

Palmer, Jerry. 2009. "News Gathering and Dissemination." In *Routledge Encyclopedia of Translation Studies*, edited by Mona Baker and Gabriela Saldanha, 186-89. London: Routledge.

Perspectives: Studies in Translatology. 2015. "Culture and Translation." Special issue, volume 23, number 4, guest-edited by Kyle Conway.

Risku, Hanna. 2002. "Situatedness in Translation Studies." *Cognitive Systems Research* 3 (3): 523-33.

Schäffner, Christina. 2008. "'The Prime Minister Said ...': Voices in Translated Political Texts." *Synaps Fagspråk, Kommunikasjon, Kulturkunnskap* 22: 3-25.

— 2012. "Rethinking Transediting." *Meta* 57 (4): 866-83.

— 2018. "Language, Interpreting, and Translation in News Media." In *The Routledge Handbook of Translation Studies and Linguistics*, edited by Kirsten Malmkjaer, 327-41. London: Routledge.

Stetting, Karen. 1989. "Transediting: A New Term for Coping with the Grey Area between Editing and Translating." In *Proceedings from the Fourth Nordic Conference for English Studies*, edited by Graham Caie, Kirsten Haastrup, Arnt Lykke Jakobsen, Jørgen Erik Nielsen, Jørgen Sevaldsen, Henrik Specht, and Arne Zettersten, 371-82. Copenhagen: University of Copenhagen.

The Guardian. 2011. News and Media Editorial Code. https://www.theguardian.com/info/2015/aug/05/the-guardians-editorial-code.

Toury, Gideon. 1995. *Descriptive Translation Studies and Beyond.* Amsterdam: John Benjamins.
— 2012. *Descriptive Translation Studies – and Beyond. Revised edition.* Amsterdam: John Benjamins.
Tymoczko, Maria. 2007. *Enlarging Translation, Empowering Translators.* Manchester: St Jerome.
UK Government. 2015. Knowledge Transfer Partnerships: What They Are and How to Apply. https://www.gov.uk/guidance/knowledge-transfer-partnerships-what-they-are-and-how-to-apply#what-is-a-knowledge-transfer-partnership
Valdeón, Roberto A. 2009. "Translating Informative and Persuasive Texts." *Perspectives: Studies in Translatology* 17 (2): 77-81.
— 2015. "Fifteen Years of Journalistic Translation Research and more." *Perspectives: Studies in Translatology* 23 (4): 634-62.
van Doorslaer, Luc. 2009. "How Language and (Non-)translation Impact on Media Newsrooms. The Case of Newspapers in Belgium." *Perspectives: Studies in Translatology* 17 (2): 83-92.
— 2010. "Journalism and Translation." In *Handbook of Translation Studies,* vol. 1, edited by Yves Gambier and Luc van Doorslaer, 180-84. Amsterdam: John Benjamins.
— 2012. "Translating, Narrating and Constructing Images in Journalism with a Test Case on Representation in Flemish TV News." *Meta* 57 (4): 1046-59.
—, and Laurence Raw. 2016. "Adaptation Studies and Translation Studies: Very Interactive yet Distinct." In *Border Crossings: Translation Studies and Other Disciplines,* edited by Yves Gambier and Luc van Doorslaer, 189-204. Amsterdam: John Benjamins.
Venuti, Lawrence. 1995. *The Translator's Invisibility: A History of Translation.* London: Routledge.
— 2019. *Theses on Translation: An Organon for the Current Moment.* Pittsburgh: FlugSchriften.
Vermeer, Hans J. 1996. *A Skopos Theory of Translation (Some Arguments for and against).* Heidelberg: TEXTconTEXT.
Vuorinen, Erkka. 1997. "News Translation as Gatekeeping." In *Translation as Intercultural Communication. Selected Papers from the EST Congress – Prague 1995,* edited by Mary Snell-Hornby, Zuzana Jettmarova, and Klaus Kaindl, 161-71. Amsterdam: John Benjamins.
Wolf, Michaela. 2002. "Translation Activity between Culture, Society and the Individual: Towards a Sociology of Translation." *CTIS Occasional Papers* 2: 33-43.

Russian bears on the move, or how national images are transferred

Pieter Boulogne & Luc van Doorslaer

Abstract

This chapter studies how animal images are socially constructed as representations of national or cultural identity, and how they function when they are transferred to other linguistic and cultural areas. While symbol and image attribution are essentially variable and changeable, they potentially carry a high degree of national and cultural image projection. The case study under investigation is that of the bear, which has been used as a symbol for several countries, regions and other collectivities. Whereas features such as wildness and strength often reappear, a bear can also be associated with softer characteristics such as kindness and friendliness. This chapter analyzes the different adaptations of the bear in relation to Russia. On the one hand, especially in the West, a negative hetero-image was/is used, mainly in a context of armed conflicts and geopolitical tensions, and on the other, in today's Russia, positive auto-images are used, for instance in the logo of the political party United Russia. These diverging contextualizations and interpretations illustrate the flexibility of image attribution through cultural, geographical or temporal transfer.

1. Introduction

In order to make their potential enemies tremble and shake with fear, nations and countries have cultivated the habit of putting frightening animals on their coats of arms. In the Belgian northern and southern regions of Flanders and Wallonia, for example, the official flags are adorned with an indomitable black lion and a perky red rooster respectively. However, not all will agree that these regions, individually or even taken together, are particularly frightening. According to the current Western dominant public narrative – to use the term proposed by Baker (2006) – Russia is a much more frightening state. Since 1993, the coat of arms of the Russian Federation has displayed a double-headed eagle. In 1917, the Bolsheviks had wrung both its necks, but the tsarist bird of prey turned out to be a phoenix. Russia shares it with quite a few other countries that present themselves as heirs to the Byzantine Empire, such as Serbia and Montenegro. Albania, the Holy Roman Empire of the German Nation, the German Empire, and the Austrian Empire have also claimed the same monstrous bird as their national animal. Perhaps it is partly due to this heraldic inflation that the double-headed eagle in practice hardly functions as Russia's national symbol. In fact, the bird must bow both its heads to make another animal come first: a bear.

Today, the Russian bear seems to lurk around everywhere – he seems omnipresent. This observation applies to the image that Russia cultivates of itself (auto-image), as well as to the image that other nations have of Russia (hetero-image). In Russia, the image of the Russian bear is mentioned on an everyday basis by political scientists, journalists and marketers. In 2012, the image was found to be a vivid factor in Russia's domestic and foreign policy (Rjabov[1] and De Lazari 2012, 5). Outside Russia, it functions as an allegory that helps to shape the way people relate to Russia and/or to the Russians. The Russian bear regularly shows his head in advertising, plays, films and computer games, and in speeches by Western authorities. He has become an indispensable figure of both Western mass culture and Western journalism (ibid.).

Drawing on transfer studies as well as imagological insights, this chapter aims to trace back the Russian bear. The transfer concept applied here is based on transfer as used by Göpferich (2007, 2010). It relates explicitly to transfer studies (mainly flourishing in the German tradition of the "Transferwissenschaften"), includes both intralingual and interlingual translation, and describes its decisive feature as "to make, what is transferred, cognitively accessible in the target culture" (Göpferich 2007, 33). Transfer studies has major common ground with more extended object perspectives on and in translation studies, as it investigates "the principles, methods and strategies of making knowledge accessible in a selective and sustained way in the wake of a flood of information and knowledge explosion" (Gerd Antos, quoted and translated in Göpferich 2007, 33).

We investigate the roots of the Russian bear image and the historical functions it has fulfilled within and outside of Russia. This also implies that the image has been transferred between different cultural and linguistic areas. For instance, there is clearly also a contemporary Western interpretation of the image that can be challenged. Rather than exhaustiveness, our aim is to uncover the most significant stages of the course that the image has taken,

---

1   In this chapter, while referring to secondary literature, ISO 9 is used for the transliteration of Cyrillic characters into Latin characters.

within and outside of Russia, since its very creation. However, before diving into the Russian bear's mouth, we first aim to gain a deeper understanding of what it is that makes animal symbols so popular for national and other usages.

2. The use of images for creating and expressing symbolic value

The eagle – be it double-headed or just single-headed – is certainly among the most frequently used animal symbols. It represents, by association, not only countries or nations, but is also applied in other forms of contemporary popular culture and astrology. For many years, the soccer teams of Benfica Lisbon (Portugal) and Eintracht Frankfurt (Germany) have been using a living eagle as mascot at all their home matches. Besides an obvious reference to both clubs' logos, where an eagle is prominently present, it is also an attempt to impress the opponent. It is no coincidence that the names of the two eagles are Vitória and Attila, both referring to supposed invincibility and strength. Astrological sources refer to eagles as symbols of "power and freedom – the stamina to unearth your capabilities and the liberty to move ahead triumphantly", as well as to characteristics such as "focused, adventurous, vibrant, benign and grounded" (both quotes from 'Eagle Meaning and Symbolism'). Moreover, it is one of the animals with symbolic value in many different cultures, as transferred through the ages and worldwide.

Animals are just one of the possible elements used in national symbols, because of their association with certain features. Nevertheless, these features are also socially constructed, being partly dependent on historical, cultural, religious and sometimes individual circumstances, and as such are poly-interpretable. Especially for younger states or communities that cannot rely on the historical dimension, it is nearly impossible to create such symbols appealing to all members of the group. In such younger states, "we see disputes over national symbols unfolding along several axes: among ethnic groups; among socio-ideological groups; and among groups with different attitudes towards other states and supranational organizations" (Kolstø 2006, 680).

Symbols share this characteristic of constructedness and variability with national and cultural images, with which they interact. In his typology, Mitchell (1986) distinguished between graphical, optical, perceptual, verbal and mental images. The imagological usage of 'image' can sometimes be related to the perceptual and verbal categories or to visual depiction, yet the main application is that of the mental imagination, a "mental or discursive representation or reputation of a person, group, ethnicity or 'nation'" (Leerssen

2007, 342). Such representations in this case are not social or factual realities, but imputed characteristics, and are as such imagined. Exactly this imputed nature of the features turns images into mobile, changeable and multi-usable discursive constructs. Symbols that are chosen to function as an image of national or cultural identity are just one possible expression of the multi-layered character of images. Although they are often presented as 'essential', they can also be changed relatively smoothly into a different symbol, as for instance has happened with the Russian eagle and bear.

Figure 1. *Steirische Völkertafel* or Styrian Table of Nations[2]

The classic *Völkertafel* (Table of Nations, see figure 1), an eighteenth-century Austrian painting that is a well-known source for historical ethnotyping, made explicit use of animals as one of the categories typifying ten different European nationalities. If we solely focus on the line where the comparison with animals is made, we find the following ten associations. Spaniard: elephant, Frenchman: fox, Italian: lynx, German: lion, Englishman: horse, Swede: ox, Pole: bear, Hungarian: wolf, Russian: donkey, Turk or Greek: cat.

2 Source: https://commons.wikimedia.org/wiki/File:V%C3%B6lkertafel.jpg. See page for author / public domain.

The eighteenth-century association of Poles with a bear and of Russians with a donkey illustrates the variability and changeability of symbol and image attribution. Moreover, the chosen animals only take on additional significance in relation to the other characteristics mentioned in the descriptions of the table. For the Pole, these are features such as being boorish, more cruel, mediocre and impetuous, whereas the Russian is characterized as malicious, most cruel, very callous and cumbersome. Although the *Völkertafel* is a mixture of factual and sarcastic features, in general it attributes more negative characterizations to Eastern European nations, which might explain why several of the traits of Poles and Russians seem to be at least partly overlapping.

To some degree, this relates to the many sources showing ethnocentrism from a Western or Southern European perspective. The assumed superior civility was expressed by the use of the word 'barbarians' for foreigners coming from either the North or the East:

> The history of the relations between settled Western European nations and the invaders from the North, the East, or Asia shows that any fresh wave (Teutons, Goths, Vandals, Huns, Avars, Tartars, Turks, Moors, Vikings and so on), took on the name and function of the barbarian. (Beller 2007, 267)

However, this does not mean that ethnocentrism in representation or designation was a (Western) European monopoly. Beller (2007) also mentions examples of non-European cultures, such as the Chinese, the Indian or the Muslim Arab, describing strangers with very denigrating terminology and expressing a similar idea of the superiority of their own civilization.

Whereas the cultural self vs. other categorization and imagination have existed for millennia, the specific national content and interpretation is much younger and a result of the rise of nationalism and nation-state thinking starting in the Napoleonic period. The visualization of national signs and symbols accompanied these new and quickly dominant categories of conceptualization. Pictorial stereotyping on a national basis became popular, particularly in combination with the new cult of national history and national myths. A case in point were history paintings:

> Important victories, heroic defeats, resistance against oppressors, heroes, formative historic incidents functioned as themes to give the nation a canonical vision of its past underpinning present and future. (Flacke 2007, 381)

The creation of mythical and heroic figures for constructing the identity of a specific community was in itself not new, yet it was the first time that such narratives were adopted in a process of national affiliation. Besides the use of history paintings, many patriotic and commemorative monuments were also created to be present in the public space, to impress and instruct through their image and visual presence. The French Revolution had set the tone for expressing shared national pride and glorifying national grandeur. This is the basis for the national and cultural projection process underlying identity building, and leads to discursive products as studied by imagology.

The nineteenth century in particular generated several pseudo-scientific currents, such as phrenology, relating group characteristics to physical appearance, in some cases also to the temperament of animals and their physical or facial features. Such a "correlation of physiognomically expressed characters with ethnicity" (Agazzi 2007, 398) affected not only science, but also many products of figurative art and literature. They artistically expressed certain interpretations of evolutionary theories that pseudo-scientifically rationalized European ethnocentrism. Moreover, quite a lot of racial thought was developed in the wake of French diplomat and writer Arthur de Gobineau's *Essai sur l'inégalité des races humaines* (1853, Essay on the Inequality of the Human Races), eventually leading to the "aberrations of nazi pseudo-science" (Agazzi 2007, 399).

Partly related to the effect of visual images is also the value of symbols, which "signify something representing something else by way of analogy" (Jourdan 2007, 434). A visual image such as an animal on a flag or an emblem aims to connect to related characteristics that are supposedly intrinsic *within* them. However, the establishment of analogy is, although not completely arbitrary, at least ambiguous in itself. Let us apply this to the eagle example mentioned before. Under certain circumstances, an eagle may evoke associations with triumph and freedom. At the same time, it will connect to other features as well, just as freedom may also be symbolized by a unicorn or a leopard. Every symbolic association is open to alternative interpretations. Only when conventionalized or socialized to a larger extent (for instance within a national, cultural, political or religious community), does the sign become more powerful.

> Symbols play an important social role, rendering abstract principles concrete (power, glory, virtues, community), and accordingly they have an important role in grouping individuals around a common focus of identification. They can impose or evoke unanimity by sending out the vaguest of messages. Thus the French tricolour invites recognition and identification from all the French, as does the hammer and sickle for all communists. But alongside its identitarian function, symbols have the power to persuade or to enjoin: the symbols of power indicate when authority resides and commands respect. (Jourdan 2007, 436)

3. The bear of the North?

The image of the bear and its potentially divergent interpretations are a meaningful illustration of both the vagueness and the common focus of identification as mentioned above.

The bear used to be particularly *feared* in Europe. This is illustrated by the conventional wisdom that the English word 'bear' stems from the Germanic word for *brown*, from which the German and Dutch words *Bär* and *beer* may also have been derived. The word is believed to have functioned as a taboo avoidance term: Germanic peoples supposedly feared that speaking the animal's true name aloud might cause it to appear and therefore just said 'the brown one'. This is why some call the word 'bear' the oldest-known euphemism in the history of the English language (Silver 2011). This is actually more a theory than a proven fact, but it is clear that as recently as the seventeenth century, Western Europe associated the "Russian bear" with "a land of unknowns—wild, untamed, and full of dangers" (Platoff 2012, 105). This perception shows interesting parallels with many nature-related tropes and images that were used throughout past centuries for imagologically representing 'the North', be it for Scandinavia, Iceland or, more recently, Alaska. We will now elucidate some recurrent features essentially establishing the imagery of the North. These characteristics and tropes can serve as a basis for a comparison with the views on and imagological usages of the 'Russian bear'.

Probably the most salient feature attributed to the North is that of *wilderness* and the desolate character of nature (for instance, as described in Duffy 2009). The vast undeveloped lands and the rich wildlife are perceived as "[b]eautiful and big, cold and scary" (Pursell and Hogan 2009, 191). The paradoxical combination of scary impressiveness and attractive or unknown beauty is in itself fertile ground for imagological variation. The positive accentuation of the unspoiled character (as a counterforce to existing 'decadent' tendencies) is an element that was frequently used for introducing innovation through cultural policies as well. Van Doorslaer (2006) describes, for instance, how German literature imported translations from Scandinavia and Flanders at the end of the nineteenth and the beginning of the twentieth century, mainly referring to the so-called unspoiled qualities of the regions and their literary production. In the case of Alaska, Pursell and Hogan (2009) relate the control of wild nature to contemporary constructions of masculinity and the ability to dominate nature.

A second characteristic of the North plays to the tension between *civilized and uncivilized*. Historically, this is also partly related to the North-South polarity, taking into account the "common late-Baroque belief in the inferiority of the uncultivated North compared to the cultivated South" (Schaer 2009, 132). Iceland is a case in point, illustrating that this belief fundamentally changed in the nineteenth century. Whereas for centuries inhabitants of Iceland were represented as "an uncivilized, half-animal, half-human people" (Ísleifsson 2009, 149), the descriptions became much more positive starting from the nineteenth century, "and writers started to present Icelanders as innocent, noble savages, living on what their native soil had to offer" (150). Being uncivilized and noble are again two sides of the same coin.

A third interesting feature is that of *folklore* (related to the common folk) as an important constituent element of cultural identity. In Nordic countries, the common folk often referred to professions such as peasants and fishermen, in a close relationship and exchange with the forces of nature: local culture and closeness to nature were interdependent. Authenticity was related to local beliefs and traditions, local language and tales such as the sagas. Icelandic folklore databases sometimes mention "odd character stories" as a separate search category (Schram 2009, 252). Those protagonists had experiences between the archaic wild and the modern, as though they were closely connected to the local roots and to the supernatural at the same time.

> These humorous characters, which a local narrator called with some warmth 'these wild beasts', could of course be perceived as something other than a representation of region or nation. But the context of representation is already within the storytelling situation. In that light these "wild" archaic masculine heroes or antiheroes can be seen as representations of a traditional and proud nation in control of, or rather in communion with, their wild northern nature. (Schram 2009, 254-255)

Last but not least, the constructed identity often contains elements of *nostalgia* for landscape and nature, which can simultaneously be presented as a sometimes implicit, sometimes explicit criticism of more modern consumer culture. Nostalgia is an emotional reaction to feelings of loss, such as lost places or lost traditions. Seen from that perspective, it is obviously partly related to the folklore feature. Both reflective nostalgia and restorative nostalgia (the types of behavior distinguished by Boym, and referred to in Pursell and Hogan 2009, 195-196) are applied. Whereas the former deals with individual and collective memory, the latter seeks to rebuild that imagined community.

4. In the footsteps of 'the Russian bear' as a hetero-image

Although today's Russia tends to imagine itself as a bear, this figure actually originated outside of Russia, as a hetero-image. The Western European association of the animal with Russia, which in view of the then wide distribution of bears in this region seems not far-fetched, goes back to the Middle Ages. Back then, Russia was already suffering from an unfortunate reputation in Western Europe: "Russia was considered a backward, sparsely populated realm of nobles and serfs, with little political organization and no cultural or intellectual achievement" (Naarden and Leerssen 2007, 227). In this context, at the end of the seventeenth century, the prominent philosopher of the German Enlightenment, Gottfried Leibniz, oxymoronically nicknamed the Russians "baptized bears" (Žakovska 2012, 169). In addition, the image of Russia as a bear was popularized by the famous traveler Francesco Algarotti, who in his acclaimed *Letters about Russia* in 1739 described Russia as a large white bear (De Lazari and Rjabov 2012, 151).

Figure 2. *L'Ours du nord* (1854) by Honoré Daumier[3]

---

3   Lithograph on wove paper. Source: http://portlandartmuseum.us/mwebcgi/mweb.exe?request=record;id=25 Public domain.

The true starting gun for the mutual association of bears and Russia, however, was fired in England, where bears were often written about when Russia came up. In the early seventeenth century, Shakespeare wrote in *Macbeth* (Act 3, Scene 4, 102-109) about "the rugged Russian bear", which he used as an imagery for danger to life:

> What man dare, I dare.
> Approach thou like the rugged Russian bear,
> The armed rhinoceros, or th' Hyrcan tiger;
> Take any shape but that, and my firm nerves
> Shall never tremble.

The English caricature culture in the eighteenth century played a key role in the creation of the transnational imagination of Russia as a bear. Between 1737 and 1836, more than a hundred different satirical engravings with a Russian bear were made in Europe. The vast majority were published in England, where, thanks to freedom of the press, caricatures flourished (Uspenskij 2012, 87). The inspiration for these engravings was the widespread import of bears from Russia for entertainment purposes. Most of these engravings were created during the Napoleonic wars (1803-1814), when Russia became actively involved in a large-scale armed international conflict and repeatedly threatened the interests of England. Notably, during the Russo-French coalition, the British enjoyed caricatures which portrayed the Russian emperor Alexander I as a tamed, muzzled bear walking on the leash of his boss Napoleon (Uspenskij 2012, 92). By association, the image of the tamed bear became not just a surrogate of the Russian tsar, but of Russia itself.

The geopolitical caricature of Russia as a bear, now losing its alleged tamed nature, was consolidated in the course of the nineteenth century (Cykalov 2012, 107). On the eve of the Crimean War, for example, the London-based satirical magazine *Punch* brought out a print on which a crowned bear hugged a turkey with a fez, with the caption underneath: "Turkey in danger" (Cykalov 2012, 109). In the period between 1863-1886, *Punch* actively competed with the Victorian weekly magazine *Fun* to provide the readership with political caricatures of Russian bears (Rossomachin and Chrustalev 2012, 126).

During the Crimean War, France, fighting alongside the British, also developed a taste for Russian bear prints. For example, in April 1854, the French satirical magazine *Charivari* published a print of an upright crowned white bear with a torch and sword, before which a mass of people knelt on the ground. The caption read: "L'Ours du nord, le plus désagréable de tous les ours connus" (see figure 2; Cykalov 2012, 113). When, at the end of the nineteenth century, the German unification pushed France and Russia into each other's arms – which was felt as a very uncomfortable diplomatic change of course – the Paris press printed caricatures of a seductive young woman with a Phrygian cap, thus recognizable as the French goddess of liberty, Marianne, sharing a bed with a Russian bear (Cykalov 2012, 121).

Given the dominant position of French and English culture in the nineteenth century, it is only logical that the image of the Russian bear was then transferred to other European nations. For example, the Spanish press published an illustration of the Russian bear in 1836, on the occasion of the fifth anniversary of the failed Polish November uprising in London (Garsija Sala 2012, 141). The Russian bear then symbolized "strength, bulk, aggression, danger, barbarism and despotism" (Garsija Sala 2012, 142).

After 1917, Russia's already-negative reputation in Western Europe deteriorated even further as a result of the Russian Revolution. According to Naarden and Leerssen (2007, 229), "[t]he Western image of Russia reverted to the fog of the Crimean War and abruptly reactivated the full resin of the Oriental despotism 'modality'." During the Spanish civil war, when the anti-Soviet propaganda machine was running at full speed, the Spanish written press embraced the Russian bear as a standard propaganda figure. In the same spirit, anti-Russian and anti-communist sentiments colored the caricatures of the Russian bear in the Polish press during and in the aftermath of the 1920 Soviet-Polish war (De Lazari and Rjabov 2012, 155), in the German press during both World Wars and in the 1930s (Žakovska 2012), and in the American written press, academic world and film industry during the Cold War (Rjabov 2012).

Clearly, in the eyes of the Western press, by engaging with communism, the Russian bear had become even more uncivilized than he already was – and in some cases also more pitiful, if he was seen as a symbol for the oppressed Russian people (De Lazari and Rjabov 2012, 164). This is how Rjabov (2012, 179) summarizes its discursive function:

> Communist Russia was presented as The Other, as the lowest and as dangerous. This presentation was achieved through various discursive practices: the opposition of normal versus deviant, civilized versus barbaric, western versus eastern, free versus totalitarian, human versus inhuman; the bear metaphor played an active role in the production of these oppositions. (Our translation from Russian)

On the eve of the fall of the Soviet Union, the narrative that shaped Reagan's presidential campaign in 1984 played a central role in the demonization of the Russian bear. The alleged existence of a Russian bear became in itself an argument to invest more money in the arms race:

> There is a bear in the woods. For some people the bear is easy to see. Others don't see it at all. Some people say the bear is tame. Others say it's vicious and dangerous. Since no one can really be sure who's right, isn't it smart to be as strong as the bear? If there is a bear... (quoted from Novikova 2012, 190)

After the fall of the Soviet Union, when Russia lost control over the former Soviet States, the image of the aggressive Russian bear had lost its relevance. However, it did not completely disappear. In the Norwegian press, which traditionally had a good relationship with Russia, the stereotypical image of the great, dangerous Russian bear, even though it appeared to be doomed in the 1990s, was used as an argument to advocate for accession to the European Union, to defend NATO membership or to conclude a bilateral military cooperation agreement with the United States (Otsbo 2012, 212-213). Interestingly, in less frequent cases, the image was used to evoke sympathy for Russia. From 2007, Norwegian analysts began to report an awakening Russian bear (Otsbo 2012, 214). When, in 2008, the five-day war between Russia and Georgia broke out in South Ossetia, the use of the image of the Russian bear in the Norwegian press grew exponentially (Otsbo 2012, 218). This observation is in line with Rjabov (2012, 175), who states that the image of the Russian bear in the context of the said international conflict was a factor in the 2008 US presidential election.

Today, when the geopolitical tensions, hostilities and political rivalries between Russia and the NATO member states, as a result of Euromaidan, the annexation of Crimea, the civil war in Eastern Ukraine and the conflicting interests in Syria, have intensified to such an extent that analysts call them a Second Cold War, the winged word "there is a bear in the woods" seems no less relevant than when Reagan coined it. In the current Anglophone press, there is no escaping the image of the aggressive Russian bear, even though he no longer wears a communist hat. During the Vice Presidential debate against Democratic nominee Hillary Clinton's running mate Tim Kaine, Donald Trump's running mate Mike Pence quoted an "old proverb" about Russia that he appears to have made up: "the Russian bear never dies, it just hibernates" (Polygraph 2016).

Given the dominant position of the Anglophone press agencies in Europe, it is logical that this has implications for the press in smaller countries and regions, such as Flanders. The search term "Russian bear" in the online version of the high-quality Flemish newspaper *De Standaard* yields more than 300 hits. While some articles are about Russian bears in the literal sense of the word, in the vast majority of cases it is about metaphorical use. The Russian army in particular, the threat of their warships, nuclear weapons and bombers are subjects in which the bear likes to be taken out of the stable. In addition, news coverage in football and other sports matches, which eagerly uses war metaphors, appears to embrace the bear metaphor with disconcerting regularity.

In the Globish-speaking academic world too, the hetero-image of the aggressive Russian bear is alive and kicking. A search for the words "Russian bear" yields the following hits on the academic search engine Limo: "The elephant and the bear: the European Union, Russia and their near abroads", "The Dying Bear: Russia's Demographic Disaster", "The dragon and the bear: inside China and Russia today", "Carlsberg in Russia: Bear with us", "RUSSIA & UKRAINE: Bear fight", "The Claws of the Bear: Russia's Targeted Killing Program", "Escaping the Bear Hug: Russia, Ukraine and European Gas", "Facing up to the bear: confronting Putin's Russia", "Russia's Eurasian bear hug", "The emerging Russian bear: integrating the Soviet Union into the world economy", and so forth.

Here, it should be noted that traditionally the image of the Russian bear was particularly successful in countries that did not belong to the Slavic world or the Eastern bloc. In Latvia, for example, which had been part of the Russian Empire and of the Soviet Empire for centuries, the bear has been positively noted. For this reason, in the post-Soviet period the caricature of Russia as an aggressive bear was rarely used (Novikova 2012, 191). In Czech culture from the second half of the nineteenth and first half of the twentieth century, the image of the Russian bear was almost non-existent. Kolja (2012, 230) explains this absence by pointing out that the Czech elite was Russophile, whereas the metaphor in question was intended in the first place to evoke negative associations. The image did not occur in the Soviet period either, not even after the bloody suppressed Prague Spring of 1968 (Kolja 2012, 231). However, since the five-day war between Russia and Georgia in 2008, the image has often been used in the Czech as well as in the Slovak press, which is an indication that the image has undergone a globalization process over the past decade.

Understandably, the image of the Russian bear, initially forged in the context of English military propaganda and in various geographical regions outside of Russia, takes shape in accordance with the region's historical relationship to Russia. For example, Sweden swears by the credo "Do not bully the Russian bear", which can be explained by referring to the Swedish complex of the Battle of Poltava, lost against Peter the Great in 1709, which resulted in significant territory loss (Benjaš 2012, 243). That notwithstanding, there is a common thread in all of these Russian bear images: in today's international media, they reinforce the dominant public narrative that Putin's Russia poses a real military threat that would be dangerous to underestimate. As such, the image of the Russian bear de facto functions as an argument to strengthen NATO – which suits certain policy-makers. As De Lazari and Rjabov (2012, 154) put it, "[i]f the Russian bear did not exist, it would be necessary to invent it" (our translation from Russian).

5. In the footsteps of 'the Russian bear' as an auto-image

In the previous part, we have seen that the image of Russia as a bear has an origin that lies outside Russia, and that it historically and presently evokes negative associations outside Russia. Nevertheless, the image is also used for internal consumption in today's Russia (Timofeev 2012, 313). The Russian term Русский медведь ('the Russian bear') is now as well-established as its English equivalent. According to Rjabova (2012, 338), "the Russian bear has become an organic part of the current historical and political situation in Russia." As can be expected, the connotations are thoroughly different, not to say contradictory.

Figure 3. A stamp with Misha, the Olympic mascot of the USSR[4]

To explain why the bear today has other connotations in Russia than in the rest of Europe, we first have to take a look at the bear cult that has existed for quite some time. In Russia, the bear has never played a neutral role in the

---

4   Source: https://commons.wikimedia.org/wiki/File:1980_USSR_stamp_Olympic_mascot.jpg. This work is not an object of copyright according to article 1259 of Book IV of the Civil Code of the Russian Federation No. 230-FZ of December 18, 2006.

collective consciousness. It has been standing on a pedestal for many centuries, in the first place as an animal whose *strength* inspires fear. Just like in other Christian countries, this fear was cultivated in Russia through the Bible, in which the allegorical bear is presented as a threat to the equally allegorical herd of sheep (Vojcechovska 2012, 13). In the Middle Ages, in the sixteenth and seventeenth centuries, the bear was placed with various attributes on the coats of arms of Novgorod, Perm and Yaroslav (Pčelov 2012, 21; 61), possibly under the influence of Finnish motives. Folklore studies, too, testify to the respected position of the bear in Russia: at the end of the nineteenth and the beginning of the twentieth century, the bear was regularly referred to by farmers in Siberia as 'lord' (*chozyain*) or 'grandfather' (*dedushka*) (Fursova 2012, 72).

The mutual association in Russia of that country with the bear is also influenced by the respected role that the animal traditionally plays in Russian folk tales: that of "the strong and just ruler of the forest" (Krivcova 2012, 325; our translation from Russian). Incidentally, that role is comparable to the part of the wolf in the fairy tale Little Red Riding Hood. There is, however, a difference: the Russian bear does not try to eat the girl that is lost in the forest. He prefers to marry her, provided that she can prove she is a good housewife (Žepnikovska 2012, 66). In this way, the bear plays an ambivalent role: he is a death threat to the main character, and therefore should be feared, but he is also her savior, and therefore should be admired. His benevolence is "dependent on the extent to which people show themselves familiar with the rules of how to interact with him" (ibid., 71; our translation from Russian).

Paintings have also contributed to the anchoring of the bear in the Russian national self-consciousness. The most popular painting with bears among Russians is doubtless *Morning in a Pine Forest* (1889) by the Russian artists Ivan Shishkin and Konstantin Savitsky, showing a mother bear with three lovely youngsters. According to Krivcova (2012, 326), these bears can be considered an archetype, "the essence of what exists forever for Russians, of what is unshakable, indisputable and undeniable, a symbol of tradition and stability" (our translation from Russian).

Yet the bear as a symbol of Russia was not a part of the Soviet culture for a long time. Of course, the Soviet authorities were well aware of the role played by the image in the West during the Cold War. In the Soviet propaganda poster art, which particularly flourished during the Civil War after the Revolution and during the Second World War, no bears were used to depict Russia. According to Rjabov (2012, 184), the Soviets were annoyed by the entire bear propaganda. The image abroad of the wild, backward and aggressive Russian bear was not very flattering, and even contradicted the self-image of a peaceful Soviet

Union. Understandably, Russia choose to ignore the hetero-image. Eventually a counter-offensive was launched, radically changing the strategy: when, at the end of the Cold War, the Soviet Union was allowed to host the Olympic Games in 1980, it was no coincidence that, out of all the animals, a bear was chosen as the official mascot (see figure 3). Interestingly, the bear features to be transferred were chosen in a very selective way: they chose not a frightening full-grown bear, but a young, cute and cuddly one. The ever-smiling bear cub was given the name Misha, which is an affectionately charged variant of Mikhail (a typical bear name in Russian fairy tales). In a communiqué, the organizational committee pointed out that the bear was chosen as a symbol of the characteristics typical of sportsmen, such as strength, perseverance and courage (Rjabov 2012, 185). In so doing, drawing on the positive associations with bears existing in Russian culture for centuries, the hetero-image of the aggressive Russian bear was reversed into a more flattering auto-image, which in turn was transferred to the world to become a new hetero-image. It is interesting to note that the only thing the Russian bear of the Soviets has in common with the Russian bear of Western Europe is his strength.

After the fall of the Soviet Union, under the influence of cultural globalization, Russian marketers quickly realized the brand potential of the Russian bear for the Russian market, both as a visual image and as a name. It was extensively used to market Russian consumption products, in particular alcoholic drinks such as vodka and beer, as well as restaurants, cafés, hairdressers, beauty salons, transport companies, advertising agencies and all kinds of businesses (Timofeev 2012, 316). This trend is still ongoing. You can walk into a random store in Moscow and find T-shirts, mugs, key rings and other gadgets with a bear mascot. According to Fursova (2012, 83), the image of the bear in Russia is today cultivated and disseminated through various channels, such as decoration, architecture, advertising and the like. In post-Soviet art as well, reference is made to the bear metaphor, albeit on a much smaller scale. Krivcova (2012, 332-333) points out that, here, it is often linked to the alleged mysterious Russian soul. It also often aims to refer to Russia's pre-revolutionary culture – which is a more important source of inspiration for the contemporary Russian national identity than the Soviet past. Thanks to such a selective use of bear images, the bear, as sociological research shows, has become one of the most popular unofficial symbols of twenty-first-century Russia (Rjabova 2012, 339).

According to the sociological surveys by Rjabova (2012, 346), in twenty-first-century Russia, the bear image is outspokenly positive, thanks to associations with strength (81%), a good nature (41%) and a lack of calculation (13%). It is therefore logical that Russian politicians embraced it in their electoral campaigns (Krivcova 2012, 325). The choice of Russia's largest political party, United Russia, to use the animal in its official emblem speaks volumes about the extent to which the bear is considered suitable for internal use. In 2008, when Dmitri Medvedev – whose name itself, as it happens, is derived from the Russian word meaning 'bear' – was a candidate for the presidential elections on behalf of the United Russia party, the bear dominated the party's advertisements in the mass media (Timofeev 2012, 321). Ironically, given the way in which the government party United Russia is depicted in the foreign press (as being responsible for election fraud, corruption, silencing the opposition, etc.), outside Russia this only confirms the existing image of the unreliable, imperialist Russian bear. Clearly, Russia's reputation abroad undermines the Russian bear's chances of becoming a successful means of promoting the country's soft power.

The Russian bear is not only a hetero-image and an auto-image, it is also a meta-image, that is, a projected self-image. Russians are well aware of the fact that the Russian bear is commonplace in the West, and that it functions in quite a different, much more negative way than in Russia itself. Interestingly, Russian respondents tend to believe that the image in the West primarily serves to evoke associations with strength (58%), backwardness (43%), rudeness (37%) and aggressiveness (25%), while American respondents tend to think that the Russian bear in the West serves to evoke associations with aggressiveness (76.6%), strength (63.6%), cruelty (50.6%) and barbarism (26%) (Rjabova 2012, 343). The contemporary Russian authorities are aware that a field of tension exists between the Russian bear as a hetero-image and as an auto-image. For example, Mikhail Lesin, when he was Minister of Media, said in 2001 that the country needed to cultivate a new image, or otherwise "Russians would always look like bears" (De Lazari and Rjabov 2012, 154). In 2009, during an interview with the German newspaper *Handelsblatt*, Putin himself declared, as Prime Minister of the Russian Federation: "Man bastelt in Europa am Bild des russischen Bären, der alle verschlucken will" (Rinke 2009; "In Europe, people are working on the image of the Russian Bear, who wants to swallow everybody").

6. *Masha and the Bear* as soft power?

Today, the aggressive Russian bear image is so widespread in the Western media that it seems irreversible and unwavering. Clearly, it is beyond Russia's power to eradicate the unflattering Western image of the Russian bear. At the same time, the mascot of the 1980 Olympic Games serves as a reminder that it is still possible to export a different, softer image of a Russian bear; one that is not an offender, but a sweet teddy bear. Recently, yet another example of such a bear has successfully emerged, along with a small but noisy girl: that of *Masha and the Bear*.

As a matter of fact, the bear character of this animation series is a charming and sweet friend, more a victim than an offender. Interestingly, as a result of the cartoon's international success – the English-language version now has more than 4 million subscribers on YouTube, and 40 billion views across 13 channels in various languages – the cartoon has raised geopolitical polemics. On several occasions, it was accused of being "Kremlin propaganda" (Sneyers 2018, 65). In 2017, the German newspaper *Neues Deutschland* reported that "according to the Head of [the] National Security department of Lithuania, Darius Jauniškis, the children's cartoon *Masha and the Bear* constitutes a threat to national security, as part of the Kremlin's 'hybrid war against the free world'" (Sinchougova 2017). The Estonian media expert Priit Hõbemägi has also claimed, in the Estonian weekly *Eesti Ekspress*, that Masha and the Bear are representatives of Russia's soft power (Propastop 2017). Similar accusations were repeated in 2018, in *The Times*, which prompted the Russian Embassy in the UK to comment derisively as follows:

> How UK can find salvation from *Masha and the Bear*? Launch an Anti-Cartoon Excellence Centre somewhere in the Baltic [sic]? Place all cartoonists on EU sanction list? Clearly a decisive – and a very expensive – approach is needed! (Russkiy Mir 2018)

It seems indeed far-fetched to regard *Masha and the Bear* as a calculated soft power tool. However, at the same time, it also seems quite reasonable to recognize its potential to function as a counter-narrative to the dominant Western public narrative of Russia as the land of military aggression: by convincingly showing that Russia is still a country of great cultural richness, *Masha and the Bear* invites the Western audiences to question and adjust their existing dominant images about Russia.

7. Conclusion

The examples above have shown that animal images and symbols are originally empty signifiers, but that cultural meanings are attributed to them. This feature of instability and flexibility inevitably leads to changes in meaning and reception when such images are transferred culturally, geographically or temporally. In this sense, they perfectly illustrate the transfer concept as described by Göpferich, since "the decisive feature of the transfer concept (…) is to make what is transferred cognitively (and, in some cases, also emotionally) accessible or more accessible and/or enjoyable for a specific audience in the target culture" (Göpferich 2010, 375). Because of the differences between (desired) accessibility in different cultures, the national and cultural projection process develops along dissimilar lines. It also explains why certain characteristics of the Russian bear (wildness, uncivilized) can be developed more strongly in the Western hetero-image than others (such as folklore and nostalgia).

Drawing on imagological insights, we have demonstrated that there is nothing natural about the stereotypical transnational image of the aggressive Russian bear, which as a dominant public narrative seems indispensable in Western popular culture and journalism: this image was literally made by human hands, but not in one day.

The image of the bear, traditionally associated with strength and nature-linked images, has never been neutral. This applies all the more to its function as a surrogate for Russia, in the West historically stereotyped as a backward, sparsely populated country: it emerged as an outspokenly negative hetero-image, in a context of armed conflicts and geopolitical tensions. The caricature of the Russian bear became commonplace in the following centuries. It turned out to be instrumental to the construction of a European identity, which relied to a large extent on the exclusion of Russia (De Lazari and Rjabov 2012, 152). Rjabov (2012, 187) points out that the bear metaphor, as a "meaningful component of the archives of Western discourse about Russia, is used to momentarily evoke all associations: a bloodthirsty, barbaric, retarded, aggressive country" (our translation from Russian).

In Russia, the bear slowly found its way into mainstream culture, but it took until the end of the Cold War before it became a symbol for the Russian nation as a whole. In the Middle Ages, the bear image was frequently used as a symbol for a city or region through heraldry. He also played a prominent, albeit ambiguous, role in Russian fairy tales. In Russia itself, the foreign national image of the Russian bear was transferred from the West, but only after an adaptation process, in accordance with national interests and under the influence of the existing, more admirative images of bears. He was stripped of all his characteristics, apart from his strength. Instead of the muzzled or aggressive bear, a more sympathetic, reliable bear was introduced, potentially even with a high level of cuddliness. During the past two to three decades, the bear has grown into a positive auto-image in Russia, and has even become the logo of the leading Russian political party, United Russia.

We are thus dealing with two quite different Russian bears, designed for quite different receiving cultural systems: one aggressive, ready to tear up Europe, and one loyal, on whose shoulders the Russians can lean. These bears were designed for different receiving communities and are not supposed to be reconciled, but their mutual confrontation in a globalized world is unavoidable, as (elements of) features are transferred transnationally and transculturally.

A type of bear such as in *Masha and the Bear*, produced in Russia, but successfully transferred to the entire world, has the potential to group individuals and to create alternative recognition and symbolization patterns. Bear-linked associations such as natural power and strength are complemented by cuteness and softness, not only broadening the interpretation scale, but also boosting the sympathy level. Traditional associations with fear and wilderness are relativized and partly questioned by softer patterns of civilization. It remains doubtful, however, that Masha's bear will turn out to be strong enough to compete with the army of Russian bear images that still are being transferred around the world.

Acknowledgement

This work was supported by the University of Tartu Astra Project Per Aspera and grant number PHVLC19917.

References

Agazzi, Elena. 2007. "Physiognomy." In *Imagology. The Cultural Construction and Literary Representation of National Characters*, edited by Manfred Beller and Joep Leerssen, 398-400. Amsterdam: Rodopi.
Baker, Mona. 2006. *Translation and Conflict. A Narrative Account*. London: Routledge.
Beller, Manfred. 2007. "Barbarian." In *Imagology. The Cultural Construction and Literary Representation of National Characters*, edited by Manfred Beller and Joep Leerssen, 266-270. Amsterdam: Rodopi.
Benjaš, Michal. 2012. "Ne draznit' medvedja! Obraz Rosii v švedskich SMI (Eskiz problem)." In *Russkij Medved'. Istorija, semiotika, politika*, edited by Oleg Rjabov and Andžej de Lazari, 243-250. Moscow: Novoe literaturnoe obozrenie.
Cykalov, Dmitrij. 2012. "Russkij medved' v evropejskoj karikature vtoroj poloviny XIX – načala XX veka." In *Russkij Medved'. Istorija, semiotika, politika*, edited by Oleg Rjabov and Andžej de Lazari, 105-124. Moscow: Novoe literaturnoe obozrenie.

De Lazari, Andžej, and Oleg Rjabov. 2012. "Dva medvedja: gosudarstvo i narod v pol'skoj mežvoennoj karikature." In *Russkij Medved'. Istorija, semiotika, politika*, edited by Oleg Rjabov and Andžej de Lazari, 150-166. Moscow: Novoe literaturnoe obozrenie.

Duffy, Annie. 2009. "The Natural Resource Industry Visual Impact Paradox: A Perspective on Alaskan Imagery and Art." In *Images of the North. Histories – Identities – Ideas*, edited by Sverrir Jakobsson, 139-148. Amsterdam: Rodopi.

'Eagle Meaning and Symbolism'. https://www.theastrologyweb.com/spirit-animals/eagle-meaning-symbolism (accessed 20 Oct 2019).

Flacke, Monika. 2007. "National History Visualized." In *Imagology. The Cultural Construction and Literary Representation of National Characters*, edited by Manfred Beller and Joep Leerssen, 381-383. Amsterdam: Rodopi.

Fursova, Elena. 2012. "Perežitki kul'ta medved'ja v verovanijach krest'jan Sibiri: tradicii i transformacii." In *Russkij Medved'. Istorija, semiotika, politika*, edited by Oleg Rjabov and Andžej de Lazari, 72-84. Moscow: Novoe literaturnoe obozrenie.

Garsija Sala, Ivan. 2012. "Otgoloski medvež'ego ryčanija: Rossijskaja imperija kak belyj medved' v ispanskoj presse." In *Russkij Medved'. Istorija, semiotika, politika*, edited by Oleg Rjabov and Andžej de Lazari, 140-149. Mosow: Novoe literaturnoe obozrenie.

Göpferich, Susanne. 2007. "Translation Studies and Transfer Studies: A Plea for Widening the Scope of Translation Studies." In *Doubts and Directions in Translation Studies*, edited by Yves Gambier, Miriam Shlesinger, and Radegundis Stolze, 27-39. Amsterdam: John Benjamins.

— 2010. "Transfer and Transfer Studies." In *Handbook of Translation Studies*, vol. 1, edited by Yves Gambier and Luc van Doorslaer, 374-377. Amsterdam: John Benjamins.

Ísleifsson, Sumarliði R. 2009. "Icelandic national images in the 19th and 20th centuries." In *Images of the North. Histories – Identities – Ideas*, edited by Sverrir Jakobsson, 149-158. Amsterdam: Rodopi.

Jourdan, Annie. 2007. "Symbol." In *Imagology. The Cultural Construction and Literary Representation of National Characters*, edited by Manfred Beller and Joep Leerssen, 434-437. Amsterdam: Rodopi.

Kolja, Adam F. 2012. "Rossija-medved' v sovremmenoj češskoj i slovackoj publicistike." In *Russkij Medved'. Istorija, semiotika, politika*, edited by Oleg Rjabov and Andžej de Lazari, 225-242. Moscow: Novoe literaturnoe obozrenie.

Kolstø, Pål. 2006. "National Symbols as Signs of Unity And Division." *Ethnic and Racial Studies* 29 (4): 676-701.

Krivcova, Ljudmila. 2012. "Medved' v postsovetskom iskusstve: semantika i pragmatika obraza." In *Russkij Medved'. Istorija, semiotika, politika*, edited by Oleg Rjabov and Andžej de Lazari, 324-337. Moscow: Novoe literaturnoe obozrenie.

Leerssen, Joep. 2007. "Image." In *Imagology. The Cultural Construction and Literary Representation of National Characters*, edited by Manfred Beller and Joep Leerssen, 342-344. Amsterdam: Rodopi.

Mitchell, W.J.T. 1986. *Iconology. Image, Text, Ideology*. Chicago: University of Chicago Press.

Naarden, Bruno, and Joep Leerssen. 2007. "Russians." In *Imagology. The Cultural Construction and Literary Representation of National Characters*, edited by Manfred Beller and Joep Leerssen, 226-229. Amsterdam: Rodopi.

Novikova, Irina. 2012. "V teni rejganovskogo zverja: 'razchristannyj' medved' i 'čužoj' medvežonok v latvijskom mediaprostranstve 1990-2000-x godov." In *Russkij Medved'. Istorija, semiotika, politika*, edited by Oleg Rjabov and Andžej de Lazari, 190-207. Moscow: Novoe literaturnoe obozrenie.

Otsbo, Jardar. 2012. "'Russkij medved'' prosnulsja! Čto delat'? 'Russkij medved'' kak argument v norvežskoj presse 1998-2008 godov." In *Russkij Medved'. Istorija, semiotika, politika*, edited by Oleg Rjabov and Andžej de Lazari, 208-224. Moscow: Novoe literaturnoe obozrenie.

Pčelov, Evgenij. 2012. "Medvedi v starinnoj russkoj geral'dike: semantika obrazov." In *Russkij Medved'. Istorija, semiotika, politika*, edited by Oleg Rjabov and Andžej de Lazari, 29-61. Moscow: Novoe literaturnoe obozrenie.

Platoff, Anne M. 2012. "The 'Forward Russia' Flag: Examining the Changing Use of the Bear as a Symbol of Russia." *Raven* 19: 99-126.

Polygraph. 2016. "'Old Proverb' States that 'Russian Bear Never Dies'." *Polygraph*, Oct 7, 2016. https://www.polygraph.info/a/united-states-mike-pence-presidential-debate-russian-proverb/28091135.html.

Propastop. 2017. "Masha, Bear, and Propaganda." *Propastop*. https://www.propastop.org/eng/2017/05/22/masha-bear-and-propaganda/.

Pursell, Timothy, and Maureen P. Hogan. 2009. "Alaska's Eternal Frontier: Rural Masculinity and Landscape Nostalgia." In *Images of the North. Histories – Identities – Ideas*, edited by Sverrir Jakobsson, 191-203. Amsterdam: Rodopi.

Rinke, Andreas. 2009. "Europa bastelt am Bild des russischen Bären. Interview mit Wladimir Putin." *Handelsblatt*, Sep 14, 2009. https://www.handelsblatt.com/politik/international/interview-mit-wladimir-putin-europa-bastelt-am-bild-des-russischen-baeren/3258312.html?ticket=ST-6009722-sxFSqznrNgxLYSLAAtgo-ap6.

Rjabov, Oleg. 2012. "'V lesu est' medved'': medvež'ja metafora kak oružie Cholodnoj vojny." In *Russkij Medved'. Istorija, semiotika, politika*, edited by Oleg Rjabov and Andžej de Lazari, 175-189. Moscow: Novoe literaturnoe obozrenie.

Rjabov, Oleg, and Andžej de Lazari. 2012. "Predislovie." In *Russkij Medved'. Istorija, semiotika, politika*, edited by Oleg Rjabov and Andžej de Lazari, 5-8. Moscow: Novoe literaturnoe obozrenie.

Rjabova, Tat'jana. 2012. "Medved' kak simvol Rossii: socialigičeskoe izmerenie." In *Russkij Medved'. Istorija, semiotika, politika*, edited by Oleg Rjabov and Andžej de Lazari, 338-353. Moscow: Novoe literaturnoe obozrenie.

Rossomachin, Andrej, and Denis Chrustalev. 2012. "'Russkie medvedi' iz žurnala 'Fan'." In *Russkij Medved'. Istorija, semiotika, politika*, edited by Oleg Rjabov and Andžej de Lazari, 126-139. Moscow: Novoe literaturnoe obozrenie.

Russkiy Mir, 2018. "*The Times* accuses popular *Masha and the Bear* animation for 'Kremlin propaganda'." *Russkiy Mir Foundation*. https://russkiymir.ru/en/news/249042/.

Schaer, Karin. 2009. "From Hell to Homeland: Eggert Ólafsson's *Reise igiennem Island* and the Construction of Icelandic Identity." In *Images of the North. Histories – Identities – Ideas*, edited by Sverrir Jakobsson, 131-138. Amsterdam: Rodopi.

Schram, Kristinn. 2009. "The Wild North: the Narrative Cultures of Image Construction in Media and Everyday Life." In *Images of the North. Histories – Identities – Ideas*, edited by Sverrir Jakobsson, 249-260. Amsterdam: Rodopi.

Silver, Alexandra. 2011. "Hooking Up and Using the John: Why Do We Use So Many Euphemisms?" *Time*. http://content.time.com/time/arts/article/0,8599,2041313,00.html

Sinchougova, Irina. 2017. "*Masha And The Bear* Is Russian Aggression – Lithuania Warns Germany." Fort Ross News. https://www.fort-russ.com/2017/04/masha-and-bear-is-russian-aggression/.

Sneyers, Hanne. 2018. *Masha en de Russische beer. De totstandkoming van de populaire Russische animatieserie Maša i Medved'*. Master's thesis KU Leuven. Supervisor: Pieter Boulogne.

Timofeev, Michail. 2012. "Russkij medved'/Russian Bear: potrebitel'skie svojstva." In *Russkij Medved'. Istorija, semiotika, politika*, edited by Oleg Rjabov and Andžej de Lazari, 313-323. Moscow: Novoe literaturnoe obozrenie.

Uspenskij, Vasilij. 2012. "Tipologija izobraženij 'russkich medvedej' v evropejskoj karikature XVIII – pervoj treti XIX veka." In *Russkij Medved'. Istorija, semiotika, politika*, edited by Oleg Rjabov and Andžej de Lazari, 87-104. Moscow: Novoe literaturnoe obozrenie.

van Doorslaer, Luc. 2006. "Ideologisch inspiriertes Idyll: deutsche Übersetzungen der flämischen Literatur unter der Flamenpolitik des Ersten Weltkriegs." In *Übersetzen, translating, traduire: Towards a 'Social Turn'?*, edited by Michaela Wolf, 307-316. Münster: LIT.

Vojcechovska, Kalina. 2012. "Ljutnyj zver' i obrazec zabotlivosti: obraz medved'ja v Biblii i apokrifach." In *Russkij Medved'. Istorija, semiotika, politika*, edited by Oleg Rjabov and Andžej de Lazari, 11-28. Moscow: Novoe literaturnoe obozrenie.

Žakovska, Magdalena. 2012. "Izobraženie Rossii-medvedja v nemeckoj karikature 1914-1945 godov." In *Russkij Medved'. Istorija, semiotika, politika*, edited by Oleg Rjabov and Andžej de Lazari, 167-174. Moscow: Novoe literaturnoe obozrenie.

Žepnikovska, Ivona. 2012. "Medvedv' v russkoj volšebnoj skazke: eskiz issledovanija problem." In *Russkij Medved'. Istorija, semiotika, politika*, edited by Oleg Rjabov and Andžej de Lazari, 62-71. Moscow: Novoe literaturnoe obozrenie.

Legal transfer and translation

The translation of legal and administrative texts in Flanders and Northern Italy during the French Revolution and the Napoleonic period

Michael Schreiber

Abstract

The language policy of the French Revolution is known today especially for the imposition of the national language. In my contribution, I want to focus on a less known aspect: legal transfer and translation. From 1790 onwards, several decrees stipulated the translation of laws and decrees into the regional languages in France. Later, this translation policy was extended to other countries and regions under French rule. This chapter considers the case of Belgium, annexed by France in October 1795, and Northern Italy, under French influence beginning with Napoleon's campaign in Italy (1796-1797), and focuses in particular on Milan and Genoa. In Belgium, many administrative, legal and political texts were translated from French into Flemish. The overall function of the translation of legal and administrative texts was not to give the Flemish language an official status, but to propagate the message of revolutionary France to Flemish-speaking citizens. In Northern Italy, the situation depended on the region or city. The city of Milan was the capital of several states under French influence, which each had Italian as its official language. In Milan, the French Civil Code and the other Napoleonic codes were translated into Italian and transferred to other Italian regions. Genoa was the capital of the Ligurian Republic (1797-1805), before the territory of this 'sister republic' was annexed by the French Empire. After the annexation, the French language became the official language, but many bilingual texts remained published. Comparing the translational settings in Belgium and Northern Italy, this chapter answers the following questions: How were the translations organized? What evidence of translation strategies can be found in these translations? What were the consequences of these translations for the target languages and cultures?

1. Introduction

The language policy of the French Revolution is known today especially for the imposition of French as the national language. In my contribution, I will be focusing on a lesser-known aspect: the translation of legal and administrative texts in the context of legal transfer. From 1790 on, several decrees stipulated the translation of laws and decrees into the regional languages in France. Later, this translation policy was extended to other countries and regions under French rule. I will consider the cases of the Southern Netherlands, annexed by France in October 1795, where I will be focusing on the Flemish-speaking territory, especially the *départements* Escaut (capital: Ghent) and Lys (capital: Bruges), and Northern Italy, under French influence since Napoleon's campaign in Italy (1796-1797), where I will be focusing on Milan and Genoa. The translation processes in this period are part of an ideological and legal transfer.[1] I will focus here mainly on legal transfer which is connected to the exportation of the French legal system (Heirbaut and Gerkens 2011; Soleil 2014). With regard to the rendering of rhetoric devices, ideological transfer will be discussed as well.

In the Southern Netherlands, many legal and administrative texts were translated from French into Flemish.[2] The overall function of these translations was not to give the Flemish language an official status, but to propagate the message of revolutionary France to Flemish-speaking citizens, to implement the legal and administrative transfer linked to the annexation and to introduce the French legal and administrative system in the annexed territory, including the introduction of French administrative structures, especially the *départements*. In official French texts the annexed territory was often referred to as *nouveaux départements* or *(neuf) départements réunis* (Dubois 2005, 119). This avoided the reference to a 'Belgian' identity.[3]

In Northern Italy, the situation depended on the region or city. The city of Milan was the capital of several states under French influence, all with Italian

---

1 According to D'hulst (2012, 140), the notion of transfer can refer to different products, e.g. "books or texts, ideas, attitudes, world views, etc." and include different types of changes on the transferred products.
2 I use the term *Flemish* for the Dutch language in the Southern Netherlands during the French period according to the usage of the adjectives *flamand* and *vlaams* in the texts of our corpus. The texts are not written in dialect, but they show the orthographical features which were used in the Southern Netherlands, with some variations, since orthography was not yet standardized (Rutten and Vosters 2011).
3 However, in some texts of our corpus from 1790 to 1794, thus before the annexation, the term *Belgique* is used.

as the official language. In Milan, the French Civil Code (*Code Napoléon*) was translated into Italian. Genoa was the capital of the Ligurian Republic (1797-1805), before the territory of this 'sister republic' was annexed by the French Empire. After the annexation, the French language became the official language, but many bilingual texts continued to be published.

The bilingual publication of the texts of our corpus and the fact that most texts are not explicitly marked as translations leads us to the question of directionality (D'hulst and van Gerwen 2018). In the texts of our corpus there are some hints that in most cases the French texts served as source text (Schreiber 2019, 818-819): The French text is published on the left side, and the Flemish and Italian texts contain many interferences from French. Furthermore, in some cases, the French text had been published before (e.g., the revolutionary laws and decrees which were translated into Flemish after the annexation).

In comparing the translation settings in the Southern Netherlands and Northern Italy, I will try to answer the following questions: How were the translations organized? What was their function in the context of legal and administrative transfer? What evidence of translation strategies and techniques can be found in the translations? What were the consequences of these translations for the target languages, especially in the field of legal language?

The data for the analyses were collected within the scope of two research projects funded by the *Deutsche Forschungsgemeinschaft*, which dealt specifically with the translation policies in Belgium during the French period (D'hulst and Schreiber 2014; Schreiber 2016; Ingelbeen and Schreiber 2018) and with the translation of legal, administrative and political texts in Northern Italy during the Napoleonic period (Hartmann, forthcoming; Nikolic and Schreiber, forthcoming).

2. Historical background

The French period in the former Austrian Netherlands began with the first French occupation, from December 1792 to March 1793, before the territory was again conquered by Austria. During this brief period, there was not yet a systematic language policy (Deneckere 1954, 109-10). After the territory had been occupied again by France in June 1794, it was annexed to the French Republic on 1 October 1795. As the new *départements* were an integral part of the French state, the official language was French. However, since many inhabitants of the Flemish *départements* did not understand sufficient French, a decree of 13 October 1795[4] allowed the translation of laws and decrees into Flemish in districts where a translation was necessary (RAB, Scheldedepartement 2009). Two years later, in November 1797, an official translation policy[5] was introduced through the creation of the *Bulletin flamand*, a bilingual, French-Flemish version of the *Bulletin des lois*, edited and translated in the French Ministry of Justice (D'hulst 2015). Furthermore, there were many regional translations of administrative texts, especially on the level of the *départements* (D'hulst and Schreiber 2014).

In Italy, the political situation differed according to the region. The cities of Milan and Genoa and their regions were chosen for the present study because they stand as examples for different translation settings within the same historical period.

Milan was, subsequently, the capital of several states under French influence: the Transpadane Republic (1796-97), the Cisalpine Republic (1797-1802), the Italian Republic (1802-05) – three so-called 'sister republics', whose political and administrative structures depended on the French model – and, finally, the Kingdom of Italy (1805-14), where the French emperor functioned as king. In all of these states, Italian was the official language. In Milan, the French Civil Code and the other Napoleonic codes were translated into Italian and later transferred to other Italian regions (Hartmann, forthcoming).

Genoa was the capital of the Ligurian Republic (1797-1805), before the territory of this 'sister republic', where Italian had been the official language, was annexed by the French Empire and divided into four Departments. After the annexation, French became the official language. Regional and local translations were often restricted to administrative texts (Schreiber 2020).

3. Organization of translation activities and functions of translations

With regard to the organization of translation activities and the function of translations, we can draw three main distinctions:

1. According to van Gerwen (2019, 29), we can distinguish between official, semi-official and non-official translations: *Official* translations are organized and published by an official institution, e.g., the government of a state or a

---

4   For practical reasons, all dates are indicated according to the Gregorian calendar (not to the calendar of the French Revolution which was valid in France and the annexed regions).
5   The term *translation policy* is understood here in a restricted sense (Meylaerts 2011, 163), referring to translation in official institutional settings.

region. *Semi-official* translations are made by individual experts having an official function, e.g., lawyers or civil servants, and published by a non-official institution, e.g., a commercial publishing house. *Non-official* translations are made by laymen, e.g., journalists, and printed in a publication for a broad audience, e.g., in a newspaper or journal.

2. Following geographical and political criteria, we can distinguish local, regional, national and, today, supra-national translations or translation policies. The distinction between the national and the regional level is, in the period of our study, less clear than it might seem: Whereas the Southern Netherlands, from October 1795 on, were part of the *Grande Nation*, the Italian 'sister republics' were, politically speaking, satellites of the French Republic, but, *de jure*, states on their own (Soleil 2014, 160-64).

3. With regard to the functions of the translation of legal (or administrative) texts, we can distinguish, according to Wiesmann (2009, 280), two main categories: performative and informative translations. The translation of a legal text is *performative* if it functions as a legal text within the legal system of the target culture. If the target text does not fulfill this official function, the translation is *informative*.

If we apply these distinctions to the texts of our corpus, we find different constellations, e.g., the following:

In the Southern Netherlands, between October 1795 and October 1797, the translation policy was regional, semi-official and informative: according to the decree of 13 October 1795, which regulates the publication of laws in the Belgian *départements*, French was the official language, and regional translations were allowed under certain circumstances only:

> Les arrondissemens où une autre langue que celle française est tellement usitée, qu'il y auroit de l'inconvénient à ne point faire de traduction, pourront en faire faire pour l'instruction de leurs Administrés, et en distribuer des exemplaires par-tout où besoin sera, sans cependant excéder le nombre qu'ils jugeront strictement nécessaire, et sans que cela retarde l'envoi des exemplaires français. (RAB, Scheldedepartement 2009)[6]
> (Districts where a language other than French is so widely used that there is the inconvenience of not making a translation, may have one made for the instruction of their constituents, and distribute copies wherever necessary, without however exceeding the number they consider strictly necessary, and without this delaying the dispatch of French copies.)

---

6 All quotations are given in the original orthography. Variants and errors are not marked or corrected.

The situation changed in November 1797 when the bilingual *Bulletin flamand* became an example of an official translation at the national level. The French *Bulletin des lois* was translated by full-time translators working for a translation office in the Ministry of Justice. The bilingual bulletin was published, as was the monolingual French one, by the French state. However, only the French text was legally valid. Hence, the translation function is still informative. Furthermore, the French authorities hoped that within ten years, all Flemish-speaking citizens would learn enough French so that translations into Flemish would no longer be necessary (D'hulst 2015, 98).

Between March 1803 and March 1804, the *Bulletin flamand* included the first Flemish translation of the *Code civil* (Heirbaut 2004, 222). As the other texts of the *Bulletin flamand*, this translation was official and informative. This translation of the *Code civil* was followed by two other translations which were both published in 1806 in Ghent: one, semi-official, by Norbert Cornelissen (the Flemish translator of the *Bulletin flamand*, who published a corrected version of his own translation), and one by P.J. Lorio, a private translator (van Gerwen 2019, 133-34).

The first Italian translation of the Civil Code, translated under the supervision of a commission of legal experts in Milan, was, on the contrary, official and performative: Since Italian was the official language of the Kingdom of Italy, the Italian translation was legally valid, but not the French original nor its translation into Latin, which had also been edited in Milan. This was regulated by a decree of the emperor and king of 16 January 1806:

> Art. I. Les traductions du *Code Napoléon* [the translations of the Civil Code into Italian and Latin] faites par les Jurisconsultes nommés par le Grand Juge, Ministre de la Justice, sont approuvées.
> II. Le *Code Napoléon* sera mis en activité, à compter du premier jour du mois d'avril. La seule traduction italienne pourra être citée et avoir force de loi dans les Tribunaux. (ASM, Atti ufficiali 1806)
> (Art. I. The translations of the Code Napoleon [the translations of the Civil Code into Italian and Latin] made by the Jurisconsults appointed by the Grand Judge, Minister of Justice, are approved.
> II. The Code Napoleon will be put into operation, as from the first day of April. Only the Italian translation may be cited and have the force of law in the Courts.)

Regional and local translations in the Southern Netherlands or Italy could be official or non-official. Official translations were often organized at the level of the Departments (in the Southern Netherlands and in Liguria after the annexation by the French Empire), e.g., the translation of regional decrees published by the administration of the Department. However, there were no official translation offices at this level. The translations were probably done by administrative employees, not by full-time translators, as they were at the national level (Ingelbeen and Schreiber 2018, 78).

Non-official translations included translations made by journalists for local newspapers. In some cases, however, a private newspaper could gain an official function: In Genoa, the newspaper *Gazzetta di Genova*, formerly monolingual Italian, achieved the status of an official journal of the Department of Genoa in June 1809 and became increasingly bilingual. From No. 44 (dated 3 June 1809) on, the title of the newspaper was followed by the sentence: "Les Actes du Gouvernement dans le Département de Gênes, insérés dans cette Feuille, sont officiels" (*Gazzetta di Genova* 1809, No. 44; "The Acts of the Government in the Department of Genoa, inserted in this Sheet, are official"). However, only the most important texts were translated into Italian to assure communication with the local population. A letter from the prefect of Genoa to the mayors of the Department concerning the situation of the military conscripts in the Department was followed by an explanation about the necessity of a translation: "L'importance de cette lettre, nous a paru exiger qu'elle soit écrite dans les deux langues. Nous en donnerons dans ce numéro et le suivant la traduction en langue italienne" (*Gazzetta di Genova* 1809, No. 44; "The importance of this letter seemed to us to require that it be written in both languages. In this and the next issue, we will give the Italian translation of the letter").

4. Analyses of selected texts

In this section, I will take a look at archival material from the Southern Netherlands and Italy, focusing on bilingual texts collected by Lieven D'hulst (Beveren, RAB), Sarah Hartmann (Milan, ASM) and Jelena Nikolic (Genoa, ASG). For a full account of the more than 1,500 bilingual texts collected and digitized within the two research projects mentioned above, see the databases DFG_BE (French-Flemish) and DFG_IT (French-Italian).

For the present publication, I will focus on three features: text structure, terminology and rhetoric. The translation of text structure and terminology is part of legal transfer, the rendering of rhetorical features can be seen as a part of ideological transfer. But before analyzing these features, I will consider the translation strategies in the translations.

4.1 Translation strategies as a part of legal and ideological transfer

The overall strategy of most of the translations in our corpus is a 'literal' translation of the source text. This can be explained by the authoritative character of the source texts (mostly legal or administrative texts), the publication form (mostly bilingual) and the overall function of legal transfer (the French legal system was applied to a new territory).

Šarčević (1997, 25) defines different degrees of literalness in the field of legal translation. She defines a *strict literal translation* (also called *word-for-word translation*) as a translation where "the words of the source text are translated literally into the target language and even the grammatical forms and word order of the source text are retained", while a *literal translation* is a translation where "the basic unit of translation is still the word; however, basic transformations (changes in syntax) are permitted to respect the rules of grammar in the target language." For Šarčević, the use of the translation strategy depends on the status of the target text and the period. According to her, strict literalness in legal translation dominated until the seventeenth century,[7] followed by a period of literalness in the eighteenth and nineteenth centuries, and later on, by less literal strategies (Šarčević 1997, 23-53). I will argue in the following sections that the application of a translation strategy also depends on the target language.

4.2 Text structure

An important feature that can be found in many legal or administrative texts of our corpus is the so-called *phrase unique*, the construction of a text (or a part of a text) in one long sentence, a norm that was introduced during the French Revolution in the judgments of the *Cour de cassation* (Court of Cassation) and then transferred to other legal text types (Schreiber 2017). In the texts of our corpus, the *phrase unique* typically has the following structure:

Part	Syntactical structure
Author or institution	Subject of the matrix clause
Legal norms ('visa')	Subordinate clause(s), introduced by *vu*
Arguments ('motifs')	Subordinate clause(s), introduced by *considérant que*
Report(s)	Subordinate clause(s), marked by *sur* or *entendu*

---

7   This statement is sharply criticized by Lavigne (2006).

Decision Verb of the matrix clause, e.g., *arrête*
Tenor (divided into articles) Object of the matrix clause (mostly main clauses)

This structure is applied with some variations. Neither the *visa* nor the *motifs* or the reports are obligatory. The following example, taken from a decree of the Schelde Department of 2 May 1799 shows the full *phrase unique* structure:

L'ADMINISTRATION CENTRALE DU DÉPARTEMENT DE L'ESCAUT
Vu la Loi du 3 Nivôse dernier, sur le mode d'assiete, de perception & de dégrevement, dans l'intérieur des Départemens, de la Contribution personelle, mobiliaire & somptuaire;
Vu l'article V de ladite Loi qui enjoint aux Administrations centrales de déterminer le prix moyen de la journée de travail dans chaque Canton;
Vu que ce n'est qu'après avoir fixé le prix moyen de la journée de travail que les Administrations centrales peuvent régler sur cette base la Contribution personnelle de chaque Canton;
Considérant qu'il est instant, pour la prompte répartition des Contributions, que cette Administration s'occupe de cet objet important,
Sur le rapport de son troisième bureau, & le Commissaires du Directoire exécutif entendu,
ARRÊTE: (...)

DE CENTRAELE ADMINISTRATIE VON HET DEPARTEMENT DER SCHELDE
Gezien de Wet von den derden Nivose laestleden, nopens het pointen, ontfangen en ontlasten van de personeele, mobiliaire en somptuaire Contributien in het inwendig der Departementen; (...)
Gezien den V artikel van de gezeyde Wet, die aen de Departements-Administratien aenbevelt van voor elk Canton de weerde van eenen daghuer-loon te bepaelen;
Gemerkt dat het op de weerde van den gemeynen loon van eene daghuere is dat de Centrale Administratie de verdeeling der personeele Contributie moet vestigen;
Overwegende dat het voorde spoedige verdeeling der Contributien aenbelangt dat deze Administratie zig aenstonds met deze gewigtige werking ophoude,
Op het Rapport van haeren derden Bureau, en den Commissaris van de uytwerkende magt gehoort,
BESLUYT: (...) (RAB, Scheldedepartement I3/447)

(THE CENTRAL ADMINISTRATION OF THE SCHELDT DEPARTMENT
In view of the Law of 3 Nivôse dernier, on the method of assessment, collection & relief, within the Departments, of the personal, movable & sumptuary Contribution;
Having regard to Article V of the said Law which enjoins the Central Administrations to determine the average price of the working day in each Canton;
Considering that it is only after having fixed the average price of the working day that the Central Administrations can pay the Personal Contribution of each Canton on this basis;
Considering that it is at this moment, for the prompt distribution of the Contributions, that this Administration is dealing with this important matter,
On the report of its third bureau, & the Statutory Auditors of the Executive Management Board having been heard,
STATES: (...))

The text structure is maintained in the translation, even if this contradicts the normal word order in Flemish, which would be as follows: "Gezien (...), overwegende dat (...), besluyt de Centraele Administratie (...)" (with inversion of the subject).

The connectives introducing the different parts are mostly translated literally. The first two forms of *vu*, introducing the *visa*, are translated by *gezien*, as in most of our texts. The third form of *vu* (followed by *que*) does not introduce a legal norm, as in the classical *phrase unique*, but an argument. Therefore, it has been translated by *gemerkt dat*, one of the equivalents of *considérant que*. The connective *considérant que* is translated by *overwegende dat*, the most frequent equivalent in our corpus.[8] The clause about the reports is translated literally as well.

Let us now take a look at one French-Italian example from our Milan corpus, a decree of 2 July 1996:

LES AGENS MILITAIRES DE LA LOMBARDIE
Vu les Représentations de la Municipalité de Milan, déléguée pour la confection des Rôles de la contribution Militaire, des quelles il résulte

---

8   Other equivalents include *in aendagt nemende dat, aenmerkende dat, bemerkende dat, (aen) gemerkt dat, overdenkende dat, considereerende dat* (Ingelbeen and Schreiber 2018, 76).

qu'une somme d'environt 70000. se trouve répartie sur environ 910. individus pauvres (...)
Considérant que le principe fondamental de l'arrête 2. Messidor touchant le levée de la contribution Militaire est de n'atteindre que les gens aisés et d'épargner ceux dont les revenus sont essentiellement necessaires à leur subsistance.
Considérant de plus que la somme repartie sur la Ville de Milan excede de 300,000 livres celles qui avoit été présumée d'abord d'après un calcul erroné.
ARRÊTENT (...)

GLI AGENTI MILITARI DELLA LOMBARDIA
In vista delle rimostranze della Municipalità di Milano delegata per la formazione dei Ruoli della Contribuzione Militare, dalle quali risulta che una somma di circa lir. 70000 trovasi ripartita sopra circa 910. individui poveri (...)
Considerando che il principio fondamentale dell'Arresto dei 2. Messidoro relativo alla riscossione della Contribuzione Militare è che non debba cadere se non se sulle persone agiate, e di risparmiare quelli, le di cui entrate sono essenzialmente necessarie alla loro sussistenza.
Considerando di più che la somma stata ripartita sopra la Città di Milano eccede di 300,000. lire quella che era stata supposta da prima per un calcolo erroneo.
ARRESTANO (...) (ASM, Taverna 21)

(THE MILITARY AGENTS OF LOMBARDY
Having regard to the Representations of the Municipality of Milan, delegated for the preparation of the Roles of the Military Contribution, from which it results that a sum of about 70,000. is distributed among about 910 poor individuals (...)
Considering that the fundamental principle of the decree 2. Messidor concerning the levying of the Military contribution is to reach only the well-to-do and to save those whose income is essentially necessary for their subsistence.
Considering moreover that the sum distributed to the City of Milan exceeds by 300,000 pounds that which was first presumed on the basis of an erroneous calculation.
STATE (...))

Again, the text structure is maintained. This is easier in Italian than in Flemish, because the normal Italian word order does not differ much from the French word order.

The form *vu* is not translated by *visto/-a* or *veduto/-a*, as in most of our texts, but by *in vista*, because *vu* does not introduce a legal norm here, but refers to a delegation that gave a report. The two occurrences of *considérant que* are translated literally by *considerando che* as in all of our texts. Given the close relationship of the two Romance languages, there is often one exact equivalent for a French term in the Italian lexicon, which is rarely the case in Flemish.

In the Napoleonic Empire and the Kingdom of Italy, the structure of the decrees changes when the monarch is the subject of the text. The *motifs* are less frequent now, which keeps the texts short and apodictic, and the subject pronoun is *nous* (the *pluralis majestatis*), as in the following example of our French-Flemish corpus, a decree of 7 February 1808:

NAPOLEON, Empereur des Français, Roi d'Italie et Protecteur de la Confédération du Rhin.
Sur le rapport de notre Ministre de l'Intérieur, vu le traité du 11 Novembre 1807. Notre Conseil d'état entendu, nous avons décrété et décrétons ce qui suit: (...)

NAPOLEON, Keizer der Franschen, Koning van Italien en Beschermer der Ryn-Confederatie.
Op het rapport van onzen Minister van Binnenlandsche zaken, gezien het Traktaat van den 11 November 1807.
Gehoord onzen Staatsraad, hebben wy gedecreteerd en decreteeren het volgende: (...) (RAB, Scheldedepartement 3074)

(NAPOLEON, Emperor of the French, King of Italy and Protector of the Confederation of the Rhine.
On the report of our Minister of the Interior, having regard to the treaty of November 11, 1807.
Our Council of State heard, we have decreed and decree the following: (...))

The textual and syntactic structure is maintained in the translation, with one exception: the word order of the first part of the decision is adapted to the syntax of the target language: *nous avons décrété – hebben wy gedecreteerd*. The participles *vu* and *entendu* are translated literally by *gezien* and *gehoord*.

In the Kingdom of Italy, the Viceroy Eugene (Eugène de Beauharnais), uses the same monarchic style, with reverence to his stepfather Napoléon, as in the following decree of 14 October 1805, printed with the Italian text on the left side:

> Eugenio Vice-Re d'Italia, Arcicancelliere di Stato dell'Imperio Francese a tutti quelli che vedranno le presenti, salute:
> Noi abbiamo in virtù dell'Autorità che ci è stata delegata dall'Altissimo, ed Augustissimo Imperatore e Re NAPOLEONE I. nostro graziosissimo Sovrano decretato ed ordinato quanto segue: (....)
>
> EUGÉNE Vice Roi d'Italie, Archichancelier d'État de l'Empire Français, à tous ceux qui les présentes verront, salut:
> Nous en vertu de l'Autorité qui nous a été déléguée par le très haut et très Auguste Empereur et Roi NAPOLEON I, notre très honoré beau-père et gracieux Souverain, avons décrété et ordonné ce qui suit: (...) (ASM, Atti ufficiali 1805)
>
> (EUGENE Vice King of Italy, State Archchancellor of the French Empire, to all those present greetings:
> We, by virtue of the Authority delegated to us by the Most High and Most Augustus Emperor and King Napoleon I, our most honored father-in-law and gracious Sovereign, have decreed and ordained the following: (...))

The order of the two text versions, which include neither *visa* nor *motifs*, does not imply that the Italian text is the source text, but it underlines that Italian is the official language of the Kingdom of Italy.[9] Structurally, the two versions are very similar, but not strictly literal: the place of the auxiliary verb of the decision (*abbiamo – avons*) is different in this case.[10]

In both target languages, the literal rendering of the *phrase unique* structure is due to the transfer of the norms of French legal text types.

4.3 Terminology

In the field of legal, administrative and political terminology, the difference between the Flemish and the Italian target texts is particularly striking, especially with regard to terminological consistency. Let us take a look at some examples.

---

9   The quotation is taken from the official Bulletin of the Italian Kingdom. In many cases, the French version was *de facto* the source text which had been translated for this Bulletin.
10 In other texts, the Italian word order follows the French model.

The French word *domicile* (residency) is rendered in Italian almost exclusively by the cognate *domicilio*, occasionally by *abitazione*. In our Flemish corpus, we can find ten different terms which occur at least twice (plus a dozen *hapax legomana*): the Gallicism *domicilie* and the Germanic forms *woonplaets* (most frequent equivalent), *woonste, wooning, woonsteden, woonhuyze, woonachtig (zijn), huyzen, huisvesting* and *verblijf(plaets)* (Ingelbeen and Schreiber 2018, 65-66).

The French term *contribution* (tax) is rendered by *contribuzione* in the Italian texts, with one graphical variation: *contribuzion*. In the Flemish target texts, we find the Gallicism *contributie* and the Germanic terms *belasting* and *last*. When we look at the compound term *contribution foncière* (land tax), we can find even more variants: the Gallicism *fonciere contributie* (the most frequent form), the Germanic forms *grondbelastung, grondlast* and *grondschatting*, and the hybrid forms *grondelyke contributie* and *grondcontributie* (Ingelbeen and Schreiber 2018, 67). The Italian texts show only two equivalents: *contribuzione fondiaria* and *contribuzione territoriale*.

The phrase *au profit de* (for the benefit of) is rendered by two Italian equivalents: *a profitto di* (the most frequent form) and *a benifizio di*. In our Flemish texts, we can find the following renderings: *ten profyte van* (the most frequent form), *ten voordeele van, tot des selfs voordeel, ten behoeve van* and *tot nut der* (Ingelbeen and Schreiber 2018, 67-68). If we look at the context in which this phrase is used, the variation of the Flemish text increases. Many texts about requisitions include expressions like *confisqué(s) au profit de (la République)* (confiscated for the benefit of (the Republic)). In our Flemish texts, we can find three kinds of renderings for the verb form and the following phrase: two Gallicisms: *geconfisqueert ten profyte van*; two Germanic forms: *verbeurt ten behoeve van*; one Germanic form and one Gallicism: *verbeurt tot profyte van* (RAB, Scheldedepartement 7006).

In some cases, the Germanic form and the corresponding Gallicism cannot be regarded as synonyms in Flemish: The expression *la Grande Nation* (the Great Nation), which refers, at that time, to the French state with its occupied and annexed territories (Godechot 2004), is often rendered literally by *de groote Natie*, but sometimes by *het groot volk* (the great people), which does not have the same political connotation. In the Italian translations, there are two variants which only differ at the morphological level: *la Gran Nazione* and *la Grande Nazione*. In other cases, there are semantic differences between the Germanic variants in Flemish: The French term *royalisme*, which, in our texts, refers to royalist enemies of the French Republic, is rendered by the Gallicism *royalismus*, and the Germanic forms *koningsgezinde* and *koningsgezindheyd*, which have the same connotation. In some texts, however, we find the term *koningdom*, which is a politically neutral term referring to monarchy. Another interesting case is the term *civisme*, which refers here to loyalty towards the French state (GR). In our Flemish translations, we find the Gallicisms *civismus* and *civism*, as well as several Germanic equivalents with a positive connotation: *borgerliefde, landsliefde, trouw aen 't Vaderland*, but also the more neutral term *borgerlykheyd*, which does not have the same political connotations (WNT, s.v. *burgerlijkheid*). The Italian equivalent is the term *civismo*, which was borrowed from French during the Revolutionary period with the same positive connotation (Leso 1991, 218).

In total, the Flemish corpus is marked by considerable lexical variety and hybridity, which is much less present in the Italian corpus. How can we explain these differences between the Flemish and the Italian translations?

1. Since French and Italian are Romance languages, there is, by definition, a strong lexical relationship. This is particularly obvious in our translations, where the intention was to produce a literal version. As Flemish is a Germanic language, of which the lexicon had been influenced by French during the time of our study, there are often two or more translation techniques, even within a literal translation: one Gallicism and one or more Germanic equivalents.

2. The Flemish (or Dutch) language became definitely co-official with French in Belgium as late as in 1898 (Martyn 2005, 281). Before that date, Flemish was nevertheless used in legal and administrative contexts, especially in translations from French, even before the French period (D'hulst 2017), but there was no standardized legal language.[11] In Italy, legal texts were frequently written in Latin until the eighteenth century (Monti 2008). In the period of our project, however, Italian was already the official language in different states, including the Italian 'sister republics' and the Kingdom of Italy. Thus, Italian was not yet fully standardized as a legal language, but was more developed than Flemish.

3. Our Flemish corpus consists mainly of regional translations of short legal and administrative texts. The translators were not full-time translators and hence probably paid less attention to terminological coherence than a professional translator would have done (Ingelbeen and Schreiber 2018, 78). Our Italian corpus includes numerous short texts, too, but also the Italian versions of the Napoleonic codes. These translations had been supervised by a commission of legal experts, for whom terminological consistency was important (Hartmann, forthcoming).

---

11   Therefore, the official translations during the nineteenth century in Belgium show a similar lexical variation (van Gerwen 2019, 120).

4.4 Rhetoric

Even if rhetorical texts *sensu stricto*, e.g., political speeches, play only a secondary role in our corpus, rhetorical devices are present in many texts. I will illustrate this by focusing on three devices: metaphors, superlatives and adjectives in a marked position. The rendering of rhetorical devices can be interpreted as part of an ideological transfer. The recipients should be convinced by the message of the revolutionary texts.

In our texts, metaphors are used with a positive or a negative connotation. One example of a metaphor with a positive connotation is the family metaphor, referring to the *Grande Nation* with its annexed territories. In a proclamation of 7 December 1796, Bouteville, commissioner of the French government in the Southern Netherlands, calls the inhabitants of the annexed *département* "nos frères, si solemnellement admis au sein de la famille" ("our brothers, so solemnly admitted to the bosom of the family"); this is translated literally into Flemish by "onze broeders, zoo plegtiglyk aenveerd in den schoot der familie" (RAB, Scheldedepartement 2007). In a letter to the inhabitants of Lombardy, General Despinoy, commandant in Milan during the Italian campaign, calls the inhabitants of that region "enfans de la grande famille" ("children of the big family"), translated into Italian by "figliuoli della gran Famiglia" (ASM, Taverna 21). Positive metaphors are also used referring to the French governance, e.g., *douceur* (sweetness). In a proclamation to the people of Lombardy of 29 May 1796, Saliceti, commissioner of the French government, states: "les Français (...) vouloient vous faire partager les douceurs de la liberté" ("the French (...) wanted to share with you the sweetness of freedom"), translated as follows: "i Francesi (...) volevano varvi divider con essi le dolcezze della libertà" (ASM, Taverna 21). A similar metaphor is used by Du Bosch, commissioner of the government of the Schelde Department, in a speech of 18 February 1796. He speaks about "toutes les douceurs d'une prospérité" ("all the comforts of prosperity"). In the translation, the (abstract) sweetness metaphor is rendered in a more concrete way as "sweet fruits": "zoete vrugten van een voorspoed" (RAB, Scheldedepartement 2010).

Metaphors with a negative connotation are used, among other things, referring to difficult moments, sometimes with a euphemistic function. In several texts, times of trouble are referred to with the meteorological metaphor *orage* (thunderstorm). In a proclamation of 10 January 1797, the central administration of the Schelde Department mentions "des momens d'orage" ("stormy times"), which was translated as "eenige onstuymige oogenblikken" (RAB, Scheldedepartement 2007), transferring the noun *orage* into the adjective *onstuymig* (stormy). In a speech addressed to the

King of Italy, the French ambassador Gingueni speaks about "les orages qui ont troublé ma patrie" ("the storms that have troubled my homeland"), which was literally translated into Italian as "le procelle, che han turbata la mia Patria" (ASM, Taverna 27). In the same speech, the ambassador uses a medical metaphor, referring to the results of war times as wounds which had to be healed: "je ne veux point rouvrir des plaies, que le tems, la paix et la concorde peuvent seuls guerir" ("I don't want to reopen wounds that only time, peace and concord can heal"), translated, again literally, by "non voglio riaprire delle piaghe, cui il tempo, la pace, e la concordia ponno da lor sole guarire" (ASM, Taverna 27). In a letter dated 25 August 1799 to the inhabitants of the Schelde Department, the commissioner of the government in Ghent, Van Wambeke, uses a similar metaphor: "Le Directoire, pénétré de la pénible situation du Département de l'Escaut, a voulu sonder les plaies & appliquer le remède" ("The Directoire, aware of the distressing situation of the Scheldt Department, wanted to probe the wounds & apply the remedy"), which was translated literally by "Het Directorie bewogen door den treurigen toestand van het Departement van de Schelde, heeft de wonde willen peylen en den geneés-middel toebereyden" (RAB, Scheldedepartement 2055). In general, most metaphors are translated more or less literally in both target languages (see also Schreiber 2015).

As metaphors, superlatives can be used with a positive and a negative meaning. In a speech given on 28 September 1796, the President of the general administration of Lombardy, Sommariva, praises Napoleon Bonaparte, who had announced the reopening of the University of Pavia, with the following words: "Ce trait surtout doit former de ce Héros l'éloge le plus grand, le plus surprenant, tel enfin comm'il est difficile d'en rencontrer un pareil dans l'Histoire" ("This trait above all must form the greatest, most surprising praise of this Hero, such as it is difficult to find one like him in History"), which had been translated as follows: "Questo tra i tanti è un tratto, che formerà di codesto Eroe gli elogi i più singolari, i più grandi, come che le istorie non ci offrono con tanta facilità gli eguali" (ASM, Taverna 23). Here, the noun *éloge* is pluralized in translation (*elogi*), the position of the adjectives has been changed, and the meaning of the adjective *surprenant* (surprising) has been modified into *singolare* (unique). The emotional style, however, has been maintained. In our next example, Napoleon, now emperor, is again referred to with a superlative. The quotation is taken from a proclamation, addressed to the inhabitants of the town Vlissingen on 7 February 1808, formerly a part of Holland, now annexed to the French Empire: "vous passez sous la domination du plus grand des Monarques" ("you come under the dominion of the greatest of Monarchs"), which has been translated literally: "Gy gaat dus over onder de beheersching van den grootsten der Monarken" (RAB, Scheldedepartement 3074).

However, it was not only people who could be referred to with superlatives. In the decree of 9 December 1800, General Brune, head of the French Army of Italy, describes his own duties as follows: "Le devoir le plus sacré du Général en chef est de pourvoir aux besoins de l'Armée" ("The General-in-Chief's most sacred duty is to provide for the needs of the Army"), translated literally as "Il dovere il più sacro del Generale in Capo è di provvedere ai bisogni dell'Armata" (ASM, Taverna 33). If it is the holiest duty of a General to care about his army, what is the holiest duty of the citizens? The answer is: to pay taxes, according to Du Bosch, commissioner of the government in the Schelde Department, in a message sent on 16 May 1797: "De ces devoirs, le plus sacré de tous c'est l'acquittement des contributions" ("Of these duties, the most sacred of all is the payment of contributions"), translated literally as: "Van deze pligten is de geheyligste van alle het betaelen der Contributien" (RAB, Scheldedepartement 2007). In general, the texts dealing with taxes are very persuasive, since it was difficult to collect the taxes from the (often poor) population of an occupied country.

In the following examples, superlatives are used with a negative connotation. In a message to the citizens of Milan, delivered on 28 May 1796, General Despinoy denounces the traitorous attitude of the enemies of the French Republic with the following words: "La trahison la plus insigne, l'hipocrisie la plus profonde" ("The most inglorious betrayal, the deepest hypocrisy"), translated word by word: "Il tradimento il più insigne, l'ipocrisie la più profonda" (ASM, Taverna 21). In his speech on 18 February 1796, Bosch, commissioner of the government of the Schelde Department, combines one of the above-quoted metaphors with a superlative, when he denounces the consequences of insubordination as "la plaie la plus profonde" ("the deepest wound"), translated as "een alderdiepste wonde" (RAB, Scheldedepartement 2010). Here, the superlative *diepst* is intensified by the prefix *alder-* (= *aller-*). In general, the translators did not have severe problems with the rhetorical functions of superlatives.

Another rhetorical device that can be found frequently in our texts is the marked position of attributive adjectives. In French, some adjectives which would normally be placed after the noun can be placed in front of a noun to express an intensification or a subjective component (Maingueneau 1994, 214). In Italian, the situation is similar (Ramaglia 2011, 30). As in the case of metaphors and superlatives, this device can be used with a positive or a negative connotation. French-Italian examples with positive connotations include the following: "nos braves marins" ("our brave mariners") – "nostri bravi marinari" (ASG, Archivio Segreto 185), "son invincible armée" ("his invincible army") – "la sua invincibile armata" (ASG, Preffetura Francese 550), "une sage administration" ("a wise administration") – "una saggia amministrazione" (ASM, Taverna 21), "les brillantes destinées de la République Française" ("the brilliant destinies of the French Republic") – "i luminosi destini della Repubblica Francese" (ASM, Taverna 31), "l'immortel BONAPARTE" ("the immortal BONAPARTE") – "l'immortal BONAPARTE" (ASM, Taverna 34). The following examples express a negative meaning: "exécrable assassinat" ("vile murder") – "esecrabile assassinio" (ASG, Repubblica Ligure 626), "les perfides insinuations du fanatisme" ("the perfidious insinuations of fanaticism") – "le perfide insinuazioni del fanatismo" (ASM, Taverna 21), "les vils émissaires des rois" ("the vile emissaries of kings") – "dai vili emissarj dei re" (ASM, Taverna 27), "leur fâcheuse intention" ("their malicious intent") – "lor cattiva intenzione" (*Gazzetta di Genova* 1809, No. 44). We even found some rare examples where the Italian translator placed a positively or negatively connoted adjective in front of a noun, where this was not the case in the French source text: "des gouvernements amis et généreux" ("friendly and generous governments") – "dei generosi ed amici governi" (ASM, Melzi restituito 4), "les insinuations perfides des nos ennemis" ("the perfidious insinuations of our enemies") – "le perfide insinuazioni dei nostri nimici" (ASG, Prefettura Francese 550).

For the Flemish translators, the situation was different. Since the position in front of the noun is the unmarked place of the attributive adjective in Dutch – with rare exceptions (Geerts et al. 1984, 700) – a word-for-word translation of the French construction cannot have the same rhetorical effect. Nevertheless, most of the translations are literal. Here are some examples of positively and negatively connoted adjectives: "le sublime orgueil" ("the sublime pride") – "de doorlugtige hoogmoed", "ces immortels défenseurs du genre humain" ("these immortal defenders of the human race") – "die onsterfelyke verdedigers van het menschelk gelagt" (RAB, Scheldedepartement 2007), "les bienfaisantes intentions du Directoire" ("the benevolent intentions of the Directoire") – "de weldoende uytzigten van 't Directorie", "braves & loyaux Habitans de la Commune de Gand" ("brave & loyal Inhabitants of the Municipality of Ghent") – "moedige en deftige Inwoonders der Commune van Gend" (RAB, Scheldedepartement 2055), "brillantes destinées" ("shiny destinies") – "de glansryk schikkingen" (RAB, Scheldedepartement 3074); "la stupide ignorance" ("stupid ignorance") – "de domme onwetendheyd", "ses vils détracteurs" ("its vile detractors") – "de veragtelyke lasteraars", "les perfides insinuations" ("the perfidious insinuations") – "deze trouwlooze redeneeringen", "ces horribles carnages" ("these horrible carnages") – "die schrikkelyke moordereyen", "cette affreuse boucherie" ("this dreadful slaughter") – "deze afgryzelyke vleeschbanke" (RAB, Scheldepartement 2007). But what could be an adequate solution for this translation problem? In the following example, the translator chose a noun with a negative connotation (*saemenrottinge*; 'mob' for *coalition*), which could be interpreted as a compensation for the reduced rhetorical effect: "l'exécrable et monstrueuse coalition" ("the vile and monstrous mob") – "de vervaerelyke en afgryzelyke saemenrottinge" (RAB, Scheldedepartement 2007). However, this is an isolated example.

5. Conclusion

Since the period in which the translations of our corpus were produced was relatively short, one might ask if it was perhaps too short to have a lasting influence on the target languages and cultures. This question cannot be answered globally, but only with regard to both target languages and the analyzed linguistic fields. In the field of text structure, it can be observed that the Southern Netherlands and Italy are among the countries that adopted the *phrase unique* structure for several legal text types, e.g., judgments (Gorla 1968, vol. 1, 22-24). Thus, translations during the Napoleonic period could have been a factor in this development.

In the field of legal, administrative and political terminology, the situations of Flemish and Italian differ notably. As we have seen, the Flemish translations are marked by a high level of variation. Therefore, I would not state that the translations had a lasting influence in this field in Flemish. In the Italian texts, there is less terminological variation. According to Zolli, some Gallicisms of the Napoleonic period were adopted, e.g., the loan word *procedura* and the loan translation *processo verbale* (Zolli 1974, 104, 129). However, neither Zolli (1974) nor Leso (1991) discuss the role of translations. According to the first results of our project, a translational influence seems probable, e.g., in the case of the translated Napoleonic codes (Hartmann, forthcoming).

In the rhetorical domain, I would not go so far as to state that there was a lasting influence. The rhetorical devices analyzed above are not restricted to the period of the French Revolution, so it would be difficult to find clear evidence for a translational influence on the level of rhetorical devices that would go beyond the lexical influence in the area of political terminology.

Going back to the topic of legal transfer, I would like to conclude with two important, more general, observations: In both countries, the Southern Netherlands and Italy, the importation of the French legal system, which began in the Napoleonic period, had a lasting influence. In Italy, the Civil

Code of 1865 is based on the Code Napoléon (Cavagnoli and Ioriatti Ferrari 2009, 147). In Belgium, the French influence is even stronger. According to Heirbaut and Gerkens, Belgium is "even more faithful to its French heritage than France itself. Its judicial organisation is still closer to the Napoleonic model" (2011, 17). Without legal translation, these structural transfers of the legal system would not have been possible.

Sources

ASG: Archivio di Stato di Genova. Genoa.
ASM: Archivio di Stato di Milano. Milan.
DFG_BE: "DFG-Projekt Belgien." http://uepol.zdv.uni-mainz.de.
DFG_IT: "DFG-Projekt Italien." http://uepol.zdv.uni-mainz.de:8080.
Gazzetta di Genova. 1809. No. 44. Genoa.
RAB: Rijksarchief te Antwerpen-Beveren. Beveren.

References

Cavagnoli, Stefania, and Elena Ioriatti Ferrari. 2009. *Tradurre il diritto. Nozioni di diritto e di linguistica giuridica*. Padova: CEDAM.
Deneckere, Marcel. 1954. *Histoire de la langue française dans les Flandres (1770-1823)*. Ghent: Romanica Gandensia.
D'hulst, Lieven. 2012. "(Re)Locating Translation History: From Assumed Translation to Assumed Transfer." *Translation Studies* 5 (2): 139-155.
— 2015. "'Localiser' des traductions nationales au tournant du XVIIIe siècle: le Bulletin des lois en versions flamande et hollandaise sous la période française (1797-1813)." In *Übersetzung und Nationenbildung*, edited by Dilek Dizdar, Andreas Gipper, and Michael Schreiber, 93-108. Berlin: Frank & Timme.
— 2017. "Traduire sous des régimes hégémoniques en Belgique: une politique de longue durée?" *Parallèles* 29 (1): 19-33. https://doi.org/10.17462/para.2017.01.03.
—, and Michael Schreiber. 2014. "Vers une historiographie des politiques des traductions en Belgique durant la période française." *Target. International Journal of Translation Studies* 26 (1): 3-32. https://doi.org/10.1075/target.26.1.01hul.
—, and Heleen van Gerwen. 2018. "Translation Space In Nineteenth-Century Belgium: Rethinking Translation and Transfer Directions." *Perspectives* 26 (4): 495-508. https://doi.org/10.1080/0907676X.2017.1402940.
Dubois, Sébastien. 2005. *L'invention de la Belgique. Genèse d'un État-Nation 1648-1830*. Brussels: Racine.

Geerts, G., W. Haeseryn, J. de Rooij, and M.C. van den Toorn. 1984. *Algemene Nederlandse Spraakkunst*. Groningen: Wolters-Noordhoff and Leuven: Wolters.

Godechot, Jacques. 2004. *La Grande Nation. L'expansion révolutionnaire de la France dans le monde de 1789 à 1799*. 2nd edition. Paris: Aubier.

Gorla, Gino. 1968. *Lo stile delle sentenze. Ricerca storico-comparativa e Testi commentati*. Rome: Foro Italiano (2 vols).

GR: *Le Grand Robert de la langue française*. 2005. Online edition. Paris: Le Robert.

Hartmann, Sarah. Forthcoming. "Die Übersetzung der Napoleonischen Gesetzbücher ins Italienische." *Parallèles*.

Heirbaut, Dirk. 2004. "Editing and Translating the Code civil in Belgium, 1804-2004." *Tijdschrift voor Rechtsgeschiedenis* 72: 215-229.

—, and Jean-François Gerkens. 2011. "In the Shadow of France. Legal Acculturation And Legal Transplants in the Southern Netherlands / Belgium." In *Legal Culture and Legal Transplants. Reports to the XVIIIth International Congress of Comparative Law*, vol. 1, 1-35. Washington: International Academy of Comparative Law.

Ingelbeen, Caroline and Michael Schreiber. 2018. "Übersetzungspolitik in Belgien während der französischen Epoche: Lexikalische und phraseologische Untersuchungen." *Moderne Sprachen* 62 (1): 59-80.

Lavigne, Claire-Hélène. 2006. "Literalness and Legal Translation: Myth and False Premises." In *Charting the Future of Translation History*, edited by Georges L. Bastin and Paul F. Bandia, 145-62. Ottawa: University of Ottawa Press.

Leso, Erasmo. 1991. *Lingua e Rivoluzione. Ricerche sul vocabolario politico italiano del Triennio Rivoluzionario 1796-1799*. Venice: Istituto Veneto di Scienze, Lettere ed Arti.

Maingueneau, Dominique. 1994. *Précis de grammaire pour les concours*. New edition. Paris: Dunod.

Martyn, Georges. 2005. "Het Burgerlijk Wetboek en de evolutie van de 'Vlaamse' rechtstaal in België." In: *Napoleons nalatenschap. Tweehonderd jaar Burgerlijk Wetboek in België*, edited by Dirk Heirbaut and Georges Martyn, 271-300. Mechelen: Kluwer.

Meylaerts, Reine. 2011. "Translation Policy." In *Handbook of Translation Studies*, vol. 2, edited by Yves Gambier and Luc van Doorslaer, 163-68. Amsterdam: Benjamins. https://doi.org/10.1075/hts.2.tra10.

Monti, Annamaria. 2008. "Tra latino e volgare: il linguaggio giuridico in età medioevale e moderna." In *Europa e linguaggi giuridici*, edited by Barbara Pozzo and Marina Timoteo, 31-82. Milan: Giuffrè.

Nikolic, Jelena and Michael Schreiber. Forthcoming. "Juristische, administrative und politische Fachübersetzungen während der Napoleonischen Epoche. Projektbeschreibung und erste Ergebnisse am Beispiel von Genua." *Parallèles*.

Ramaglia, Francesca. 2011. "Aggettivi." In *Enciclopedia dell'italiano*, edited by Raffaele Simone, 29-32. Rome: Treccani.

Rutten, Gijsbert and Rik Vosters. 2011. "Chaos and standards: Orthography in the Southern Netherlands (1720–1830)." *Multilingua* 29: 417-438.

Šarčević, Susan. 1997. *New Approach to Legal Translation*. The Hague: Kluwer.

Schreiber, Michael. 2015. "*Quel spectacle majestueux présente dans ce jour la grande nation!* – Die Rhetorik der Französischen Revolution in Übersetzungen." In *Wissenstransfer und Translation*, edited by Alberto Gil and Robert Kirstein, 261-272. St. Ingbert: Röhrig.

— 2016. "Covert Multilingualism: The Case of the Translation Policy in France and Belgium during the French Revolution and the Napoleonic Era." *Across Languages and Cultures* 17: 123-136. https://doi.org/10.1556/084.2016:17.1.6.

— 2017. "*La phrase unique*: Die Ein-Satz-Struktur in Texten der Französischen Revolution und deren Übersetzungen." In *Sprachvergleich und Übersetzung. Die romanischen Sprachen im Kontrast zum Deutschen*, edited by Wolfgang Dahmen, Günter Holtus, Johannes Kramer, Michael Metzeltin, Christina Ossenkop, Wolfgang Schweickard, and Otto Winkelmann, 81-98. Tübingen: Narr.

— 2019. "*Dans les deux langues* – Zur Referenz auf Mehrsprachigkeit und Übersetzung in Texten der Französischen Revolution und der Napoleonischen Epoche." In *Comparatio delectat III. Akten der VIII. Internationalen Arbeitstagung zum romanisch-deutschen und innerromanischen Sprachvergleich*, edited by Eva Lavric, Christine Konecny, Carmen Konzett-Firth, Wolfgang Pöckl, Monika Messner, and Eduardo Jacinto García, 809-821. Berlin: Peter Lang.

— 2020. "Translation Policies in Northern Italian Cities during the Napoleonic Era: The Case of Milan, Genoa and Turin." In *Translating in Town: Local Translation Policies during the European 19th Century*, edited by Lieven D'hulst and Kaisa Koskinen, 21-40. London: Bloomsbury.

Soleil, Sylvain. 2014. *Le modèle juridique français dans le monde. Une ambition, une expansion (XVIe – XIXe siècle)*. Paris: IRJS.

van Gerwen, Heleen. 2019. *"Tous les citoyens sont censés connaître la loi." Étude des pratiques de traduction et de transfert dans le domaine juridique belge (1830-1914)*. Leuven: KU Leuven – Faculteit Letteren (doctoral dissertation).

Wiesmann, Eva. 2009."Rechtsübersetzung: Praxis – Theorie – Didaktik." In *Translationswissenschaftliches Kolloquium I*, edited by Barbara Ahrens, Lothar Černý, Monika Krein-Kühle, and Michael Schreiber, 273-294. Frankfurt: Lang.

WNT: *Woordenboek der Nederlandsche taal*. http://gtb.inl.nl/search/?owner=WNT.

Zolli, Paolo. 1974. *Saggi sulla lingua italiana dell'Ottocento*. Pisa: Pacini.

Language and translation policies in state-building processes

The case of Lithuania

Dainora Maumevičienė, Ramunė Kasperavičienė
& Yves Gambier

Abstract

The beginning of the 20th century induced geopolitical changes that triggered the formation of many modern states in Europe, including the modern state of Lithuania along with other neighboring countries. This chapter focuses on Lithuanian language policy making as an important process in the nation-building and Lithuanian identity-(re)presentation process. It gives an overview of how translation practices were interrelated with language policies in many different ways. Writers, poets, translators, editors and publishers were not only mediators within and between cultures, languages, texts and minds of the time, but also crucial agents who substantially contributed to the development of the Lithuanian identity after 1918.

The aim of this chapter is to examine the Lithuanian language policy during the first independence period (1918-1940) and until independence was regained in 1991, to determine the role of the different agents in the institutionalization of language and translation as well as the contribution of diaspora to the development and construction of Lithuanian identity. We apply historical, descriptive and reconstructive translation approaches: our analysis is based on historiographic and documentary material. The collected evidence allows us to outline the historical context and to highlight the roots and sources of the language policies, as well as the role of translation in building and preserving the national Lithuanian identity throughout most of the 20th century.

1. Introduction

The end of WWI and the beginning of the twentieth century induced many geopolitical changes that in turn triggered the formation of many modern states in Europe, such as the emergence of modern Estonia, Finland, Latvia,

Poland and Lithuania. This formation was mainly triggered by the *Spring of Nations*, a political upheaval in Europe after the revolutions of 1848, which revived a sense of nationalism, a feeling of shared identity, and the demand for free press, which had an impact on the emergence of a national language. The leaders of the newly developed state of Lithuania had to build a strong foundation for the development of the state in terms of diplomacy, policy, economy, education and culture. The new state of Lithuania had to declare Lithuanian as the state language, since it had never been established as such in the history of Lithuania before 1918. The newly adopted language policy had an impact on the use of other languages of historical, local minorities that existed in Lithuania. Moreover, it affected the position of translation and the role of translators who played an important role in state-building processes.

This chapter focuses on the creation of language policies (i.e., the use of the state language, its relationship with other local languages of minorities, multilingualism and translation policy) as an important factor in the nation-building and Lithuanian identity-(re)presentation process. Writers, translators, editors and publishers were not only mediators within and between cultures, languages, texts and minds of the time, but also crucial agents who substantially contributed to the development of Lithuanian identity. This type of research is new in Lithuania and might be described as the first attempt to analyze language policy and translation practices that existed in Lithuania in the twentieth century, in other words, from the emergence of the first independent state of Lithuania until the reestablishment of Lithuanian independence in 1990. At the same time, it is relevant for the development of both Lithuanian, as a language, and translation studies, as well as for the understanding of the position and the impact of Lithuanian intelligentsia on the language policy and history of the state.

The time span of this study is the following: from 1918 until 1939, and from 1940 until 1991.[1] The first period is related to the establishment of the modern state of Lithuania that existed until WWII. The second period covers the years from 1940 onwards, when independent Lithuania as a state ceased to exist for 50 years and had to surrender to the Soviet regime, until

---

1   Initially, the authors of this chapter planned to give an overview of the context of language policy in Lithuania over a period of one hundred years, since in 2018, Lithuania celebrated the jubilee of one hundred years of the establishment of the modern state. The particular time span was selected with the aim to explore how language policy, translation and the role of translators and other agents involved have changed and what trends could be detected. The data was collected for the period mentioned above. However, due to the vast amount of collected resources, we decided to limit our analysis in this chapter to the period from 1918 to 1991.

the declaration of the reestablishment of the second independence of the Republic of Lithuania in 1990. These periods were purposefully selected since they are marked by significant geopolitical changes in Europe, which also had a direct impact on the state-building processes in Lithuania. Furthermore, political issues became the direct causes of language policy development. This historical exploration provides insights into the status of Lithuanian alongside other languages, the significance of certain agents in terms of language policy and translation, and allows us to draw certain conclusions about these two periods.

The development of the modern state of Lithuania was built on the idea of nationalism, perceived by means of the Lithuanian identity through the use of the Lithuanian language. The perception of the language policy, therefore, is of key significance to understand the current state of Lithuania and its society. Moreover, the language policy of a state never exists outside of its politics, public policy and governance, since various political decisions have an impact on the use of language(s) in a particular territory. The term 'language policy' was not used by the leaders of the state during the development of the first independent state of Lithuania. However, decisions formulated in the legal documents of those days clearly demonstrate leaders' attempts to define the status and regulate the use of Lithuanian as the state language in relationship to the use of other languages that were and are spoken in Lithuania. In this chapter the term 'language policy' is understood as language use-related philosophy and beliefs, language management, language institutionalization as the state language and its use in various administrative, legal, educational and other settings. The term is based on the perception of language policy as described by D'hulst, O'Sullivan and Schreiber (2016, 8). Moreover, it is related to the use of other languages of ethnic minorities alongside the state language in various institutional settings and public domains. It is assumed that language policy is closely interconnected with multilingualism and translation policy. In fact, language policy and translation policy coexist, since both of them grant members of society "the right to participatory citizenship" by means of regulating important aspects of human lives and providing or restricting access to public domain and services (Meylaerts 2011, 165).

The term 'translation policy' was not used at the beginning of the twentieth century during the development of the modern state of Lithuania, yet, it might be detected since governments of modern Lithuania had to communicate with its citizens who did not speak Lithuanian. Thus, the term 'translation policy' is perceived in this study as translation institutionalization in terms of the state language; translation management and translation practices in various administrative, legal, educational and other settings; as well as agents, in other words, translators involved in translation processes. In this chapter, we consider translation practices as closely interrelated with language policy in many diverse perspectives: for example, different nation-building processes, language-policy making and other institutions impacted the types of texts that were published, the languages that different texts were translated from and to, and the standardized use of Lithuanian in translated texts.

This case study is relatively new in Lithuania since there are no articles or studies that attempt to describe language policy and the role of translation and translators in Lithuania during state-building and -development processes over a period of approximately one hundred years. Similar research on language policy and translation in Latvia has been carried out by Andrejs Veisbergs (2009, 2016, 2018), and Daniele Monticelli and Anne Lange in Estonia (2014). The three Baltic States (Estonia, Latvia and Lithuania) have undergone similar state-building processes in the twentieth century. Thus, the comparison of trends in language policy development and the role of translation could bring interesting insights for further research.

This chapter is theoretically and methodologically underpinned by research findings in publications and collections of Meylaerts (2011), D'hulst (2012), Munday (2014), D'hulst, O'Sullivan and Schreiber (2016), Du (2017), González Núñez and Meylaerts (2017), D'hulst and Gambier (2018) and others who discuss the relationship and impact of public policy and general politics on language policy, factors, settings and agents that affected the role of translation and translators. At the same time, this study applies historiographic data analysis, a historical, descriptive and reconstructive translation approach and is based on the analysis of historiographic and documentary material that was collected in archives, namely the Archive of Legal Documents at the Seimas of the Republic of Lithuania,[2] the Virtual Electronic Heritage System,[3] Archives of Martynas Mažvydas National Library,[4] Kaunas County Public Library,[5] Virtual Library at Kaunas University of Technology,[6] the Universal Lithuanian Encyclopedia,[7] and databases (Register of Legal Acts)[8]. The socio-historical research method offers theoretical explanations of past events that influence the present turn of events, as described in publications of Hamilton (1993), McDowell (2002), Leedy and Ormrod (2005), and is appropriate since it

2 http://www3.lrs.lt/pls/inter_archyvas/dokpaieska_arch.forma_l
3 www.epaveldas.lt
4 www.lnb.lt
5 www.kvb.lt
6 www.library.ktu.edu
7 http://www.vle.lt/
8 https://www.e-tar.lt/portal/en

provides a historical perspective on the origins of institutions, institutional actors and policies.

2. Historical background and conditions for state-building

The modern state of Lithuania was not established within the territory of the Grand Duchy of Lithuania that existed in Europe from the thirteenth century until the end of the eighteenth century when the territory was divided between the Russian Kingdom, the Prussian Empire and Austria. The medieval state of Lithuania occupied a large territory that extended from the Baltic to the Black Sea and used to be one of the largest countries in Europe. Within this large territory, a linguistic, cultural, ethnic and religious diversity was maintained and multilingualism existed as a natural setting. Lithuanian[9] was not officially established as the state language in the Grand Duchy of Lithuania, though the written tradition of Lithuanian was formed in the sixteenth century, with the first printed book in 1547 (Vaišnienė and Zabarskaitė 2012). Following the tradition of noblemen, Latin was used as the language of diplomacy, whereas Slavic was the administrative language, and Lithuanian served as one of the local languages. In the Commonwealth of Lithuania and Poland after 1569, Polish replaced the local Russian and the administrative Slavic language, and became the language of the noblemen and the church (Snyder 2003). After the subdivision of the Commonwealth, when Lithuania became a part of the Russian Empire (from 1815), Polish was, again, replaced by Russian as the language of politics and administration, and Lithuanian was the language of the people alongside other languages of ethnic minorities. The rebellion of 1863 triggered "linguistic Lithuanian nationalism" (Snyder 2003, 36) and the emergence of a new elite which enthusiastically studied Lithuanian and supported the idea of developing a society based on a national identity. They elevated the importance of Lithuanian and laid the foundation of the modern national Lithuanian movement, which, in turn, stipulated the establishment of the modern state of Lithuania in 1918. After WWI and before the declaration of independence, the territory of Lithuania was occupied by Germany. This context made prerequisites for Lithuanian

---

9   Lithuanian is one of the oldest living Indo-European languages and is part of the Baltic branch. The modern standard Lithuanian language was formed in the nineteenth century. Currently, the number of speakers is around 3 million people. Today Lithuanian is considered as part of the national identity and self-perception of the Lithuanians as well as "one of the core national values and objects of presenting Lithuania to the world" (Vaišnienė and Zabarskaitė 2012, 55).

activists to appeal to the German government and seek for the restoration of the independence of the Republic of Lithuania.

3. The first independence from 1918 until 1939

On February 16, 1918, the Council of Lithuania,[10] which was elected in 1917 at the Vilnius Conference, proclaimed the restoration of the independence of the Republic of Lithuania in the Act of Reinstating Independence of Lithuania. It was unanimously decided to address the governments of Russia, Germany and other states and inform them about the reestablishment of the modern and democratically arranged state of Lithuania with Vilnius as its capital. The original act of the reestablishment of independence (the original copy was found in Berlin only in 2018) was written in Lithuanian and German. However, the public announcement of the Act was illegal at the time, since the German government prohibited its publication. When Germany lost WWI, it acknowledged the independent state of Lithuania. The Lithuanian Council formed the first cabinet of the Lithuanian government, prepared the Constitution of Lithuania and established all important institutions of the state management. The work of the first government was not stable due to the fact that soon after the reestablishment of the independence, Poland occupied Vilnius and its district from April 1919 until 1939. Therefore, Kaunas became the temporary capital of Lithuania where all important state governance-related institutions were moved and new educational and cultural institutions established.

During the reestablishment of the statehood of Lithuania, the diaspora, a lot of whom were educated and wealthy people, played a significant role. Before WWI, there were approximately half a million Lithuanians in diaspora (Eidintas 2005). They fled the country and went to live in Western Europe, North and South America or Russia because of many reasons, including economic instability and the absence of a statehood. After WWI, many of them came back and contributed to the declaration and establishment of the state. However, those who stayed abroad devoted a lot of effort to establishing many new Lithuanian organizations, which helped Lithuania maintain

---

10   During the turmoil of WWI, Lithuanian activists used the opportunity to appeal to the German government and establish the independent Republic of Lithuania. In 1917, they asked for the permission of the German government to organize the Vilnius conference, an assembly of Lithuanian politicians and delegates that took place in September. The Council of Lithuania, consisting of 21 members, was elected at this conference.

its independence by publishing newspapers, journals and books (Eidintas 2005). For example, in the US, a Society for Lithuanians Abroad was active in supporting Lithuanians, financing Lithuanian schools and teachers, and raising funds to support the poor.

3.1 Language policy

After the restoration of independence, Lithuanian came to the fore and was officially granted, for the first time in history, the status of 'state language'. This was the case, not only because the state was established within the borders where Lithuanian was prevalent, but also because the first constitution had officially been approved. The underlying principles of the first provisional constitution, approved by the Council of Lithuania on November 2, 1918, of the amendments of 1919, and of the Provisional Constitution of 1920 included the fundamentals related to the governance of the state. Even though the first two documents can hardly be classified as a constitution (Machovenko 2017), they did regulate the main principles of the state management, the roles of the state-governing institutions and the rights of Lithuanian citizens. Members of the first government understood the need to politically fix the foundation for Lithuanian as the state language and entrench its usage in the most important institutions. These legal acts did not legitimize Lithuanian as the state language, but the equality of all citizens in terms of having the same rights according to Lithuanian laws, the inviolability of possessions, and the freedom of speech and religion were established. Ethnic minorities had the right to use their language in various settings. One of the most important journals in which decisions of the Lithuanian government were announced, *Laikinosios Vyriausybės žinios*, available since December 29, 1918, was published in the main local languages, namely, Lithuanian, Polish, Belorussian and Jewish. Prior to granting the official status of state language, on July 1, 1919, the Ministry of Education passed a regulation for teachers of primary schools with the requirement to follow the standard of Lithuanian as it was established in 1910 and apply it to avoid the incorrect use of grammar in educational settings.

The first Lithuanian Constitution, approved on August 1, 1922, established Lithuanian as the state language; the use of local languages (with no mention of specific languages) became regulated by law as well (Lithuanian Constitution 1922). The Lithuanian Constitution of May 25, 1928, and the last Constitution, approved on May 12, 1938, retained the same wording as the initial article. However, the latter included an amendment that regulated in which parts and institutions of Lithuania other languages could be used alongside Lithuanian. For instance, local minorities published newspapers in their own languages and used their languages in church to practice their religion. However, Lithuanian as a subject had to be taught within the same amount of lessons during the week as the number of lessons reserved for teaching the local minority language (The Law of Secondary and Higher Schools 1925, April 23).

3.2 Translation policy and translators

The language policy approved in 1920 and 1922 laid the foundation for the acknowledgement of language diversity and translation policy, even though the term 'translation policy' was not officially used. The profession of translators was institutionalized in 1920 through the law that regulated salaries of officials in national and local institutions. The law described different types of translators and the range of their salaries. For example, the subdivision between a professional translator, a translator and a proficient user of English and French, a sworn translator in courts and a translator of telegrams in the Lithuanian Editorial Office, a translator-dispatcher and a translator of foreign languages (I and II category) was made. The largest salary was paid to translators of telegrams at the Lithuanian Editorial Office, whereas a sworn translator was paid less. Moreover, the number of translators in ministries (the Ministry of Foreign Affairs, the Ministry of Finances and others) and Lithuanian consulates was also regulated by law. For example, there had to be at least two positions of translators at the Ministry of Foreign Affairs.

The main translation directions in Lithuania mainly involved the local languages, namely, Lithuanian-Polish, Lithuanian-Belorussian, Lithuanian-Jewish, Lithuanian-Russian and Lithuanian-German. In terms of official communication outside of Lithuania, our analysis of legal documents in the archives of legislation from 1918 until 1939 revealed approximately 70 examples of various agreements, contracts, ratified conventions and protocols that were officially signed in two languages: French (since the official language of diplomacy at that time was French), and Lithuanian (by means of certified translations into Lithuanian). In some cases, certified translations were made into other languages than Lithuanian. For instance, the cooperation agreement between Lithuania and Afghanistan, signed on June 3, 1933, was prepared in Lithuanian and Afghan. When corresponding with Russia, translations into Russian were used.

3.3 Translation in municipalities and courts

The law also institutionalized the use of Lithuanian in local governments and municipalities. The document, approved in 1929, stated that all documentation in local governments should be submitted in the state language. However, the same law also stipulated language diversity and indicated that other local languages could be used alongside the state language. The law of municipalities, approved in 1931, stated that all officials and officers in municipalities had to be proficient users of the Lithuanian language, both spoken and written. Bookkeeping and all records in the General ledger had to be performed in the state language. However, if other local languages were used to issue invoices, translations had to be presented, especially if asked by the Tax Inspecting Office. Military representatives operated in the Lithuanian language as the state language, yet, when men were called to military services, it had to be indicated in the application in which and in how many foreign languages they were fluent.

Translation services also had to be used in courts to represent the non-Lithuanian-speaking population. The provisional law regulating the work of Lithuanian Courts and Processes in courts, approved on January 16, 1919, controlled the use of Lithuanian by indicating that the language used in courts had to be Lithuanian. All minutes, protocols and decisions were written and announced in the state language. The lawyers had to be proficient in other local languages (Polish and Belorussian). If a person did not speak Lithuanian, services of translators of their language had to be used. The law on the functioning of the court (1933) and the civil law of 1938 determined that Lithuanian was the official language in courts, but non-Lithuanian speakers could orally present their testimonials in their native language using the service of a court interpreter. If a witness in court was a non-Lithuanian-speaking person, an interpreter had to be invited during the interrogation and all testimonials had to be recorded, both in the language of the witness and in Lithuanian.

3.4 Translation at the theater

The establishment of the theater as an institution played an important role in the process of building a modern state. The theater was seen as a place of entertainment and one of the most significant agents to educate the population and develop the feeling of national pride. Since many artists, composers, dancers and singers studied abroad, they returned to Lithuania and contributed to the establishment of the theater. Various performances of well-known operas and operettas were staged, and librettos were translated into Lithuanian. In many cases composers and art directors, together with Lithuanian poets and writers, translated librettos into Lithuanian. For instance, on December 31, 1920, the first performance staged in Lithuanian was *La traviata* by G. Verdi. The libretto of the opera was translated into Lithuanian by writers/poets B. Sruoga and F. Kirša.

3.5 The language of education and knowledge

Education was also considered as one of the strategic priorities in the development of state and nation-building. Vilnius University, established by Jesuit order in Vilnius in 1579, was closed by the order of Tsar Nikolaj after the rebellion in 1831, until 1919. However, when Vilnius was occupied by Poland (1919-1939), it became a Polish university. Since the most important institutions in the occupied capital were moved to Kaunas, the leaders of the state understood the need to educate the population. On February 16, 1919, the Lithuanian University was established in Kaunas as the first modern university in Lithuania. All the information was presented in the state language; however, the Statute of the University of Lithuania was published in 1923 in Lithuanian with a translation in English. Though the language of diplomacy in those days was French, the most important documents were translated into English, given the fact that large parts of the Lithuanian diaspora resided in the United States. Representatives of local minorities could study at the University of Lithuania, but they had to pass an entrance exam of Lithuanian and submit all their documents with translations into Lithuanian. According to the Statute, all dissertations had to be written in the state language, except for those in the fields of Humanities and Theology, where Latin was allowed.

3.6 Publishing and printing of newspapers and magazines

Between the wars, when Kaunas was the capital (1919–1939), all the intelligentsia resided in Kaunas and the major and most important publishing houses, at that time called printing houses, operated in Kaunas. New ones, such as *Kaunas printing house, Raidė, Spindulys* and *Varpas*, were established in the 1930s and 1940s. They published books and periodicals, translations of fiction books and religious literature. Some of them have been active, albeit under different names, to this day.

There were over 2000 different newspapers and periodicals in the period of independent Lithuania (Urbonas 2012). The majority of them was published in Kaunas. The first issue of the official gazette of Lithuania *Lietuvos Aidas* was published in 1917. In 1918, the gazette printed the Act of Independence of Lithuania. This official newspaper published fiction, poetry, translations and reviews of famous Lithuanian poets and writers of the time, along with official information on the actions of the government, parties and state institutions (Urbonas 2012). During the interwar period, there were a few newspapers in other languages, namely Polish, Russian, German and Yiddish, for instance *Glos Kowienski*, *Naše echo* and *Litauische Rundschau* (Urbonas 2012). A number of newspapers in Lithuanian were related to different parties. Even the Communist Party, which worked illegally until 1940, had its own newspapers. Many different newspapers were published in occupied Vilnius. However, none of them survived longer than three or four years. Since Lithuanian periodicals were persecuted by Polish occupation authorities, the names of the newspapers were often changed and published as one-off publications (Urbonas 2012).

Members of the Lithuanian diaspora in the United States were also very active in publishing. Some newspapers were published before the twentieth century, for example *Vienybė Lietuvininkų*, which is known to be the oldest Lithuanian newspaper in the United States. More newspapers appeared at the beginning of the twentieth century and later throughout the interwar period: *Darbininkas* in Brooklyn, *Draugas* in Pennsylvania, *Laisvė* in Boston, *Tiesa* in New York, *Sandara* and *Vilnis* both in Chicago, and a number of other daily, weekly and monthly newspapers and journals (Balys 1976). Newspapers and magazines greatly contributed to establishing and maintaining the Lithuanian language as the official language of the country throughout the first independence period.

3.7 Literary translators and translation

There is little research on literary translations during the first independence period. However, foundations for the quality of translation practices were already laid during that period. Since there was a lack of good translators and translations, linguists and activists, concerned with language and its proper use, paid attention to the quality of translations, mainly through articles in newspapers, where the language of translations was analyzed and suggestions for better translations were provided (Malažinskaitė 2015). The contribution of linguist Jonas Jablonskis, who translated and edited texts and taught his students how to translate properly, was of utmost importance. Another key figure in the translation practice and discourse of the time was Sofija Kymantaitė-Čiurlionienė (1886–1958), who was a teacher, writer, poet, critic, and translator as well as an active member of a women's movement and the only woman with the right to vote in the League of Nations. With the aim to analyze translations, she organized meetings of famous linguists, poets and translators at her house, which were known as 'Čiurlionienė's Saturdays'. Many times, she read her translations or asked young writers to read their writings or translations. In 1933, the newspaper *Gimtoji kalba* published Sofija Kymantaitė-Čiurlionienė's well-known treatise on translations, which laid the foundations for translation work in Lithuania. Čiurlionienė's Saturdays took place between 1926 and 1940 and may be considered as the most significant translation school in the history of Lithuanian culture (Malažinskaitė 2015). Another woman who played an important role in the promotion of the Lithuanian language and culture was Konstancija Sketerytė-Jablonskienė (1868–1948), the wife of linguist Jonas Jablonskis. She was active in writing for newspapers, editing her husband's books, and translating from Russian and Finnish, often under pseudonyms.

Persons of the highest rank were always very much concerned with the status of Lithuanian and contributed to building the modern state as well as its language policy, through translations as well. Many Lithuanian linguists, translators, publishers and editors of the time were activists whose work contributed significantly to the declaration of independence of Lithuania and some of them became members of the government and officials in different state institutions. During the independence period (1918–1940), there were 21 governments and there was at least one minister who was also a practicing translator alongside other fields of expertise. For example, the head of the first government and Prime Minister Augustinas Voldemaras, the first President of Lithuania Antanas Smetona, the Minister of Education of the 4th and the 5th government Juozas Tūbelis, the second President Aleksandras Stulginskis, and the third President Kazys Grinius cooperated in different journals, published and edited many of them and translated classical works, fiction or popular science from different languages (Eidintas 1990, 1993, 1995).

4. The period of annexed Lithuania: from 1940 to 1991

The geopolitical context and the start of WWII triggered new changes in the life cycle of the State of Lithuania. The successful economic, political, cultural and social development of a newly formed state was disrupted by the war, followed by the annexation and occupation of the Republic of Lithuania by the Soviet Union. During the war period from 1941 until 1945, the country was governed by Germany. In 1945, Lithuania became a part of the Soviet Socialist Republics until March 11, 1991, when the re-establishment of independence of the State of Lithuania was declared by the Supreme Council of Lithuania.

The upheaval had serious implications on the functioning of the state since the Republic of Lithuania ceased to exist as an independent state. All state-governing institutions were abolished. Many formal leaders, teachers, scholars, priests, lawyers, military representatives, businessmen and other people were either killed, imprisoned, persecuted by the KGB or deported from Lithuania due to their religious beliefs or resistance to communist propaganda and ideology, died in Siberia or had to flee the country. Due to the ban of the freedom of speech and religion, persecutions, genocide and alienation of property, thousands of Lithuanians emigrated to the United States, Germany, Argentina, Australia and other countries. People were deprived of their property and were pushed to join collective farms or work in industry to rebuild the Soviet countries after the victory of WWII.

Many people retreated to forests and became forest brothers and sisters who organized a partisan movement to fight against the Soviets and re-establish the independence of Lithuania. To support Lithuanian partisans in forests, the clergymen formed an underground movement where they illegally and secretly published the propaganda-free journal *Lietuvos Katalikų Bažnyčios Kronikos* that was shipped to Lithuanian communities abroad. This period can be described as the dark period of terror, persecution, exile, Soviet propaganda and severe censorship. The fall of the Iron Curtain stopped the economic, cultural and social development of the modern state of Lithuania until the period of the second independence in 1991. The situation improved only after Stalin's death and the period of the government of the Communist party leaders Nikita Chruschev and Leonid Brezhnev.

The introduction of *perestroika* reforms (1984–1990) in the domestic policy of the Soviet Union during the period when Mikhail Gorbachev was the head of the Communist party and the president of the Soviet Union led to the decentralization of the management of all the Soviet Union Republics and induced democratization and the revival of national feelings. During that period, active leaders of the Communist Party in Lithuania started the discussion about gaining the independence of the Lithuanian Communist party from the central government, which in turn led to more freedom in the management of Lithuania as a country. In this context, *Lietuvos Persitvarkymo Sąjūdis/the Reform Movement of Lithuania* appeared and its activists started raising the issue of independent Lithuania, as based on the Independence Act, signed on February 16, 1918. In 1989, members of the movement declared that Lithuania was annexed by the Soviet Union by force and required both the Soviet Union and other countries to acknowledge this.

4.1 Language policy

The geopolitical situation during and after WWII resulted in the introduction of a new and different language policy in annexed Lithuania. The Lithuanian language, which was firmly institutionalized as the state language from 1918 to 1939, was downgraded during the Soviet times and Russian became the language of administration and politics in the entire Soviet Union. The process of Russification started with the aim to erase all the historic memory of the first independence and the use of Lithuanian. The only reason why these processes of Russification in comparison with other annexed Baltic countries, Estonia and Latvia, were not so significant is the fact that the majority of Lithuanian citizens, or around 90 percent of the population, were Lithuanians, whereas the population of native language speakers in Estonia and Latvia was smaller. It was impossible to ban the usage of Lithuanian and the leaders of the Soviet Union were afraid to make such a decision. At the same time, the purposeful use of Lithuanian in various official and non-official settings became associated with the feeling of national identity and pride, as well as a weapon in the silent fight against the Russification and occupation.

Translations were widely used and everyone had to learn Russian. In nursery and secondary schools the learning and teaching of Russian was compulsory. The constitution of the Lithuanian Soviet Socialist Republic adopted in 1978, approved as the main law, stated that all citizens had equal rights in terms of their race, education, language and religion. This constitution, however, legitimized bilingualism since all citizens of Lithuania had the right to use either Lithuanian or any other language of Socialist Republics (Articles 34 and 43). At the same time, Article 103 strictly regulated the use of both Lithuanian and Russian in all the main institutions of the state directing that all laws, decisions or acts of the Supreme Council of the Lithuanian Soviet Socialist Republic and other announcements of the Chairman and Secretary had to be announced in both languages. This was done both due to censorship and the centralized government from Moscow.

4.2 Translation policy

The Constitution of the Lithuanian Soviet Socialist Republic (the main law, 1978) paved the way for translation. Although the role of translation and translators was not directly regulated and stated by the main law, translation had to be used in order to provide reports in Russian to central officials of the Soviet Union who needed to understand the local context by making sure that there was no anti-Soviet and anti-communist propaganda hidden in the channels of communication. The role of translators was only specifically mentioned in the article related to the functioning of courts. Article 156 determined that all proceedings in courts had to be carried out in Lithuanian or the language spoken by the majority of that location. If participants did not speak the language used in the proceeding, the right to get acquainted with the documentation was granted by means of using translators and interpreters.

The regime obviously affected translation directions. During the period of annexation, Russian became the dominant language for translation. This was mostly related to the development of various state-regulating documents that were based on documents of the central government in Moscow. However, the analysis of translated documents during the period of annexation indicates that various Soviet and communist propaganda-related documents, the aim of which was to educate the population in a communism- and socialism-based spirit, were also translated from German, English, French and even Latin.

4.3 Translation in districts and courts

A new administrative subdivision was introduced in the annexed Lithuania. All municipalities and local governments were replaced by district governments where Lithuanian was used. Although Russian became the language of administration, Lithuanian was the language of communication in many state management institutions, except for the KGB and military or other communist party related bodies. Military officials and soldiers used Russian as the main language of communication. However, all documents and reports that had to be delivered to the central government in Moscow had to be translated into Russian. Other languages such as English and German were also studied and learned as the languages of potential enemies, for spying reasons and because of the political persecutions of dissidents, forest brothers (partisans) and followers of resistance against the Soviet Union. On the other hand, Lithuanian was still used in media, educational settings, cultural events, publishing and printing, but severe censorship was applied to check if there were no blasphemies against the Communist party or Soviet leaders. Courts functioned in Lithuanian with translation into Russian if needed, yet cases of political prisoners and convicts were written and translated into Russian.

4.4 Translation at the theater

During the period of annexation, the theater played an important role and became a place of resistance against Soviet ideology and communism. During the period of the independent Republic of Lithuania, many performances and librettos were translated into Lithuanian. However, in annexed Lithuania, many art directors wisely staged performances and plays with metaphorically hidden Soviet-ideology criticism and used translations of scenarios to twist and manipulate the meaning and the message they aimed to deliver to the audience. However, many such performances were banned and art directors had to leave Lithuania due to their persecution. For example, a well-known art director Jonas Jurašas had to emigrate from Lithuania because his performance *Barbora* used religious symbolism of the virgin Mary and thus was shown only once. Only those art directors and creators who conceded to Soviet ideology received awards and were acknowledged.

Interviews with current representatives and heads of the National Kaunas Drama Theater disclosed the fact that a translation booth was fixed at the theater during Soviet times with the sole intention to censor the work of art directors and actors. Soviet functionaries understood the power of art and culture in the education of society and attempted to use theater and literature for the development of a true 'Soviet person'.

4.5 The language of education and knowledge

The constitution of annexed Lithuania regulated language use in educational establishments in Lithuania. Although Lithuanian or the language of ethnic minorities had to be used as the main language of instruction within the entire education system, the learning and teaching of Russian was imposed and required. Children from the age of 3 were supposed to study Russian in nurseries. In all state-controlled secondary schools, Russian was taught alongside Lithuanian. In addition to this, communism-based education was strongly imposed in schools. Every child had to become Lenin's grandchild, a pioneer and a young communist follower. The oath to Lenin and the Soviet Union had to be sworn in Russian. Military development and special classrooms in schools were compulsory with the aim to get ready for the nuclear war with the main enemy, the USA. Without such education, secondary school graduates could not get access to universities, institutes or other establishments of higher education.[11]

---

11   Since two of the authors of this chapter grew up in the regime, their personal memories serve as testimony of the situation and the context described above.

During the WWII period, many educational institutions, established in the times of independent Lithuania, were closed and their performance was disrupted. After WWII, Vilnius University was re-opened as a state-controlled university, but the University of Lithuania in Kaunas was destroyed. The faculties of Medicine, Agriculture and Engineering served as the background for the establishment of Kaunas Polytechnic Institute, the Academy of Lithuanian Agriculture and Kaunas Medicine Institute (at the moment all the institutions operate as state universities in Lithuania). The language policy implied that the study curricula of establishments of higher education also had to include the study of Russian, the theories of Marxism and Leninism, and Political Economy. In addition to this, military departments were established in all institutions of higher education. Translation was not directly used since the majority of professors and students were fluent in Russian. However, the most important documentation, student and professor files, as well as reports had to be presented in Russian. At the same time, authorities of higher educational establishments in Lithuania understood the aim of Soviet functionaries to erase all features of Lithuanianism and tried to avoid and bypass certain requirements of the regime by refusing to include the studies of Marxism and Leninism or Russian in the study curriculum. Soviet ideology and Russification were very much rejected in higher education. Therefore, the occupants tried to eliminate and suppress national awareness and the Lithuanian identity by destroying higher education and exiling and firing professors, students and administration of universities, institutes and colleges, or incriminating them with anti-Soviet action. Professors and students from the faculties of philosophy, philology, history, and, in general, the humanities (the academics who were the first to raise the self-consciousness of the nation) were immediate targets. They were followed, charged with fabricated crimes, fired, punished or even arrested. Later, in the 1960s, the institutes that sought to survive had to teach students only in Russian (Nakas 2008). However, many university and secondary school students refused to attend classes of Russian in protest against the Russification policy: they ignored classes of Marxism, Leninism and political history since these were taught in Russian and by teachers from Russia, tore down posters that were in Russian, got involved in underground activities and created various secret revolutionary organizations (Nakas 2008).

Before WWII, many great minds and the intelligentsia of the independent Lithuania were educated in western countries, where they obtained their higher education at universities like Sorbonne (France), Halle and Leipzig (Germany) and Vienna (Austria). Yet, during the Soviet period, possibilities to study abroad were ruled out. The only way to get a higher education was at the universities of Lithuania or the Soviet Union. Doctoral dissertations had to be defended not only in Lithuania, but also in Moscow or Leningrad. Russian gradually became the language of science. This was also reinforced by the fact that there was a huge scarcity of books in other languages. Only dissidents managed to illegally procure books published in the United States or Western Europe (Zulumskytė 2014).

4.6 Publishing, printing and distribution of books and the role of diaspora

During and after WWII, approximately 60 to 70 thousand (out of almost 3 million[12]) Lithuanian people fled the country to Germany, the United States, Australia and other countries. Activists, including writers, poets, publishers and translators, formed Lithuanian communities abroad. The Lithuanian World Community, now active in more than 40 countries, was established in 1958 along with other Lithuanian communities, which were concerned with the preservation and protection of Lithuanian traditions, culture and language. The ways of doing that were numerous: many books were published, including the famous multi-volume Lithuanian encyclopedia published in Boston; the Department of Lithuanian was established at the Illinois University, Chicago; the radio station *America's Voice* has been broadcasted since 1951 in Lithuanian as well as other radio stations such as *Laisvoji Europa* (Free Europe) and *Laisvė* (Freedom) (Kmita 2009).

Many Lithuanian writers, philosophers and linguists, for example Marija Gimbutienė, Algirdas Julius Greimas and others studied and worked at European universities, created poetry and literature, published newspapers and journals (Paplauskienė 2011). American Lithuanians managed to secretly bring the journals to occupied Lithuania and, thus, keep the hope of freedom. Many famous and significant works of literature and poetry were written and published in the US and made available in Lithuania after 1991. Translation was practiced by poets and writers in diaspora. Some former officials at the Lithuanian Foreign Affairs Ministry and embassies abroad became translators after they moved to the West during WWII and ultimately to the US.

Many famous Lithuanian writers, poets, publishers and translators were exiled to Siberia after the war, where supposedly many of their works disappeared and have never been published, such as those of poet, editor and translator Jonas

---

12 According to the data of the census, there were 2 950 000 people in the Lithuanian Soviet Republic in 1940 (Stanaitis and Adlys 1973).

Graičiūnas and writer, editor and translator Juozas Keliuotis. Some translators fought for independence as partisans, for example Bronius Krivickas, who stayed in the forest for more than five years, managed to write poetry himself and also translated Goethe's poetry (more than 80 poems) (Gasiliūnas 2007).

New state-regulated publishing houses were established in Lithuania right after its occupation in 1940, such as the State Publishing House of Soviet Lithuania, which mainly published books of Soviet authors. One of the first publications was Stalin's Constitution of Soviet Lithuania (Prunskis 1957). At the beginning of the 1970s, the Press Committee was established, which controlled and regulated the entire book production, printing and market.

4.7 Literary translators and translation

In literature, poetry, cinema, theater and other forms of art, there was an intensive censorship. Writers were forced to depict the communist future and to devote their works to exaltation of Soviet principles and standards. Especially cinema was seen as an instrument to propagate Soviet ideology. Before Stalin's death in 1953, the majority of translations were done from Russian. Yet, severe censorship was applied to make sure that there was nothing against Soviets and communism. Books that were translated from English had forewords and explanations, indicating that the protagonists were in support of communism and socialism. Russian as the pivotal language was often the only possibility to translate masterpieces of European and American writers.

Many Russian books were translated by those Lithuanian writers and poets who could not publish themselves because of their anti-communist ideas. After 1953, there was a decline in translations from Russian, along with an increase in publications of Lithuanian authors, mostly those whose works could be explained within Soviet ideology (Grinius 1959). Famous Lithuanian authors such as Vydūnas, Jurgis Baltrušaitis, Maironis, Vincas Krėvė and Vincas Kudirka were ignored and not published at all or only those works that did not compromise the Soviet ideology were published. In the 1950s and 1960s, Lithuanian authors in diaspora were not even mentioned and never published, which shows how strict the Soviet censorship was.

4.8 The role of the church in language policy and translation

When Lithuania was annexed in 1945, the human right of practicing certain religions was banned. The church as an institution could not function, and although the constitution of 1978 declared the freedom of religion, many churches in Lithuania were turned into storage houses, sports halls, galleries or manufacturing sites. The highest church authorities, priests, monks and nuns were exiled to Siberia, persecuted by the KGB or imprisoned. However, churches in remote areas and regions functioned, where people secretly took part in services and ceremonies. The church became an agent of resistance against the Soviet regime, government and ideology and at the same time the institution that fought for Lithuanian independence, aimed to maintain the Lithuanian identity and language and supported partisan movement. One of the representatives of the Church's deeds was the secret publication and translation of the periodical *Lietuvos Katalikų Bažnyčios Kronikos*. The journal was published underground and distributed via churches to Lithuanians in Lithuania and Lithuanian societies abroad that could translate and transmit the message behind the Iron Curtain. The journal was published in Lithuanian and described crimes and terror of the Soviet regime. The diaspora could become acquainted with the real context in Lithuania and at the same time financially support the publication of the journal. Moreover, the news in the periodical was secretly sent to Vatican City, which has never acknowledged the annexation of Lithuania, and the Lithuanian consulate functioned there until the independence of Lithuania was restored for the second time in 1991. Many religious books were translated from other languages such as Polish, Italian and English, published in other European countries and brought to Lithuania.

4.9 Channels of mass media

In annexed Lithuania, officially published magazines, journals and news via other channels of communication were examined due to censorship. All channels of communication had to show the benefits of the Soviet regime and communism against wild capitalism. The language of various channels of communication was Lithuanian. For example, TV and radio shows were broadcasted in Lithuanian; yet, the most important news was followed by the Russian news show *Vremia (Time)*. The news was broadcasted in Russian with no translation into Lithuanian. Foreign movies and shows from the US and Western Europe were banned. Performances and films that were staged in Moscow or other film studios were shown in the entire Soviet Union. The Russian language dominated in all productions with subtitles into Lithuanian. Only cartoons for children were dubbed.

5. The role of different associations and committees throughout the century

During the first independence period and the Soviet occupation, many institutions played a crucial role in establishing the language policy and consequently translation practices, helping to build the national identity and the modern state. Some of those institutions were illegal in different periods; some had to change their names in order to function, or had to work underground. A few associations and societies were created already at the end of the nineteenth century, such as the society *Sietynas*, which existed from 1892 until 1927. The society supported book smugglers who brought books that were translated and published outside Lithuania and distributed newspapers in Lithuanian when Latin orthography was banned (Merkys 1975). The *Lithuanian Scientific Society*, now considered to be the predecessor of the *Lithuanian Research Council*, worked between 1907 and 1940. Many famous writers, linguists and translators who also contributed to the establishment of Lithuanian independence and building of the modern state were members of this society. The main objectives of this society were the study and the popularization of the Lithuanian language (Jurginis 1975). The Lithuanian Education Society *Rytas* (1913–1940) considerably contributed to Lithuanian language education, its popularization and spread.

One of the associations that played a major role in Lithuanian language and identity preservation and strengthening is the *Lithuanian Language Society*, which was established in 1935. In different periods, the *Society* existed in Lithuania (1935–1940), Germany (1946–1949), the United States (1950–1968), and in Lithuania again (1989 up to present) (Sabaliauskas 2008). Between 1967 and 1989, the *Society* could not function under its original name in Lithuania because Soviet authorities did not allow the re-establishment of the *Society*. Pupkis (2010) claims that the practices and activities of the *Society* established during the first independence could not be ignored and undervalued even during the Soviet period. The *Society* had a number of sections, including those of the language of press, language of schools, as well as a committee on theater language (Pupkis 2010). The section of the language of translations decided on important language issues to be used in translations published in Lithuanian and, thus, played a regulating role in translation practices. Many famous linguists, pedagogues and translators were members of the *Society*. They created the first language standardization theory and many other theoretical and practical language standardization documents, like Lithuanization principles on writing and translating names, surnames and place names (ibid.). Since many members of the *Society* fled

Lithuania to other European countries and the United States during the war and afterwards, they understood the threats to the Lithuanian language abroad and re-established the work of the *Society*, first in Germany and later in the United States (Pečkus 1994), where the journal *Gimtoji kalba* was again published. In 1989, the activities of the *Society* were renewed in Vilnius. The *Lithuanian Language Society* significantly contributed to Lithuanian language standardization, language policy-making and, consequently, translation practices and policy for over 80 years. Its contributions and significance are only partially uncovered and researched.

6. Final implications and conclusions

This chapter is one of the first studies attempting to give an overview of language policy and translation practices in Lithuania over the past 100 years, thus contributing to the field of translation studies in terms of raising awareness on the mutual impact of translation and language policies on the building and development of a small state, fighting for its status and language preservation. Although a lot of microdata is still to be examined, the collected evidence allows us to outline the historical context and to highlight the roots and the sources of the language policy as well as the role of translation in building and preserving the national Lithuanian identity throughout almost the entire nineteenth century. The main contributors and agents of Lithuanization, the current Lithuanian language status in terms of language policy and consequently to Lithuanian independence were many: writers, poets, translators, publishers, editors, teachers, scholars, the clergy, the diaspora as well as various committees and associations, both formal and informal, legal and illegal, within and outside the country.

Yet, certain issues still remain unanswered. In Jeremy Munday's (2014) words, details may help to uncover many important specific interactions between individuals and institutions. For this reason, focusing on microhistories is one of the ways to give deserved credit to those people and events without which current Lithuanian identity, self-perception of the nation and the statehood would not have been possible. Analysis of extra-textual material, including that obtained through interviews with contributors that are still alive, or manuscripts, working papers and paratexts would be of utmost value in determining the crucial agents who helped to build Lithuania as a free nation.

One of the limitations of this study is the insufficient availability and accessibility of archives. Fortunately, there is a huge amount of archives that have been digitized and are available to the academic community and the public. Yet, much of the archival material, including manuscripts and printed documents, is stored in many different places across the world or were either destroyed, or taken away from Lithuania when the Soviet army left Lithuania and returned the occupied TV tower in 1991. Although Lithuanian researchers have often acknowledged the importance of accessibility of archives and devoted great efforts to making them available to the public, they have also realized that only a small part of the existing archives, especially those that have been collected and stored abroad, are effectively used in research (Lankutis 2006). Moreover, valuable material within the country may remain inaccessible because it was stored in personal archives which were lost over time (ibid.). Therefore, it is extremely hard to see the full picture, to understand the links between different people and events, and to process contradicting data, especially data relating to the Soviet period, which was marked by propaganda and censorship.

The time span chosen for the purposes of this study – 100 years – allows us to overview and acknowledge the most crucial and essential events and actors whose contributions to Lithuanian language preservation and policymaking may not be appreciated in a study of such a short length. Therefore, further research and joint efforts, taking into consideration not only freely available data but also private personal archives and those scattered around the world, are needed.

Sources

Algų nustatymo centralinių ir vietos įstaigų valdininkams įstatymas. *Vyriausybės žinios*, 1920-05-11, no. 30-344.
Civilinės teisenos įstatymas. Ministerių kabinetas, 1938-01-01.
Laikinasis Lietuvos Teismų ir jų Darbo Sutvarkymas, Laikinosios Vyriausybės žinios, 1919-01-16, no. 2.
Lietuvos Valstybės Laikinosios Konstitucijos Pamatiniai Dėsniai (Valstybės tarybos priimta 1918 m. lapkričio mėn. 2 d.). *Lietuvos aidas*, 1918-11-13, 130(178).
Lietuvos Valstybės Laikinosios Konstitucijos Pamatiniai Dėsniai. Lietuvos valstybės tarybos priimti 1919 m. balandžio mėn. 4 d. *Priedėlis prie Laikinosios Vyriausybės žinių Nr. 6/24a*.
Laikinoji Lietuvos Valstybės Konstitucija. *Laikinosios Vyriausybės žinios*, 1920-06-12, no. 37-407.
1918 vasario 16 d. Lietuvos Valstybės nepriklausomybės aktas. *Lietuvos aidas*, 1918-02-19, 22 (70).

Lietuvos Valstybės Konstitucija. *Vyriausybės žinios*, 1922-08-06, no. 100-799. http://www3.lrs.lt/pls/inter_archyvas/dokpaieska_arch.showdoc_l?p_id=112956&p_tr2=2

Lietuvos Valstybės Konstitucija. *Vyriausybės žinios*, 1928-05-25, no. 275-1788. http://www3.lrs.lt/pls/inter_archyvas/dokpaieska_arch.showdoc_l?p_id=113394&p_tr2=2.

Lietuvos Valstybės Konstitucija. *Vyriausybės žinios*, 1938-05-12, no, 608-4271. http://www3.lrs.lt/pls/inter_archyvas/dokpaieska_arch.showdoc_l?p_id=113395&p_tr2=2

Lietuvos Tarybų Socialistinės Respublikos Konstitucija (Pagrindinis Įstatymas). *Vyriausybės žinios*, 1978-01-01, no. 11-130. https://e-seimas.lrs.lt/portal/legalAct/lt/TAD/00ca15b024e611e58a4198cd62929b7a?jfwid=1bc6m4z0e3

Prekybos, pramonės, kredito ir amato pelno mokesčio įstatymas, *Vyriausybės žinios*, 1924-08-20, no. 168-1180.

Prekybos, pramonės ir kredito įstaigų sąskaitybos knygų įstatymas. *Vyriausybės žinios*, 1924-09-10, no. 171-1190.

Teismų santvarkos įstatymas. *Vyriausybės žinios*, 1933-07-11, no. 419-2900

Vietos savivaldybės įstatymas. *Vyriausybės žinios*, 1931-05-02, no. 356-2419

Vidurinių ir aukštesnių mokyklų įstatymas. *Vyriausybės žinios*, 1925-04-23, no. 190-1289.

References

Balys, Jonas. 1976. "The American Lithuanian Press." *Lituanus – Lithuanian Quarterly Journal of Arts and Sciences* 22, no. 1 (Spring). http://www.lituanus.org/1976/76_1_02.htm.

D'hulst, Lieven. 2012. "(Re)Locating Translation History: From Assumed Translation to Assumed Transfer." *Translation Studies* 5 (2): 139-155.

—, Carol O'Sullivan, and Michael Scheiber. 2016. "Translation Policies: What's in a Name." In *Politics, Policy and Power in Translation History*, edited by Lieven D'hulst, Carol O'Sullivan, and Michael Scheiber, 7–13. Berlin: Frank & Timme.

—, and Yves Gambier, eds. 2018. *A History of Modern Translation Knowledge: Sources, Concepts, Effects*. Amsterdam: Benjamins.

Du, An. 2017. "Translating in Linguistically Diverse Societies: Translation Policy in the United Kingdom." Review of González Núñez 2016. *Language and Intercultural Communication* 18 (3): 351-353.

Eidintas, Alfonsas. 1990. *Antanas Smetona*. Vilnius: Mintis.

— 1993. *Kazys Grinius: ministras-pirmininkas ir prezidentas*. Vilnius: Mintis.

— 1995. *Aleksandras Stulginskis: Lietuvos Prezidentas – Gulago kalinys*. Vilnius: Mintis.

Eidintas, Alfonsas. 2005. *Lithuanian Emigration to the United States, 1868–1950*. Vilnius: Mokslo ir enciklopedijų leidybos institutas.

González Núñez, Gabriel, and Meylaerts, Reine, eds. 2017. *Translation and Public Policy: Interdisciplinary Perspectives and Case Studies*. New York: Routledge.

Grinius, Jonas. 1959. "Literatūra ir menas okupuotoje Lietuvoje po Stalino mirties." *Aidai*, 2 (117). http://www.aidai.eu/index.php?option=com_content&view=article&id=6599:po&catid=397:195902&Itemid=450

Hamilton, Diane, B. 1993. "The Idea of History and the History of Ideas." *The Journal of Nursing Scholarship* 25 (1): 45–48. https://doi.org/10.1111/j.1547-5069.1993.tb00752.x

Jurginis, Juozas. 1975. "Lietuvių mokslo draugija." In *Mokslo, kultūros ir švietimo draugijos*, edited by V. Merkys, 37–118. Vilnius: Mokslas.

Kmita, Rimantas. 2009. *Ištrūkimas iš fabriko. Modernėjanti lietuvių poezija XX a. 7–9 dešimtmečiais*. Vilnius: Lietuvių literatūros ir tautosakos institutas.

Leedy, Paul, D., and Ormrod, Jeanne, E. 2005. *Practical Research: Planning and Design*. Upper Saddle River, N.J.: Prentice Hall.

Machovenko, Jevgenij. 2017. "1918 m. lapkričio 2 d. ir 1919 m. balandžio 4 d. Lietuvos konstituciniai aktai – dvi atskiros konstitucijos ar dvi to paties konstitucinio akto redakcijos? (The Lithuanian Constitutional Acts of November 2, 1918 and of April 4, 1919 – two separate constitutions or two versions of the same act?)." *Teisė*, no 104: 37–51. http://www.zurnalai.vu.lt/teise/article/view/10844.

Malažinskaitė, Erika. 2015. "Grožinės literatūros vertimas tarpukario Lietuvoje: nuo lietuvinimo tendencijos iki ekvivalentiškumo paieškų (Literary Translation in Interwar Lithuania: From the Tendency to Lithuannianize to the Quest for Equivalence)." *Colloquia*, no. 35: 71–88.

McDowell, Bill. 2002. *Historical Research: A Guide*. London: Longman.

Merkys, Vytautas. 1975. "Sietyno" draugija ir jos byla." In *Mokslo, kultūros ir švietimo draugijos*. 9–36. Vilnius: Mokslas.

Meylaerts, Reine. 2011. "Translation Policy." In *Handbook for Translation Studies*. Volume 2, edited by Yves Gambier and Luc van Doorslaer, 163–168. Amsterdam: John Benjamins. https://doi.org/10.1075/hts.2.tra10.

Monticelli, Daniele, and Anne Lange. 2014. "Translation and Totalitarianism: The Case of Soviet Estonia." *The Translator* 20 (1): 95–111. https://doi.org/0.1080/13556509.2014.899096.

Munday, Jeremy. 2014. "Using Primary Sources to Produce a Microhistory of Translation and Translators: Theoretical and Methodological Concerns." *The Translator* 20 (1): 64–80. https://doi.org/10.1080/13556509.2014.899094.

Nakas, Algimantas. 2008. *Vardan Lietuvos: Pasipriešinimas okupacijoms aukštosiose mokyklose 1940-1991 metais*. Vilnius: Technika.

Paplauskienė, Virginija. 2011. *Liūnė Sutema: gyvenimo ir kūrybos keliais*. Monografija. Vilnius: Vilniaus universitetas.

Pečkus, Kęstutis. 1994. "Lietuvių kalbos draugija tremtyje." *Kultūros barai* 11: 73–74.
Pupkis, Aldonas. 2010. *Lietuvių kalbos normintojai ir puoselėtojai*. Vilnius: Mokslo ir enciklopedijų leidybos centras.
Prunskis, Juozas. 1957. "Amerikiniai lietuvių laikraščiai." In *Kovos metai dėl savosios spaudos*, edited by Vytautas Bagdanavičius, Petras Jonikas, and Juozas Švaistas Balčiūnas, 297–314. Čikaga: Draugas.
Sabaliauskas, Algirdas. 2008. "Lietuvių kalbos draugija." In *Visuotinė lietuvių enciklopedija*. https://www.vle.lt/Straipsnis/Lietuviu-kalbos-draugija-15356
Snyder, Thimothy. 2003. *The Reconstruction of Nations: Poland, Ukraine, Lithuania, Belorus, 1569-1999*. Yale: Yale University Press.
Stanaitis, Algirdas, and Petras Adlys. 1973. *Lietuvos TSR gyventojai*. Vilnius: Mintis.
Urbonas, Vytautas. 2012. "Lietuvių periodinė spauda: Raidos istorija ir dabartis." (Lithuanian Periodical Press: The History of its Development and the Present) *Gimtasai Kraštas* 5: 42–61. http://www.ziemgala.lt/saugykla/pdf/7-urbonas.pdf
Vaišnienė, Daiva, and Zabarskaitė, Jolanta. 2012. "The Lithuanian Language in the Digital Age // Lietuvių kalba skaitmeniniame amžiuje." In *META-NET White Paper Series*, edited by Georg Rehm and Hans Uszkoreit. Springer.
Veisbergs, Andrejs. 2009. "Translation Language: The Major Force in Shaping Modern Latvian." *Vertimo Studijos* 2: 54–70. Vilnius: Universito Leidykla.
— 2016. "Translation during the German Occupation in Latvia. *Translation und "Drittes Reich"*, edited by Dörte Andress and Larisa Schippel, 237–256. Berlin: Frank & Timme.
— 2018. "The Translation Scene in Latvia (Latvian SSR) during the Stalinist Years." *Vertimo studijos* 11: 76–99. Vilnius: Vilniaus universito leidykla.
Zulumskytė, Aušrinė. 2014. "Aukštųjų mokyklų sistema Lietuvoje 1940–1990 metais: raidos bruožai." *Tiltai* 1: 105–120. Klaipėda: Klaipėdos universitetas.

Transfer troubles

Andrew Chesterman

Abstract
This chapter offers a critique of the view that translation can usefully be seen as a kind of transfer. The transfer metaphor is very old (in the West); indeed, Latin "translatio" exactly matches Greek "metafora." But it has serious disadvantages, costs as well as benefits. All metaphors are in fact metonymic: they select some part of their object to be highlighted but hide other parts. Seeing translation as transfer highlights some notion of equivalence, something that is carried across, something that remains somehow intact. But by highlighting movement across a border, this view hides the fact that a translation itself does not actually move (*pace* Pym), but is a new text derived from an original under certain constraints. The original (or source) usually remains in place, and a new text is created, for a new group of receivers, that is in some relevant respect similar to it. This view sees translation as an additive or duplicative activity, not one of transfer. To highlight this aspect, other metaphors are needed, such as might be borrowed from genetics: genes duplicate, with mutations; so do memes (Dawkins etc.). It is ideas that can move, carried by new texts in new languages. Translation can thus be profitably viewed as a memetic activity, in contrast to a transfer one. On this view, the notion of divergent similarity becomes central, as do relevance constraints. The view offers a realistic way of conceptualizing equivalence, has different consequences from the transfer view, and raises different kinds of research questions.

Metaphors of translation abound. It may be that the more metaphors we can make use of, the broader our perspective. But we need to be explicit about what our metaphors highlight, and what they hide. Furthermore, translation itself is increasingly used metaphorically, e.g. in postmodern "post-translation studies" (Gentzler et al.), but these metaphorical approaches seem to underestimate the metonymic nature of metaphor, and the costs of using any one metaphor exclusively. How might Bohr's complementarity principle, whereby we need e.g. to see light as both particles and waves, be applied in translation research?

1. Translatio = μεταφορά

In much of the Western tradition, the understanding of translation is grounded in the transfer metaphor. Indeed, translation is predominantly conceptualized *as* a metaphor: Latin *trans-latio* exactly matches Greek *meta-fora*, with the sense of *carrying* something *across*: a message, a meaning ... Trans-lating is trans-ferring (from Latin *ferre* 'to carry', past participle *latum*). However, theoretical developments have modified this equation in some respects. For one thing, the contemporary consensus seems to be that translation is best seen as a *type* of transfer: transfer is thus given a wider sense than translation.

One scholar making this point is Itamar Even-Zohar (1990), who embeds (literary) translation theory within a more general polysystemic theory of cultural transfer. He describes polysystems, and the transfer processes which influence them, as being dynamic. And this dynamism involves change: transfer implies transformation (see e.g., Even-Zohar 1990, 20). In his 1990 publication, Even-Zohar does not offer an explicit definition of the term 'transfer'. But he does in a later paper (1997). Here, the context is the construction of a 'culture repertoire', which comes about (he argues) either via invention or importation. When imported cultural goods become integrated in the importing culture, we get transfer.

> I would like to call the state of integrated importation in a home repertoire 'transfer'. Transfer, in short, is the process whereby imported goods are integrated into a home repertoire, and the consequences generated by this integration. (Even-Zohar 1997, 358-359)

This definition is not without its problems. Transfer appears to be seen both as a state and a process; and it is explicitly linked to the effect of integration – very much a target-oriented view. The definition is broad, in that it purports to cover many kinds of cultural importation; however, its scope is restricted by the reservation in the next sentence, which states that "not all imported goods result in such 'transfers'" (Even-Zohar 1997, 359). But is transfer only to be judged *a posteriori*? If so, what is the degree of integration, and the required time interval, that justifies calling an imported item a transfer? (On this query, see also Pym 1998 and Pym 2004, 13.) And what about the perspective of the exporting culture? The metaphorical status of 'transfer' is not discussed.

Even-Zohar's view that transfer is a broader category than translation, and includes translation, is illustrated by Rachel Weissbrod (2004), with examples of different kinds of adaptation: to a new kind of audience, a new time, a different semiotic system, and so on. Like Even-Zohar, she expands Roman Jakobson's (1959) classic tripartite categorization of intralingual, interlingual and intersemiotic translation to also include the transfer of models (e.g., literary models). She does not question the appropriateness of the transfer metaphor itself.

Lieven D'hulst (2012) also takes transfer – and specifically cultural transfer – as an 'umbrella concept' that includes translation. He acknowledges that cultural transfer is a vague and abstract concept, however, which allows different scholars from different fields to selectively foreground semantic features that they find most useful in a given context. (I return to this significant observation below.) Such features are, for example, "getting across, import, export, process, product, integration" (D'hulst 2012, 139), and, according to D'hulst, they may be "supplemented, replaced or adapted" according to the specific discipline in question. This makes the notion sound a loose one indeed, although he counters this risk by positing a central cluster of headings around which features can be grouped. These headings are: source and target poles, products, agents, carriers (or media), and techniques. His conceptualization is a broad one, encompassing all kinds of adaptation. He proposes the heuristic notion of 'assumed transfer', mirroring Toury's 'assumed translation' (Toury 1995, 35), albeit with some reservations, as a useful conceptual tool in historical research. In an intriguing endnote (note 1), D'hulst says that in this paper he will keep to general terms (such as the above-mentioned headings) "without detailing their metaphorical features" (D'hulst 2012, 151) – precisely those that interest me here.

Underlying the thinking of these scholars, and of course many others, there seems to be a general acceptance of the usefulness of seeing translation as transfer, or as a kind of transfer. The metaphor appears to capture the essence of the translation process and of what a translation is. It also allows extensions from interlingual text-based transfer to all kinds of adaptation and cultural transfer, thus enabling more powerful generalizations. Some, such as Even-Zohar (1990, 73) have suggested that sooner or later "it will turn out to be uneconomical to deal with transfer and translation separately." *Sic transit* translation studies?

However, there are also problems with the transfer metaphor. I will mention three, before offering an alternative. First problem: the hidden assumption of movement. The transfer metaphor is fundamentally based on this assumption. Texts are assumed to move. Translations are 'carried across'. A detailed statement and development of this view is to be found in Anthony Pym's book *The Moving Text* (2004) and its predecessor, *Translation and Text Transfer* (1992). Of particular interest to Pym is what he calls "the material movement of texts." His use of the transfer concept has altered to some extent over the period between these two books. The earlier volume states:

> To the extent that they require material supports, texts move in time and space. Sitting on library shelves, they move through time (…); manually, mechanically or electronically reproduced, they can be moved through space; translated, they can move from culture to culture. (Pym 1992, 128)

The later volume embeds 'transfer' within a notion of distribution, described as "a set of transfers" (Pym 2004, 12). However, this does not remove from the transfer metaphor the assumption of movement. Indeed, Pym (2004, 13-14) specifies that his use of the term 'transfer' refers to movement as change of position, "without any necessary modification to the form of whatever is moving" – a position that also appears to accept the possibility of invariance (see below). For further comments on the various senses of 'transfer' in translation research, see Shuttleworth and Cowie (1997). The "terminological mess" here (Pym's term, 2004, 13) is indeed considerable.

In some sense, of course, texts do move, carried by postmen or optical fibers or sound waves or whatever. More importantly, however, in translation there is also a sense in which texts do *not* move – a literal sense, moreover. If something moves from A to B, when it gets to B it is by definition no longer at A. But a text in culture A that is translated into culture B is not, after this process, by definition absent from culture A. The source text does not automatically disappear when it has been translated; true, it does sometimes, in special cases, but not typically. Indeed, there are several common kinds of translation where the source is manifestly still visible, alongside the translation: e.g., subtitles (where the original speech remains audible), parallel texts, interlinear translations, linguistic glosses, and double presentations (where a source language term appears alongside its translation, such as in this notice seen in New Zealand, with a Maori word in brackets: *This lake is sacred (tapu)*. The assumption of movement may often be misleading.

Second problem: the hidden assumption of invariance. If you 'carry something across', you normally assume that it is the same something that arrives on the other side. When preparing this essay, I came across a reference to a football player who was to be 'transferred' to another club. One would not expect this player to arrive in his new team in some altered state, but to be precisely the same skilled player that he had been in his previous team. Applied to translation, what remains unchanged is simplistically conceptualized as the message, the meaning, the information, and so on.

As Martín de León (2008) points out, this view is itself a manifestation of the widespread conduit metaphor of communication, with a 'container' moving through time and space and carrying within it something that arrives intact at its destination. Such a view captures something of the nature of communication, of course, but also misses a great deal. In translation, it highlights some notion of equivalence, whether dynamic or formal or some other kind. Recall the long (mainly Western) tradition of seeing the source text as sacred, not to be changed, requiring quasi-total equivalence. We can also recall the fates of Bible translators who were thought to have changed something. Such a view, however, overlooks obligatory and optional shifts, the effect of agency, a change of *skopos* (purpose), and much else. Paradoxically, the inevitability of change seems inherent to Even-Zohar's dynamic conceptualization of transfer mentioned earlier. If transfer indeed implies transformation, this clashes with the assumption of an unchanging content that is transferred. Does this conceptual inconsistency matter?

Third problem: the clash with the target metaphor. Given the predominance of the transfer metaphor, it is surprising that it clashes conceptually with another widespread metaphor, one that is particularly associated with descriptive translation studies but also plays a central role in functional theories such as Skopos Theory: the target metaphor. Here, translation is conceptualized as a dynamic relation between a source and a target, which are connected by a path. (See Martín de León 2008 for a detailed analysis.) This metaphor agrees with the movement assumption, and implicitly adds a path along which to move towards the target. However, it rejects the hidden assumption of invariance (and thus dethrones the notion of a predetermined equivalence), because it implies that the translating agent needs to adapt the message to target conditions, so that shifts of all kinds will be inevitable in order to meet the goal of the operation. Does this clash matter? What alternatives are there, to the basic transfer metaphor?

2. A memetic alternative

One alternative is to be found in memetics. In Chesterman (1997) I discussed the advantages of seeing translation in memetic terms. Memes are defined as units of cultural transmission, or units of imitation: ideas that spread (Dawkins 1976, 192). Memes, argued Richard Dawkins, are replicators, like genes. Genes propagate via (mostly) exact duplication, with occasional mutations; but memes, being cultural elements, are less constrained by sameness, and spread via imitation which can be much less constrained. If a melody spreads as a meme, for instance, it may be manifested in quite different variations, but they can all be heard as representing the same theme – in other words, the same meme. For two manifestations of some cultural unit to be counted as varieties of a given meme, there must be adequate similarity between the two, but not necessarily identity. People can tell the same joke in different ways, and in different languages, but it can still remain essentially the same joke.

A caveat: for many scholars, the very notion of a meme is metaphorical. It is a way of conceptualizing how ideas spread: like genes. There are, however, investigators who claim that memes also have a physical existence, for example, as constellations of synapses in the brain. (See further Chesterman 1997, Chapter 1, and the update in the revised edition, 2016; and for a collection of critical responses Rose and Rose 2001.) In the present context, the metaphorical view will suffice.

Translations can be seen as ways of propagating memes. Seeing translation through the lens of a memetic metaphor does not need the idea of transfer. The underlying notion here is that of sharing, spreading, propagating, duplicating-with-variation (e.g., Pym's 'distribution', above). In Darwinian terms, ideas (etc.) can be thus said to spread from one population to another, and also to evolve via inevitable mutations. According to this metaphor, the process of translation is not an equative one of replacement or substitution, such that there is a target text that somehow equates to a source one. Nor is it a transfer movement involving the transport of something from one place to another. Nor does it imply invariance. Rather, translating is seen as an *additive* operation: alongside (not instead of) one text, another is created that is *relevantly similar* to the first one: that is, in a way that is relevant to purpose, context, and so on. We might call this a similarity condition (or even, depending on your definition of the term, an equivalence condition…). When a given act of translation is carried out, the process can be formulated as follows, where 'A' denotes a cultural unit such as a text, and the arrow denotes the time interval between the situations before translation and after translation:

$$A \rightarrow A + A^1$$

After the translation process, the source text A continues to exist (usually), but now alongside a variant of it (A^1), e.g., in another language or medium. The series can of course be continued indefinitely, to include A^2, A^3 and so on, for example, as translations in different languages.

The relation between A and A^1 is one of similarity, as noted above. Similarity is a surprisingly complex concept, but a distinction can usefully be made between two basic types (see further Sovran 1992). On the one hand, we have what I have elsewhere (Chesterman 1996) called convergent similarity. This is observable when we notice something similar between two separate entities, say, a surprising resemblance between two pictures, or an analogy of some kind. For instance, I could comment that Helsinki is similar to Oslo in some respects. On the other hand, *divergent* similarity starts from a single entity: it is the relation between one thing (A) and a second, similar thing (A¹) that is somehow derived from it. Divergent similarity describes the case of translation, or, for example, duplication, or forgery.

The memetic metaphor can thus be anchored in a theory of similarity. It highlights aspects of translation that are not highlighted by the transfer metaphor: that translation is an additive process, that source texts do not normally disappear after translation, and that mutations are normal. The memetic metaphor is partly compatible with the target metaphor, in that translation spreads information (etc.) originating in a given source culture into a given target one, in an appropriately adapted form. But the memetic view does not imply movement along a path. Rather, new variants are generated to suit different conditions (i.e., target culture conditions). Being based on the notion of a shared similarity, not equative sameness (nor some strict definition of equivalence), the memetic metaphor naturally encompasses a wide range of possible variation and adaptation. Similarities can be of many kinds and degrees. And since its fundamental unit is a cultural one, it also seems eminently applicable to the analysis of translation as a part of cultural history.

It may be of interest to compare this memetic view with Gideon Toury's three 'postulates', which he proposes as a way of explicating his notion of 'assumed translation' (Toury 1995, 33–35). The Source-Text Postulate entails the existence of a source (e.g., what I have symbolized above as 'A'). The Transfer Postulate entails the existence of a second text that is derived from the source text in some way, via a process that has involved "the transference from the assumed source text of certain features that the two now share" (Toury 1995, 34). In my memetic terms: the second text (A¹) has been derived from the first (A) and is relevantly similar to it. Toury's reference to the "transference" of "certain features that the two now share" seems to imply the preservation of at least some invariance, an assumption discussed above. In the revised version of his book (Toury 2012, 29) there is a slight change here: 'transference' has been replaced by 'transfer'. The third postulate is the Relationship Postulate, which assumes, as a consequence of the Transfer Postulate, that there are "accountable relationships" between the source and target texts. In memetic terms, this too seems to be covered by the similarity condition. We will now look more closely at two kinds of conceptual relationship.

3. Metaphors are metonymic

From a hermeneutic point of view, metaphors can be taken as kinds of interpretive hypotheses: that is, like definitions and categorizations of all kinds, they can be seen as conceptual tools whose usefulness is tested pragmatically. (See Føllesdal 1979; Chesterman 2008.) They have to do with how phenomena can best be interpreted, made sense of. They are not empirical hypotheses to be tested against a truth criterion; they are hypotheses of interpretation, to be tested in terms of usefulness: by assessing the extent to which a given interpretation yields greater understanding, more significant research questions, better formulated empirical hypotheses, etc., than some other interpretation. In the previous sections, I have offered some criticism of the transfer metaphor, and suggested a memetic metaphor as an alternative. Here too, however, doubts can be raised.

All metaphors highlight some aspects of the phenomenon described and hide others – as do similes. If I say "translating is (like) changing clothes", I intend to select a particular salient feature: say, the idea that translation only changes the external form of something, not its essence, which remains unaltered; I am in fact highlighting the idea of some kind of equivalence. However, at the same time I am hiding other aspects of translating, aspects which may not be immediately relevant to the image of changing clothes, such as its economic dimension, and the media involved. Seeing translation as transfer highlights its role as a way of crossing cultural boundaries, but hides, for example, the fact that sources do not automatically vanish when they have been translated. Seeing translation as memetic replication does highlight the latter point, but this metaphor hides other aspects such as power and agency. All metaphors are in fact metonymic.

Metaphor and metonymy are of course closely related concepts. Jakobson (1956) saw them as representing two fundamental ways of thinking, metaphor being based on similarity, metonymy on contiguity and connection. Metonymy is notably more heterogeneous than metaphor, he argued. Maria Tymoczko agrees that metonymy is highly heterogeneous, but argues that it has been undervalued in translation theory. She defines metonymy as follows: "*Metonymy* is a figure of speech in which an attribute or an aspect of an entity substitutes for the entity or in which a part substitutes for the whole" (Tymoczko 1999, 42). She thus includes synecdoche, sometimes considered a separate figure, under metonymy, and I will follow suit here. Her detailed study of the translation of medieval Irish literature is theoretically grounded in a 'metonymics of translation'. In her concluding chapter, she calls for the development of a theoretical metalanguage, and for further exploration of translation metonymies themselves:

Such metonymies are to be found in the way that translation is always a partial process, whereby some but not all of the source text is transposed, and in the way that translations represent source texts by highlighting specific segments or parts, or by allowing specific attributes of the source texts to dominate and, hence, to represent the entirety of the work. (Tymoczko 1999, 282)

Both at a theoretical level and in the analysis of her empirical data, Tymoczko makes a powerful argument for the case that translation as a whole is better considered and modeled as a metonymic activity, rather than a metaphorical one. One reason is the richness of interpretation that a metonymic view allows. So many different aspects or parts can represent a given original. Tymoczko shows how a metonymic analysis can enrich postcolonial research on translation, for instance. She polemically opposes the metonymic view to the more restricted metaphorical one, "translation-as-substitution", which

breeds a discourse about translation that is dualistic, polarized, either/or, right/wrong. A metonymic approach to translation is more flexible, resulting in a discourse of both/and which recognizes varying hierarchies of privilege, overlapping and partially corresponding elements, coexisting values, and the like. (Tymoczko 1999, 283)

I agree that the metonymic approach is potentially a broader one, and eminently suitable for freer kinds of adaptations, the creation of new connections, and so on as argued and illustrated by Tymoczko. However, I think that her caricature of the metaphorical approach is something of a straw man. Also to be noted is the fact that Tymoczko is dealing with literary translation – and with good reason. (Consider, for instance, the dozens of translations and retranslations of a single poem that are collected in Douglas Hofstadter's *Le Ton beau de Marot* (1997), each with a different focus, exploiting a different constraint, reflecting a different aspect of the original – different similarities, in fact. His analysis of them is supremely metonymic.) On the other hand, Tymoczko's conclusions seem less relevant to legal, medical or technical translation, for example.

I would argue that selection is involved in the use of both metonymy and metaphor. A speaker selects not only the vehicle of the metaphor (e.g., 'changing clothes', for translation), but also the part or associated aspect that forms the basis of a metonymic figure (e.g., 'Downing Street' for the British Prime Minister). Both imply the existence of other alternatives, and both are therefore selective. I agree, however, that there is a clear distinguishing feature that separates the two figures: this is the nature of the relation they embody. In a metaphor, this relation is one of similarity, as noted by Jakobson. In metonymy, there seems to be no such constraint: any relation will serve. But there must *be* a relation, between the part or attribute and the whole – either recognizable *a priori*, or created *ad hoc*. This distinction thus explicates the way that metonymy is the more abstract and the more general of the two, and hence more heterogeneous in expression and more resistant to theorizing. A metonymic view of translation allows one to relax or stretch the similarity constraint. Metaphor highlights a similarity aspect, while metonymy picks out *any* aspect (that is, any aspect which seems interesting and relevant for a given purpose). On this view, metaphor and metonymy are not just in opposition: in the sense that metaphors also select an aspect to highlight, metaphors *are* metonymic.

4. Thou art translated!

What happens to the transfer metaphor when 'translation' is itself used in a metaphorical sense? Metonymically, quite a variety of relations can be noted, which raise more questions than answers. In *A Midsummer Night's Dream* (3.1.), when Quince the carpenter sees his friend Bottom transfigured with an ass's head, he exclaims in surprise and horror "Bless thee, Bottom, bless thee! Thou art translated!" Quince recognizes that it is still Bottom there, but somehow changed. Something has remained invariant, but what matters is the change of state; the word 'translated' highlights the change, not the invariance. Indeed, a few lines earlier another friend, Snout, has exclaimed in the same situation: "O Bottom, thou art changed!" 'Translated' here is simply a synonym of 'changed'. Note, by the way, that Bottom does not 'move', in any obvious sense. He undergoes a sudden change of state, something simply happens to him.

In the context of the Indian diaspora, Salman Rushdie (1991, 17) writes: "[h]aving been borne across the world, we are translated men." There is certainly movement here. But does he mean 'transferred', unchanged, from one place to another? Since he goes on to say that he believes that something has been gained through this 'translation', presumably some change is involved too. So the assumption of invariance is not completely maintained. The footballer 'transferred' to a new club may also change, but presumably not immediately: changes may occur over time, as the environment of the new club has an effect on the new player. In Rushdie's case too, one assumes that the changes affecting the translated men come about after their initial 'translation', perhaps as they become integrated in their new environments, as Even-Zohar might say. But suppose they resist this integration, preferring to cling to their original selves and ways of being? Have they then *not* been 'transferred'?

In biology, or more precisely biosemiotics, the term 'translation' is used in a wider sense than in translation studies, to refer to "the process of semiosic change taking place in and between all organisms, even at the cellular level" (Marais and Kull 2016, 172, as cited by van Doorslaer 2019, 227-228). There seems to be no invariance assumption here (unless the change only concerns a sign system, not whatever is conveyed by that system); what is highlighted is the notion of change, through both time and cellular space, within and between entities.

In chemistry, the metaphorical usage seems similar: "[Translation is] the unidirectional process that takes place on the ribosomes whereby the genetic information present in an mRNA is converted into a corresponding sequence of amino acids in a protein." (Chemicool Dictionary, n.d.) Here, we have a change of state, where information is "converted into" a different but corresponding form, like a change of code. Presumably, the invariance assumption does apply here, in that the "information" remains in some sense the same. Additionally, the process is said to be unidirectional. A transfer, however, can be reversed (at least in the literal sense), and a translation can be back-translated, albeit with no guarantee of automatically arriving at the precise place of departure.

In mathematics, we find an interpretation that looks like a kind of isomorphism:

> Translation is a term used in geometry to describe a function that moves an object a certain distance. The object is not altered in any other way. It is not rotated, reflected or re-sized. In a translation, every point of the object must be moved in the same direction and for the same distance. (Beddoe, n.d.)

This interpretation certainly involves both movement and the preservation of total invariance: a kind of ultimate formal equivalence. Nothing changes except the position, the environment.

In sociology, the Scandinavian institutionalist school have interestingly agreed to change their usage of the phrase "diffusion of ideas" to "translation of ideas" (see e.g., Bromley and Suárez 2015). 'Diffusion' is, interestingly, a memetic notion. The new term 'translation' is intended to stress the fact that ideas change as they spread from one place to another. So the invariance assumption is explicitly denied.

In contemporary healthcare, 'translation' has a usage which gives the concept some additional dimensions altogether, with an unusual selection of aspects. It occurs in the concept of 'knowledge translation', first defined by the Canadian Institutes of Health Research.

> Knowledge translation (KT) is defined as a dynamic and iterative process that includes synthesis, dissemination, exchange and ethically-sound application of knowledge to improve the health of Canadians, provide more effective health services and products and strengthen the health care system. (Canadian Institutes of Health Research 2004)

So here we have 'translation' meaning something like the complex and ethical (etc.) application of theory to practice, including the achievement of positive effects of several kinds. We have come quite some distance from transfer, it seems. Implied is a radical change of form, from theoretical knowledge to good practice. The knowledge itself presumably does not thereby change, and indeed remains where it was (unless there is feedback from the good practice), so is there any implied movement? The relation with the textual concept of translation has become thin indeed. How far can the relation be extended? Note the mention of dissemination: this again recalls the memetic metaphor.

What may be the ultimate step is taken by Guldin, writing about how best to understand the general state of the contemporary world:

> In this all-encompassing climate of disintegration and recombination, translation has become a general metaphor for connection, exchange, transfer and transformation. One might say that translation has become one of the essential metaphors, if not *the metaphor*, of our globalized world. (Guldin 2016, 1, emphasis original, as cited by Dam et al. 2019, 232)

Quite how 'transfer' is to be interpreted here is not clear. If translation has indeed become the general metaphor for so much, its meaning risks becoming so diluted as to be vacuous. It may be, for the people in the specific fields exemplified above, that 'translation' is simply being used as a technical term, in senses that vary across fields. But translation scholars will, I think, see all these usages as metaphorical ones. For whatever reasons, some aspect (or set of aspects) of translation has been selected to be relevant, and this aspect is then metonymically taken to be usefully represented by the term itself. There seems to be no system in the ways the term has been used metaphorically, just a variety of selected aspects, some more shared than others. More like metonymy, in fact. The concept itself, or at least the term 'translation', is becoming a meme, like a fashion, as it spreads and mutates.

The metaphorizing of translation plays a significant role in one recent trend within translation research, which its adherents call post-translation studies. This was launched by Siri Nergaard and Stefano Arduini (2011, 8-9) in the first issue of a new journal. They wrote:

> We propose the inauguration of a transdisciplinary research field with translation as an interpretive as well as an operative tool. We imagine a sort of new era that could be termed post-translation studies, where translation is viewed as fundamentally transdisciplinary, mobile and open-ended. The "post" here recognizes a fact and a conviction: new and enriching thinking on translation must take place outside the traditional discipline of translation studies.

"Translation as an interpretive tool": that is, we are encouraged to see all kinds of things *as* translation (in other words, an interpretive hypothesis is hereby proposed). Edwin Gentzler takes up the challenge:

> What if we consider the political, social, and economic structures as built upon translation? What if we view the landscape – the parks, buildings, roads, memorials, churches, schools and government organizations – not as solely monocultural, but also as a product of post-translation effects? (Gentzler 2016, 5)

In his book, Gentzler offers some fascinating empirical studies of literary translation and adaptation, at one point using 'translation' as a trope on which to base an insightful analysis of several aspects of *Hamlet*. Yes, the idea of using translation as an interpretive tool can be useful. But if one can see anything as translation or the result of translation – parks, churches, government organizations etc. – does the concept retain any meaning? Does metaphorization have no limits? What is gained, what lost?

5. Complementarity?

In the Western tradition, one can speculate that the centrality (until recent decades, in some quarters) of the concept of equivalence may have something to do with the very term 'translation' and its Indo-European cognates. After all, one of the original semantic features of the term is the assumption of something invariant which is 'carried across', although this is not always implied in use, or at least not always foregrounded.

In a number of other languages, however, the term denoting the concept of translation highlights change, not invariance. These other conceptualizations are based on different metaphors. For instance, the notion of turning underlies the word for 'translate' in Finnish (*kääntää*), and other languages too: this carries an implication of difference, rather than invariance. One can further speculate that in other cultures, terms that are not based on the idea of 'carrying something across', might correlate with a broader concept of translation, less constrained by the demands of equivalence. In still other languages, the translation word foregrounds the idea of mediation, such as Arabic *tarjamah*, related to *turguman* 'translator, interpreter', hence English 'dragoman'. However, I will not pursue this line of inquiry here (see Stecconi 2004).

And what about other metaphors for translation itself, apart from transfer or memes? Nicholas Round (2005) gives a delightful survey of the range of images that have been offered, and attempts to group them in various ways, for instance images of appropriation and bringing across (such as transfer) and images of imitation (such as recreating). Aptly, he recalls the ancient Hindu story of the six blind men and the elephant. Each touches a different part of the animal, and each gets a different image of it: the elephant is like a snake (the trunk), a fan (the ear), a tree-trunk (the leg), a wall (its side), a rope (its tail) and a spear (its tusk). Each of the images was partially right, but all conceptions of the whole were wrong. Would their joint conception of the elephant have been better if they had combined their various images? Round doubts whether such a reconciliation of different views, if possible at all, would have been much of an improvement.

However, consider the complementarity principle proposed by the physicist Niels Bohr (and now, in fact, a widespread meme). This states that in order to understand the phenomenon of light at the subatomic level we need to conceptualize it both as waves and as particles. This requires some imaginative effort, but seems to be necessary if we are to make sense of the experimental evidence. Would our understanding of translation be better, richer, if we could hold in mind more than one metaphor at the same time? Even metaphors that conceptually clash, like transfer and target? Transfer *and* memetics? Where would the upper limit be? Simply, the limit of our imagination?

To conclude: it seems at least advisable to be explicitly aware of what any given metaphor assumes, and what it hides as well as what it highlights. The transfer metaphor is not unproblematic, and is not always used in a consistent manner. And there are alternatives.

Another conclusion is the value of maintaining a critical attitude. Metaphors are indispensable tools for thinking, yes; but they are also rhetorical devices whose function is to make a claim more persuasive. A poor position, or a reinvented wheel, can be impressively marketed with the help of a good metaphor. And as D'hulst (1992, 47) points out, there is a risk that repeated metaphors can end up being taken literally, as definitions. As the map is not the territory, the metaphor is not the thing itself.

References

Beddoe, Jennifer L., n.d. "What is Translation in Math? – Definition, Examples, & Terms. Chapter 1. Lesson 15. Transcript." Accessed June 28, 2020. https://study.com/academy/lesson/what-is-translation-in-math-definition-examples-terms.html

Bromley, Patricia, and David Suárez. 2015. "Institutional Theories and Levels of Analysis: Diffusion, History and Translation." In *World Culture Recontextualized*, edited by Jürgen Schriewer, 139–160. London: Taylor and Francis.

Canadian Institutes of Health Research. 2004. "Knowledge Translation – Definition." Last modified July 28, 2016. http://www.cihr-irsc.gc.ca/e/29418.html#2

Chemicool Dictionary, n.d. "Definition of Translation." Accessed June 28, 2020. https://www.chemicool.com/definition/translation.html

Chesterman, Andrew. 1996. "On Similarity." *Target* 8 (1): 159–164.

— 1997. *Memes of Translation. The Spread of Ideas in Translation Theory*. Amsterdam: John Benjamins. (Revised edition 2016.)

— 2008. "The Status of Interpretive Hypotheses." In *Efforts and Models in Interpreting and Translation Research*, edited by Gyde Hansen, Andrew Chesterman, and Heidrun Gerzymisch Arbogast, 49–61. Amsterdam: John Benjamins.

Dam, Helle V., Matilde Nisbeth Brøgger, and Karen Korning Zethsen, eds. 2019. *Moving Boundaries in Translation Studies*. London: Routledge.

Dawkins, Richard. 1976. *The Selfish Gene*. Oxford: Oxford University Press.

D'hulst, Lieven. 1992. "Sur le rôle des métaphores en traductologie contemporaine." *Target* 4 (1): 33–51.

— 2012. "(Re)locating Translation History: From Assumed Translation to Assumed Transfer." *Translation Studies* 5 (2): 139-155.

Even-Zohar, Itamar. 1990. *Polysystem Studies*. Special issue of *Poetics Today* 11 (1). Tel Aviv: Porter Institute for Poetics and Semiotics.

— 1997. "The Making of Cultural Repertoire and the Role of Transfer." *Target* 9 (2): 355-363.

Føllesdal, Dagfinn. 1979. "Hermeneutics and the Hypothetico-Deductive Method." *Dialectica* 33 (3-4): 319–336. Also in *Readings in the Philosophy of Social Science*, 1994, edited by Michael Martin and Lee C. McIntyre, 233-245. Cambridge, MA: MIT Press.

Gentzler, Edwin. 2016. *Translation and Rewriting in the Age of Post-Translation Studies.* London: Routledge.

Guldin, Rainer. 2016. *Translation as Metaphor.* London: Routledge.

Hofstadter, Douglas R. 1997. *Le Ton beau de Marot. In Praise of the Music of Language.* New York: Basic Books.

Jakobson, Roman, 1956. "Two Aspects of Language and Two Types of Aphasic Disturbances." In *Fundamentals of Language,* edited by Roman Jakobson and Morris Halle, 53–82. The Hague: Mouton.

— 1959. "On Linguistic Aspects of Translation." In *On Translation,* edited by Reuben A. Brower, 232–239. Cambridge, MA: Harvard University Press.

Marais, Kobus, and Kalevi Kull. 2016. "Biosemiotics and Translation Studies: Challenging 'Translation'." In *Border Crossings. Translation Studies and Other Disciplines,* edited by Yves Gambier and Luc van Doorslaer, 169–188. Amsterdam: John Benjamins.

Martín de León, Celia. 1008. "Skopos and beyond. A Critical Study of Functionalism." *Target* 20 (1): 1–28.

Nergaard, Siri, and Stefano Arduini. 2011. "Translation: A New Paradigm." *Translation* 1 (1): 8–17.

Pym, Anthony. 1992. *Translation and Text Transfer.* Frankfurt am Main: Peter Lang.

— 1998. "Note on a Repertoire for Seeing Cultures." *Target* 10 (2): 357–361.

— 2004. *The Moving Text. Localization, Translation, and Distribution.* Amsterdam: John Benjamins.

Rose, Hilary, and Steven Rose, eds. *Alas Poor Darwin. Arguments against Evolutionary Psychology.* London: Vintage, 2001.

Round, Nicholas. 2005. "Translation and its Metaphors." *Skase Journal of Translation and Interpretation* 1 (1): 47–69.

Rushdie, Salman. 1991. *Imaginary Homelands: Essays and Criticism 1981–1991.* London: Granta.

Shuttleworth, Mark, and Moira Cowie. 1997. *Dictionary of Translation Studies.* Manchester: St. Jerome Publishing.

Sovran, Tamar. 1992. "Between Similarity and Sameness." *Journal of Pragmatics* 18 (4): 329–344.

Stecconi, Ubaldo. 2004. "Interpretive Semiotics and Translation Theory: The Semiotic Conditions to Translation." *Semiotica* 150: 471–489.

Toury, Gideon. 1995. *Descriptive Translation Studies and beyond.* Amsterdam: John Benjamins. (Revised edition 2012.)

Tymoczko, Maria. 1999. *Translation in a Postcolonial Context.* Manchester: St. Jerome Publishing.

van Doorslaer, Luc. 2019. "Bound to Expand. The Paradigm of Change in Translation Studies." In *Moving Boundaries in Translation Studies*, edited by Helle V. Dam, Matilde N. Brøgger, and Karen K. Zethsen, 220–230. London: Routledge.

Weissbrod, Rachel. 2004. "From Transfer to Translation." *Across Languages and Cultures* 5 (1): 23–41.

About the editors

Maud Gonne is FNRS postdoctoral fellow at University of Namur and UCLouvain. Her research interests include cultural transfers and mediators, translation and identity building, language minorities and Belgian literature. She is the author of numerous articles on these topics (see https://research-portal.unamur.be/fr/persons/maud-gonne), as well as of the monograph *Contrebande littéraire et culturelle à la Belle Époque: Le « hard labour » de Georges Eekhoud entre Anvers, Paris et Bruxelles* (Leuven University Press 2017). She is an active member of Namur Institute of Language, Text and Transmediality (NaLTT) and a CETRA associated research member.

Klaartje Merrigan holds a PhD in translation studies from KU Leuven and specializes in contemporary translation theory, literary self-translation and cultural transfer. Her current research focuses on theories of embodied cognition and psycholinguistics. She is currently active as a translator and an Employee Training and Development expert.

Reine Meylaerts is Full Professor of comparative literature and translation studies at KU Leuven where she teaches courses on European literature, comparative literature and translation and plurilingualism in literature. She is currently (2017-2021) vice-rector of research policy at KU Leuven. Her current research interests concern translation policy, intercultural mediation and transfer in multilingual cultures, past and present. She is the author of numerous articles and chapters on these topics (https://lirias.kuleuven.be/items-by-author?author=Meylaerts%2C+Reinhilde%3B+U0031976). She was director of CETRA from 2006-2014 and is now board member. She was also review editor of *Target. International Journal of Translation Studies* (2011-2017). She was coordinator of 2011-2014: FP7-PEOPLE-2010-ITN: TIME: Translation Research Training: An integrated and intersectoral model for Europe. She is former secretary general (2004-2007) of the European Society for Translation Studies (EST) and chair of the Doctoral Studies Committee of EST.

Heleen van Gerwen holds a PhD in translation studies (KU Leuven). Her PhD focuses on translation and transfer practices in the legal and administrative domains in nineteenth-century Belgium. Her current research interests include translation history, intercultural transfer, translator studies and sociocultural roles of translation in multilingual contexts. Her publications include "Translation space in nineteenth-century Belgium: rethinking translation and transfer directions" (co-authored with Lieven D'hulst, published in *Perspectives*) and "Studying the forms and functions of legal translations in history: the case of 19th-century Belgium" (published in *Translation and Interpreting: the International Journal of Translation and Interpreting Research*).

About the authors

Susan Bassnett is Professor of comparative literature at the University of Glasgow, and Professor Emerita of comparative literature at the University of Warwick. Recent publications include a special issue of *The Translator*, co-edited with David Johnston (2020) and an edited collection of essays, *World Literature and Translation* (2018). In addition to her scholarly works, Susan Bassnett is a well-known journalist and translator and also writes poetry. She is an elected fellow of the Academia Europea, the Institute of Linguists and the Royal Society of Literature. Since 2016 she has been president of the British Comparative Literature Association.

Pieter Boulogne is a part-time Assistant Professor at KU Leuven, where he teaches Russian literature and trains Russian translators and interpreters. He is the director of the CETRA – Centre for Translation Studies, which, since 1989, organizes a yearly research summer school in translation studies. His main research interests lie at the crossroads of Russian literature, descriptive translation studies and reception studies. In 2011, he received a PhD Degree in Slavonic studies from KU Leuven, with a dissertation on early translations of Dostoevsky. In the following years, he co-founded the Centre for Russian Studies and became its first coordinator, he was a lecturer of Russian at the University of Antwerp and trained public service interpreters at the Flemish Integration Agency. In addition, from 2015 until 2019, he was a Visiting Professor at Ghent University, where he taught courses on the history of Russia, Russian literature and modern Russian culture. Outside of academia, Pieter Boulogne works as a public service interpreter and as a literary translator.

Andrew Chesterman was born in England but moved to Finland in 1968 and has been based there ever since, mainly at the University of Helsinki, where his main subjects have been English and translation theory. In 2010 he retired from his post as Professor of multilingual communication, but continues to be active in translation studies, refereeing and writing. His main research interests have been in contrastive analysis; translation theory, norms, universals, and ethics; and research methodology. His most recent book is *Reflections on Translation Theory. Selected papers 1993–2014* (Benjamins, 2017). He was CETRA Professor in 1999 (KU Leuven).

Yves Chevrel is Professor Emeritus of comparative literature, Sorbonne University, and Doctor honoris causa of the university Ștefan cel Mare (Suceava, Romania). He is the author of *La littérature comparée* (PUF, 1989, 7th updated edition 2015; translated into 9 languages) and the *Guide pratique de la recherche en littérature* (with Yen-Maï Tran-Gervat, coll. «Les fondamentaux de la Sorbonne nouvelle», 2018). Co-publisher, with Jean-Yves Masson, of *Histoire des traductions en langue française* (Verdier, 2012-2019, 4 vols.). Forthcoming: «Les traductions et leur apport à la formation d'un patrimoine culturel européen», in *CompLit. Revue de la société européenne de littérature comparée*, n° 1, 2021.

Dirk Delabastita teaches English literature and literary theory at the University of Namur and is a long-time member of the CETRA team at KU Leuven. His publications engage with fields such as translation studies, wordplay studies, literary multilingualism, and the European reception of Shakespeare's works. He has co-authored several dictionaries of literary terms, including *Dictionnaire des termes littéraires* (2005) and *Algemeen Letterkundig Lexicon* (open access at http://www.dbnl.org/tekst/dela012alge01_01/). His books include *Multilingualism in the Drama of Shakespeare and His Contemporaries* (co-edited with Ton Hoenselaars, 2015) and *"Romeo and Juliet" in European Culture* (co-edited with Juan F. Cerdá and Keith Gregor, 2017).

Yves Gambier is Professor Emeritus at the University of Turku where he taught translation and interpreting (1973-2014). He is a Visiting Professor and research fellow in different universities. He has published on socio-terminology, translation studies, audio-visual translation and bilingualism in Finland. He has been involved in several European research projects and he was the general editor (2005-2017) of the Benjamins Translation Library. He was the chair of the group of experts in the project EMT/European Master's in Translation (2007-2010) and member of the EMT Board (2010-2014). He was also the vice president (1993-1998), and then president (1998- 2004) of the European Society for Translation Studies/EST. (https://orcid.org/0000-0002-1858-4281)

Maud Gonne is FNRS postdoctoral fellow at the University of Namur and UCLouvain. Her research interests include cultural transfers and mediators, translation and identity building, language minorities and Belgian literature. She is the author of numerous articles on these topics (see https://research-portal.unamur.be/fr/persons/maud-gonne), as well as of the monograph *Contrebande littéraire et culturelle à la Belle Époque: Le « hard labour » de*

Georges Eekhoud entre Anvers, Paris et Bruxelles (Leuven University Press 2017). She is an active member of the Namur Institute of Language, Text and Transmediality (NaLTT) and a CETRA associated research member.

Ramunė Kasperavičienė is Professor at the Faculty of Social Sciences, Arts and Humanities of Kaunas University of Technology (Lithuania). Her research interests include translation studies, machine translation and post-editing, translation technologies, translator training, language teaching and learning. She is currently involved in an international research project on crowdsourcing and language learning. She is editor-in-chief of the scholarly journal *Studies about Languages*. She is also a translator, interpreter and language editor.

Dainora Maumevičienė is Associate Professor at the Faculty of Social Sciences, Arts and Humanities of Kaunas University of Technology (Lithuania). Her research interests include translation studies, translation history, the role of translation in state development processes, translation technologies, localisation and Lithuanisation, modern didactics in translation and interpreting teaching. She is currently involved in an international research project concerning the gamification of study courses for students of humanities and social sciences. She also works as a translator and interpreter.

Reine Meylaerts is Full Professor of comparative literature and translation studies at KU Leuven where she teaches courses on European literature, comparative literature and translation and plurilingualism in literature. She is currently (2017-2021) vice-rector of research policy at KU Leuven. Her current research interests concern translation policy, intercultural mediation and transfer in multilingual cultures, past and present. She is the author of numerous articles and chapters on these topics (https://lirias.kuleuven.be/items-by-author?author=Meylaerts%2C+Reinhilde%3B+U0031976). She was director of CETRA from 2006 until 2014 and is now board member. She was also review editor of *Target. International Journal of Translation Studies* (2011-2017). She was coordinator of 2011-2014: FP7-PEOPLE-2010-ITN: TIME: Translation Research Training: An integrated and intersectoral model for Europe. She is former secretary general (2004-2007) of the European Society for Translation Studies (EST) and chair of the Doctoral Studies Committee of EST.

Jean-Marc Moura is Professor of French and comparative literature at the University of Paris Nanterre, France, and co-director of the Observatoire des littératures française et francophones at this university. He is a member of the Institut Universitaire de France. His current work focuses on the literary history of French-language literature and on literatures in European languages and their importance in the globalization of culture. Recently published works include *Littératures francophones et théorie postcoloniale* (1999), 3rd revised edition, Paris: PUF, 2020; with Jean-Claude Laborie and Sylvie Parizet (eds.): *Vers une histoire littéraire transatlantique*, Classiques-Garnier, 2018; with Silvia Contarini and Claire Joubert (eds.): *Penser la différence culturelle du colonial au mondial*, Mimesis, 2020.

Isabelle Nières-Chevrel is Professor Emerita of general and comparative literature, University of Rennes 2 – Haute-Bretagne. She holds a state doctorate (Amiens 1988) on *Lewis Carroll en France. 1870-1985: les ambivalences d'une réception littéraire*. Her work focuses mainly on children's and young adult's literature, e.g., *Introduction à la littérature de jeunesse, Didier jeunesse* (2009; reprinted 2010 and 2018), *Dictionnaire du livre de jeunesse* (co-edited with Jean Perrot, Editions du Cercle de la librairie, 2013). Recent publications include «Littérature d'enfance et de jeunesse» (in Yves Chevrel et al., eds. 2012, *Histoire des traductions en langue française. XIXe siècle*, Verdier), «Les livres pour l'enfance et la jeunesse» (in Yves Chevrel et al., eds., 2014, *Histoire des traductions en langue française, XVIIe-XVIIIe s.*, Verdier), and «Usage du français et traductions : la naissance d'une littérature de jeunesse dans quatre pays de langue romane», *Les Langues Néo-Latines*, n° 393, June 2020.

Christina Schäffner is Professor Emerita at Aston University, Birmingham, where she was the head of translation studies until her retirement in 2015. Her main research interests are political discourse in translation, news translation, metaphor in translation, and translation didactics, and she has published widely on these topics.

Michael Schreiber obtained his PhD in 1993 (Mainz-Germersheim) and his habilitation in 1998 (Heidelberg). He has teaching experience at universities in Heidelberg, Stuttgart, Graz, Innsbruck, Cologne and Montpellier. Since 2005 he is Professor of linguistics and translation studies (French and Italian) at the University of Mainz in Germersheim. From 2008 until 2011 and from 2013 until 2020 he was dean of the Faculty of Translation Studies, Linguistics and Cultural Studies (FTSK Germersheim). His research interests are linguistic problems of translation, translation theory, and history of translation.

ABOUT THE AUTHORS

Luc van Doorslaer is Chair Professor for translation studies at the University of Tartu (Estonia), the former president of CETRA (2014-2018), the Centre for Translation Studies at KU Leuven (Belgium), and Professor Extraordinary at Stellenbosch University (South Africa). Since 2016 he is vice president of EST, the European Society for Translation Studies. He is book series editor of 'Translation, Interpreting & Transfer' at Leuven University Press. Together with Yves Gambier, he is the editor of the online *Translation Studies Bibliography* and the four volumes of the *Handbook of Translation Studies*. Other recent books edited include *Interconnecting Translation Studies and Imagology* (2016), *Border Crossings. Translation Studies and other Disciplines* (2016) and *Methods in News Translation*, a special issue of *Across Languages and Cultures* (2018). His main research interests are: journalism and translation, ideology and translation, imagology and translation, institutionalization of translation studies.

Index

adaptation 11, 18, 21, 50, 75, 91, 92, 101, 105, 116, 121, 122, 151, 208, 209, 213, 215, 219
agent 11, 20, 28, 75, 79, 115, 118, 121, 182, 183, 189, 200, 202, 209, 211
Bâ, Ahmadou Hampâté 80
Beowulf 18, 33
biosemiotics 12, 217
border 10, 12, 26, 71, 120, 122, 187, 207
Brontë, Charlotte 16, 21, 49
Brontë, Emily 51, 94
children's literature 19, 91
complexity 13, 20, 22, 75, 107
Cronin, Michael 12
cultural translation 13
D'hulst, Lieven 33, 36, 75, 79, 107, 115, 184, 209
diffusion 217
displacement 13, 27
dissemination 11, 28, 117, 121, 127, 218
domestication 22, 66, 69
duplication 27, 211, 213
ecotranslational 12
emergence 24
entangled history 11, 61
    histoire croisée 75
equivalence 10, 104, 114, 207, 211, 219
Espagne, Michel 9, 23, 75
Even-Zohar, Itamar 9, 75, 208
exchange 10, 11, 15, 66, 75, 108, 122, 140, 218
export 122, 150, 158, 208
fictionalization 23, 80
genetics 126, 207
genetic studies 93
Genette, Gérard 91, 107
Göpferich, Susanne 10, 114, 116, 124, 127, 134, 151
heterolingualism 14, 16, 49, 56, 65
hyper-objects 12
identity 12, 26, 59, 61, 127, 136, 137, 140, 151, 158, 182
    cultural identity 140
    national identity 148, 185, 194, 201
image 9, 14, 16, 20, 22, 42, 60, 72, 134, 135, 220
    animal image 150

auto-image 17, 134, 146, 148
cultural image 16, 75, 135
hetero-image 17, 134, 141, 145, 148
images of appropriation 220
images of imitation 220
meta-image 149
national image 25, 49, 151
self-image 73, 147
visual image 138, 148
imagology 14, 138
import 26, 27, 81, 122, 139, 142, 176, 208
integration 9, 27, 208, 217
interdisciplinary 12, 13, 27, 36, 45, 75, 122, 127
interlingual 13, 120
    interlingual alienation 67
    interlingual transfer 121, 122, 209
    interlingual translation 18, 122, 127, 134, 209
interpretation 44, 71, 84, 95, 98, 114, 133, 134, 137, 139, 152, 214
    (re)interpretation 25
    reinterpretation 28
    reinterpretation processes 18
interpreter 19, 23, 79, 189, 195, 220
intersemiotic 13, 18
    intersemiotic translation 116, 209
intralingual 13
    intralingual transfer 122
    intralingual translation 18, 25, 37, 116, 122, 134, 209
Jakobson, Roman 20, 209, 214
Marais, Kobus 16
mediation 9, 13, 16, 26, 42, 61, 113, 117, 220
mediator 11, 20, 22, 61, 84, 182, 225, 228
    conciliatory mediator 23
    cultural mediator 20, 23
    intercultural mediator 20, 21, 75, 119
    multifaceted mediator 23
metaphor 14, 25, 46, 80, 113, 126, 172, 196, 208
    bear metaphor 145, 148
    family metaphor 172
    memetic metaphor 24, 212, 218
    metaphorization 13

target metaphor 211
transference metaphor 115
transfer metaphor 27, 115, 116, 207, 209
metonymy 117, 214, 218
modality 143
multimodality 12, 13, 20
   multimodal translation 18
news translation 17, 18, 26, 113, 117, 120
   transediting 13, 18, 113, 120
non-linearity 15, 17
orality 19, 39, 80, 82, 84, 88
Oyono, Ferdinand 80
paradigm of simplicity 14
plurality of roles 20, 22
process 9, 11, 12, 14, 36, 46, 113, 114, 208
   additive process 213
   cultural processes 116
   cultural transfer processes 20
   emergent process 24
   globalization process 145
   identy-(re)presentation process 182
   nation-building processes 184
   projection process 138
   self-discovery process 61
   state-building processes 19, 183
   transfer process 11, 14, 17, 49, 75, 122, 208
   transformational process 26
   translation process 21, 158, 209
   transmedial process 20
product 10-12, 14, 24, 28, 36, 91, 113, 114, 138, 209
   product-oriented studies 123
Pym, Anthony 209
reception 40, 49, 62, 100, 128, 150
re-semanticization 9, 18
similarity 213
system 10, 14, 24, 116
   cultural system 25, 152
   legal system 158, 161
   polysystem theory 9, 208
   receptor system 76

semiotic system 209
systemic approach 11
translation system 12
Toury, Gideon 75, 123, 209, 213
tradosphere 12
transculturation 13
transfer
   assumed transfer 10, 36, 75, 108, 209
   back transfer 16, 49
   knowledge transfer 127
   transfer chains 18
   transfer modes 116
   transfer space 15
   transfer strategies 24
   transfer studies 33, 36, 45, 75, 116, 122, 127, 134
   Transferwissenschaft 10, 134
transformation 9, 23, 26-28, 101, 116, 120, 122, 126, 164, 208, 211, 218
translational
   translational character 122
   translational dimension 13, 25
   translational enunciation 79, 80, 84
   translational influence 176
   translational practices 13
   translational relationships 18
translation history 10, 13, 18
translation policy 157, 160, 182, 183, 188
translation studies 9, 10, 12, 18, 27, 28, 33, 36, 45, 79, 88, 92, 108, 113, 117, 121, 122, 124, 127, 134, 202, 209, 217
   descriptive translation studies 123, 211
   linguistics-based translation studies 114
   post-translation studies 219
transmedial 14, 18, 19, 28
transposition 19, 97, 99, 104
Tymoczko, Maria 115, 214
Venuti, Lawrence 88, 114
Weissbrod, Rachel 10, 208
Werner, Michael 9, 11, 61, 75
Zimmerman, Bénédicte 11, 61, 75